Praise for *Undaunted*

T0038072

. . .

"The power of this book is that it reminds the reader that this need not be the end of your story. Broken and hopeless people can mend and regain energy, focus, meaning, and new direction to revise, redirect, and change the rest of their 'story.' This wonderful collection of insights from 'lived experience' and professionals with an array of healing 'tools' gives the reader hope. Healing is possible; there is hope for all of us."

Bruce D. Perry, MD, PhD
Principal of The Neurosequential Network
Author, with Oprah Winfrey, of the *New York Times* #1 Bestseller *What Happened to You: Conversations on Trauma, Resilience, and Healing*

. . .

"If ever there was a comprehensive roadmap for how to easily understand and heal trauma, *Undaunted Hope* is it! Replete with complex stories from real people and commentary from top experts, the reader will find a true direction of what's required should they take the leap to unwind their emotional pain. Black's years of experience in the field of dysfunctional family systems, coupled with her intelligent and compassionate voice, accompanies the reader on this journey reminding us that, 'You are not your trauma . . . healing is possible.'"

Alexandra Katehakis, PhD
Author of *Sex Addiction as Affect Dysregulation:
A Neurobiologically Informed Holistic Treatment*

. . .

"*Undaunted Hope* is an important work for anyone considering treatment, for clinicians of all ages, and for anyone who loves someone who has experienced trauma. In over twenty-five years of working with people who are hurting, I still thank Claudia for the groundbreaking way she unpacks adverse childhood events and the hope she has provided for so many."

Karen Odell-Barber, MS, CISD
Founder and Chairman, Neurologics, Inc.

. . .

"Dr. Claudia Black has made a tremendous impact on our field, and the powerful stories she shares in this book shine an inspiring light on the innovative work at The Meadows, further cementing her pioneering legacy and heart for those who suffer."

Miles Adcox
Chairman and Owner of Onsite

. . .

"*Undaunted Hope* serves as an exploration of inspiration, illuminating narratives that underscore the inherent resilience individuals possess, allowing them to courageously seek support, even in the depths of adversity. Despite life's intricacies and profound wounds, Claudia Black, a distinguished leader in our field, once again, contributes to fostering hope and healing."

Nanette Zumwalt, ICADC, CCJP, CIP
CEO of Hired Power

. . .

"In *Undaunted Hope*, Dr. Claudia Black has once again broken down potential barriers to seeking recovery. Whether you're contemplating pursuing help or are already in recovery, it is an informative and supportive guide. Dr. Black weaves together diverse individual stories of a variety of forms of compulsive behavior along with insights and impressions from experts in the field who help the reader to navigate the many tools for recovery. *Undaunted Hope* is a great resource to orient you to your options and illuminate whatever path you choose."

Nancy Sobel, PsyD, APC
Founder of Global Adolescent Project

UNDAUNTED HOPE

UNDAUNTED
HOPE

Stories of Healing from Trauma, Depression, and Addictions

Claudia Black

CENTRAL RECOVERY PRESS

LAS VEGAS

Central Recovery Press (CRP) is committed to publishing exceptional materials addressing addiction treatment, recovery, and behavioral healthcare topics.

For more information, visit www.centralrecoverypress.com.

29 28 27 26 25 24   1 2 3 4 5

Library of Congress Cataloging-in-Publication Data
Names: Black, Claudia, author.
Title: Undaunted hope : stories of healing from trauma, depression, and
    addictions / Claudia Black.
Identifiers: LCCN 2023048705 (print) | LCCN 2023048706 (ebook) | ISBN
    9781949481853 (paperback) | ISBN 9781949481860 (ebook)
Subjects: LCSH: Psychic trauma. | Depression, Mental. | Substance abuse.
Classification: LCC BF175.5.P75 B54 2024 (print) | LCC BF175.5.P75
    (ebook) | DDC 616.85/2100922--dc23/eng/20240125
LC record available at https://lccn.loc.gov/2023048705
LC ebook record available at https://lccn.loc.gov/2023048706

Photo of Claudia Black courtesy of Brad Reed Photography.

Publisher's Note
The information contained herein is not medical advice. This book is not an alternative to medical advice from your doctor or other professional healthcare provider.

Our books represent the experiences and opinions of their authors only. Every effort has been made to ensure that events, institutions, and statistics presented in our books as facts are accurate and up to date. To protect their privacy, the names of some of the people, places, and institutions in this book may have been changed.

Cover design by The Book Designers. Interior design by Sara Streifel, Think Creative Design.

To Pia Mellody, whose groundbreaking work on codependency has been the foundation to the Meadows Model for over four decades.

Your legacy will span generations of healing throughout the world.

CONTENTS

FOREWORD

Each year, innumerable people who struggle with depression, anxiety, relationship problems, or addictive behaviors go into therapy to get help. The majority of them have a history of adverse childhood experiences—physical or emotional neglect, physical or sexual abuse, family chaos, unpredictability, or inconsistency—that continue to exert an influence on how they experience themselves and the world around them.

Every person tries to cope as best as they can to manage, but how well you do that depends on how old you are, how you understand what is going on, and who is there to protect you. But no matter what resources are available, ongoing danger and trauma leave people hypervigilant for danger, or spaced out, or obsessively controlling. Still others (or even the same people) develop eating problems, addictions, or other self-injurious behaviors to deal with their emotional pain. These behaviors have their origins as self-protective mechanisms to cope with horrendous challenges that people were unable to manage any other way.

Indeed, trauma and neglect are at the root of much of their emotional pain and ineffective coping. It sometimes looks like people are drawn to trauma; every day they eagerly consume stories of wars, natural disasters, community violence, or accidents, often as if they are titillating gossip rather than serious events with concrete consequences. But these *public traumas* also have a galvanizing aspect, because typically there is a focus on what we, as a community or nation, are going to *do* about that terrible situation out there. There usually is some element of hope and a promise for a better future. However, *secret traumas*—emotional and physical neglect or sexual and physical abuse by caregivers and family members—are vastly more common than these public events and can have even more devastating effects on our bodies, minds, and brains.

One common way of dealing with trauma is to push it away and soldier on as best as you can. Blocking out miserable realities is an effective short-term way of coping. Blaming yourself for the violence or the abuse that you experienced can also be a way of dealing with what is going on—at least it gives you a (usually false) sense that there may be something you can do to keep these things from happening to you in the future. Children, in particular, often learn that it is safer to hate themselves than express anger or to run away. Or they treat even innocuous bystanders as mortal enemies. Spacing out and making yourself mentally disappear can also be a helpful coping technique, but the long-term price may be that you lose track of who you are, of what you are feeling, and of what and whom you can trust. Rage that has nowhere to go can be redirected against the self in the form of self-hatred, depression, and destructive actions.

What happened to you cannot be undone, and along the way you may have learned to numb with drugs or alcohol. Or you may have such deep shame and self-loathing that it led to attempted suicides. Or you might be experiencing an unsustainable toggling between having complete control and none at all, resulting in rapidly declining health or psychotic breaks.

It all makes sense in the context of our evolution: our minds and brains became specialized in dealing with terror and danger. Whether traumatized as children or adults, we get stuck in chronic fight, flight, or shut-down modes. Deep down that persistent sense of danger is ever present, even under the objectively most favorable conditions.

So, you now have learned much about the bad news: how trauma and neglect can profoundly mess up the housekeeping of our bodies and the integrity of our sense of self. But this also opens up the door to the good news: that by understanding the impact of trauma on the developing body, mind, and soul, these consequences *can* be dealt with—and healed.

In recovery, the goal is to reestablish ownership of your body and mind, of your *self*. This means regaining the freedom to know what you know and to feel what you feel without becoming overwhelmed, enraged, ashamed, or collapsed. This involves finding a way to become calm and focused; learning to maintain calm in response to images, thoughts, sounds, or physical sensations that remind you of a hurtful past; finding a way to be fully alive in the present and engaged with people around you; and, lastly, not having to keep secrets from yourself, including secrets about the ways you have managed to survive.

Trauma resides in the body, and body-focused therapies are essential to healing.

For change to take place, the body needs to learn that the danger has passed and how to live in the reality of the present. To heal, the body must be restored to a baseline state of safety and relaxation from which it can mobilize and take action in response to real danger. Certain trauma therapies are very good at achieving this. They decentralize the story of what happened and re-center attention on tolerating and exploring the physical sensations that are the result of the imprints of the past trauma in your sensory system. Before plunging in to the full exploration of trauma itself, you need to build the internal resources necessary to deal with sensations and emotions that were the source of feeling so overwhelmed at the time of the trauma.

Over the years, I have worked with many programs that are committed to healing trauma. About two decades ago, I was invited to consult for a private-sector inpatient addiction and mental health program known as The Meadows. Now, many years later, this treatment facility continues to acknowledge and treat post-traumatic stress and the underlying issues of primary disorders with which their clients are diagnosed. The Meadows programs take an eclectic approach, which I strongly endorse. Talk therapy can be transformative, but alone it does not always abolish flashbacks, improve concentration, stimulate vital involvement in our lives, or reduce hypersensitivity to disappointments and perceived injuries. They address these critical life skills with programs designed to help clients regain control of all aspects of their life, so they can thrive.

In addition, they understand that therapy is most effective in community. It is a safe place with safe people, where clients can find a responsive community in which to tell their story. It's where they can put their past in perspective and move forward with their lives. Finding their truth while making connections makes recovery possible.

For the past two decades, other Senior Fellows and I have influenced the incorporation of numerous modalities into their treatment system, including neurofeedback, EMDR, Somatic Experience, psychodrama, Internal Family Systems therapy, and more. I'm proud to see that our variety of techniques have helped those who are traumatized to stabilize and be calm, to lay the trauma to rest, to put words to nonverbal experiences, and to reconnect people to others.

I want to thank author Claudia Black, PhD, a colleague with whom I have shared the stage at many conferences, for the gift of her reminder: it takes a village to heal. And you, the reader, are a part of that village.

If you experienced trauma as a child, there's a strong chance that you have a childlike part living inside you that is frozen in time. You may have grown up believing that you are fundamentally unlovable, because why else would you have been treated so badly? You may have survived by denying, ignoring, or splitting off large chunks of reality, or by pushing away intense feelings. This form of short-term coping may have preserved your dignity and independence, or helped you maintain focus on critical tasks of the day. But long term, it is not a solution.

Recovery from trauma involves coming out of your emotional or physical isolation and reconnecting with fellow human beings in a safe space. You need a guide who is not afraid of your terror, who can safeguard the wholeness of you while you explore the experiences that you had to keep secret from yourself for so long.

Every survivor of trauma I have met is resilient in his or her own way, and every one of their stories inspires awe at how people cope. You will see that in the stories awaiting you in this book. And you will also find hope—which can be a part of your story too. No matter how extremely painful your history is, you *can* heal.

Bessel van der Kolk, MD
Professor of Psychiatry, Boston University School of Medicine
President, Trauma Research Foundation
Author of *The Body Keeps the Score*
Sr. Fellow

MESSAGE FROM DR. D.

My name is Michael Denicole, and I am the medical director for addiction medicine at The Meadows, a licensed psychiatric facility known for treating multiple addictive disorders, trauma, and psychiatric issues. Clients know me as Dr. D.

When individuals admit, I am usually one of the first clinicians they meet. Most arrive scared, angry, skeptical, and hopeless. It is likely their first experience living with a large number of people they do not know yet. While that can be scary, even more scary is the thought of getting through a day without the substances or behaviors they have been using for survival for many months or years.

As a person with the disease of addiction and living a life in recovery, I am able to tell them that I have been right where they are seated. I thank them for their courage and taking this huge leap of faith in being here. I have great respect for them. They are not alone here.

Those of us with this disease of addiction (and yes, it is truly a disease) or those struggling with other mental health issues have different stories of how we got to this place, but nearly all of us have similar core issues. I call these soul wounds. I speak about my experiences, strength, and hope. I tell them how I was held hostage by my disease. I tell them about my resistance in accepting my addiction, my fear and shame. I felt like I was one of the worst people ever, that I was broken and not fixable. I tell them my time in treatment was the beginning of acceptance that I may be a good person with a bad disease—not weak, bad, flawed, or broken. I tell them that this experience may truly be an opportunity to start living once again, and not just surviving. I tell them that doing this work will be difficult, but this journey will be worth it.

I ask two things of them, to stay teachable (humility) and be willing to get naked (honesty/vulnerability). If they are able to remain aware and work on those two things on a daily basis, then the treatment team will provide them tools to address their core issues. They will most definitely be a different human being on the day they complete their journey with us. Completing treatment with us is not a cure though; it's a course correction, as described in the following stories. The journey of recovery continues, one day at a time.

Respectfully,

INTRODUCTION

No matter your age, you do not have to continue to live in your pain, isolation, despair, or hopelessness. You can live your life differently.

If you are seeking answers for why your life is the way it is, how it could be different, and how to make things better, this book is for you. If you are wanting to get a handle on why someone you care about continues to make poor decisions and whether there is any hope of a bright future, this book is for you.

Perhaps you're deeply unhappy but don't know why. Maybe you're doing things that you know are hurtful—to yourself or to those you care about—but can't seem to stop. Or maybe you have a tendency to pick the wrong people to be with, who hurt you, and yet you stay, or go and find someone else who hurts you. You may feel lost or unmotivated and can't find a way out.

As hard as it may be to believe, you are not alone in having uncomfortable emotions, distressing thoughts, or shameful secrets. You are not alone in feeling out of control with whatever behaviors may be causing problems in your life. You may feel as if no one could ever understand what you're going through, or that no one would like the *real* you if you shared what is truly inside your mind and heart.

I and so many others have been in this exact place; it's a lonely, dark, frightening cave. But I'm here, along with twenty-one other storytellers, to tell you that we took the risk to reach out and ask for help. We did it, and so can you. I'm glad you are here.

Putting Words to Our Experiences

When we are in pain, we have a tendency to not talk honestly about what we are experiencing, often because we learned not to, and because we don't think people will understand. We may camouflage depression and self-loathing with beautiful posts on Instagram or TikTok, or by being at the tip-top of our game at work. We can get really good at compartmentalizing our lives so that people are not even aware that we're in trouble. At the other extreme, we can engage in such outrageous behaviors that deep shame keeps us from accepting help when it is offered.

Whatever your struggles, you do *not* have to handle them alone.

Yes, it can be scary to share with others what you are thinking, feeling, or doing. Nearly all of the storytellers felt the same way when faced with the possibility of going for treatment. They too were frightened of their own intense feelings, which was what led them—and likely you as well—to unhealthy ways of coping in the first place.

You may come from a childhood where the people you needed to rely on weren't trustworthy, so today you have a difficult time reaching out and trusting others. It's possible you didn't have any role models giving you permission to ask for help when warranted. You may have grown up uncertain of how to get even your basic needs met. So, you stayed silent.

What you are experiencing can be explained; there *are* words to describe it. There is a path out of your struggle, and it begins with willingness. Just by reading this book, you have begun.

Healing Is Possible

When our struggles with life are intense and chronic, it typically means that we were wounded in some way, likely as a result of *childhood trauma*. As a consequence, we created defenses to be able to cope. And while some of those coping mechanisms may have worked temporarily or in the beginning, in time they took on a life of their own. They led to making poor decisions that exacerbated our difficulties, which in turn negatively impacted our relationships, careers, spiritual growth, mental health, physical health, and whatever else we valued.

You or someone you care about may be stuck in this dangerous cycle. Without help, you may pile up the secrets and repeat hurtful family legacies. Please know that you can get out of the trap. You can find answers. You have worth, and your life has value. I'll say it again: help is near, and healing is possible.

What Help Can Look Like

For more than twenty-five years, I have been a consultant to Meadows Behavioral Healthcare. I first walked onto their beautiful campus in the high desert in February 1998. It was a natural fit for me professionally, and while I continue to consult to their many programs, with pride, I am the founder of the Claudia Black Young Adult Center at The Meadows.

Long before my arrival in the late 1990s, their chief nurse, Pia Mellody, today a renowned author and educator, had created a model and structure in which to explore underlying issues to the mental health, relationship, and addiction problems they were treating. This was a new era of clinical work that addressed *acute trauma* and *complex trauma*, a trauma that comes from repeated negative experience during one's growing up years. This model became the foundation of treatment sustaining itself over the past forty-five years.

The search to understand trauma has led clinicians to think differently, not only about the structure of the mind but also the processes by which it heals. Because no single modality of trauma treatment will fit everyone, the programs of Meadows Behavioral Healthcare (MBH) take an eclectic approach. They do, however, operate under the belief that everyone needs to be assessed and, if indicated, treated for trauma. Should it be ignored, then healing will not be complete.

Even before the staff had the neuroscience to understand the dynamics involved in healing from trauma, they had incorporated mindfulness practice into the programming, intuitively recognizing the need for emotion regulation. The programs use the proven methods of affirmations, yoga, expressive arts, and equine therapy. They have assisted clients in shifting their cognitive narrative about their worth and value through role play, sociometrics, gestalt modalities, and specific trauma therapies such as neurofeedback, Somatic Experiencing, Eye Movement Desensitization Reprocessing (EMDR), and Internal Family Systems therapy.

The Meadows' programs recognize that therapy is most effective when a person experiences healing in community. For this reason, it has created a climate where people feel safe from feeling shame or admonishment or judgment, where they can be honest without fear.

In my several years of work on their many campuses, I have been witness to the complexity of people's lives and to the transformation of healing. While most people do not need inpatient treatment to find answers for their problems, those who do can discover recovery and growth. This is within everyone's scope. Wherever you are on the continuum of despair, hurt, or pain, if the people we have worked with can get well, you can too.

How This Book Can Make a Difference

In this book, you'll read true stories from people in their own words. Some of the identifying details of their lives have been changed to protect privacy. All storytellers are alumni from the different Meadows Behavioral Healthcare campuses. I invited them to share about their journeys: what brought them to the point of asking for help, how they responded to the help available, and where they stand currently in their recovery. I selected these stories for you with the hope that reading about what others found helpful in treatment, and what made a difference for them, may offer direction about your own path to recovery.

In Chapter One, you will learn about trauma and how addressing it is a critical part of most healing interventions. Chapters Two through Seven feature stories from brave men and women of varying ages who found the courage to go deep and become honest with themselves and others. In Chapter Eight, you'll hear from family members of those who underwent treatment. Family members are invited to attend special programming and share at an intimate, honest level not previously thought possible. Loved ones are suffering as well, and healing takes place for them too.

Because trauma is often an underlying dynamic to a multitude of disorders, you will see that it plays a leading role in many of the narratives. As well, you'll find that alcohol and drug use are key players throughout many narratives, as people commonly use them to numb overwhelming pain when they can't find healthier answers.

As these storytellers demonstrated their capacity to make important life changes, so can you. While you may believe your own story is impossible for anyone else to relate to, I want to reiterate, as someone who has worked with all the problems in this book for more than forty-five years, that there is little that is unique as much as there is a lot that is not openly acknowledged.

In an effort to take some of the mystery out of therapy, I gathered enlightening commentary by high-level clinical staff and respected national and worldwide authorities who consult as Senior Fellows to the various campuses. Their perspectives are meant to enhance the understanding of the issues being shared and various treatment methods the alumni participated in. Their comments are not meant to be case consultations, but to offer more educational insight about certain aspects of the harrowing but ultimately hope-filled stories.

It's important to know that there is not one mental health or addiction problem that does not cross gender lines. However, because Meadows Behavioral Healthcare eating disorder and intimacy programs currently enroll only women, and because its sex addiction program currently enrolls only men, those stories are written from their respective genders.

At the end of the book, you will find a glossary with definitions of acronyms commonly used in the stories and brief explanations of the psychological and medical terms used by the commentators. You will also find more complete biographies and credentials of the Meadows Senior Fellows and contributing commentators. A brief description of each program facility is also included.

While You Read

I encourage you to find a comfortable setting in which to read. While you may have an interest in a certain chapter, be open to reading them all. It's likely that even though a storyteller isn't struggling with your same issue, they will have something to say that resonates with you. It might be their process of resistance, how they hid their problems, or what they were willing to do to get help. If you own the print version of the book, consider having a pen or highlighter nearby so you can underline passages that speak to you. You don't need to know why something touches you; by marking it, in time you will find its relevance.

The stories and your own self-reflection may bring up many feelings at different times. I encourage you to be cognizant of your breathing and to take deep breaths as you read. Deep, steady breathing allows you to stay present and to feel safe when feelings are triggered. Pace your reading. This isn't a race to finish a chapter or the book. I also encourage you to let someone you trust know you are reading this. That will make it easier to share what you will be learning about yourself or someone you care for.

As you read, my hope is that you will find some answers for yourself or someone you care about. I want you to know you are not alone. Your story is as important as the lives of the alumni you will hear from. May they inspire you to reach out and get the help you need. I applaud you for taking this journey.

CHAPTER ONE

You Weren't Meant to Heal Alone

None of us are immune from the ravages of pain, trauma, grief, fear, and, at times, the impulse to check out. We all know someone who is struggling with relationships, depression, anxiety, drugs or alcohol, or a serious problematic behavior. We notice when others have great potential that never blossoms due to self-sabotaging actions, but we may not see that same potential in ourselves. Making one poor decision after another may be a way of life. We may have secrets or are privy to the secrets of others that are fueling self-loathing. Fortunately, all of us are capable of healing and moving forward in our lives with a far greater sense of our worth.

By not being able to identify why we feel and act as we do, by thinking we "should" be able to get our act together, or by fearing what the healing process could entail, we often do nothing. It is as if we think that we are supposed to spontaneously be okay, or that the only way to deal with the hand we've been dealt is passive acceptance. Or we irrationally avoid asking for help, since we believe therapy could be better spent on someone whose situation we perceive as worse than ours.

Of course, there is always going to be someone else whose life experiences are more painful than our own, but that does not for a moment lessen the fact that we deserve our own healing. We all deserve to live without the fear or shame that so often sets us up for self-defeating behaviors. No one person's losses and pain diminish our own. We are as deserving as anyone else.

Mental Health Struggles Are More Common Than You May Realize

Sadly, mental health and addiction issues have plagued humankind from time immemorial. Today it is estimated that nearly half of Americans are struggling with a mental health issue.

The reasons for this are multifaceted. We cannot dismiss the impact of an ever-expanding population against a backdrop of greater isolation. The advent of the internet and the increased use of screens offers us anonymity and accessibility like never before; it also has given us the illusion of being better connected than ever thought possible—but virtual connection is still non-contact communication. We don't have to interact with another human. Household goods, groceries, drugs and alcohol, and weapons can all be delivered to our doorstep. We can also access entertainment, educational information, and myriad opportunities that can range from job possibilities to those things that can get us in trouble. While there are many advantages to access to the internet, the past two decades have shown a significant correlation between the number of hours spent online and depression, suicidality, and anxiety. There is no doubt it has also contributed to the escalation of many different addictive disorders, such as compulsive sexual behaviors, gaming, and gambling, wreaking havoc in the lives of many families.

The Covid-19 pandemic gave us fear and confusion and reason to hide in our homes. It also brought the deaths of hundreds of thousands of people in our country alone, leaving no one unaffected by loss. Add to that the current political divide, which is fueling outward expressions of anger and hate. All of this leads to greater disconnection from others and, for many, despairing thoughts and self-defeating behaviors.

As common as mental health and addiction problems are, we still hold an illogical stereotype of struggling with these issues. We picture a person at the end of their rope, barely hanging on, their problem blatantly exposed to the world. That may not be you. The truth is you may be very good at hiding your problems and pain. And when your behaviors are exposed, you may rationalize it by telling yourself and your loved ones that you can handle it. You may not like that your drinking, drug use, or other risky behaviors are escalating, but you don't know how to stop. The thought of getting help scares you, and you tell yourself that you're still in control. Then again, you may be starting to feel that you could use some help, but you don't know where to begin or what to ask for; you feel hopeless. This is understandable, but the help is there. You don't have to keep living the way you are.

What Lies Beneath

While there are many contributing factors, what lies beneath so many of our mental health, relationship, and addiction issues is the experience of *trauma*. The word "trauma" comes from the Greek, meaning a wound, a hurt, or a defeat. It is the result of a shock to the body, mind, or soul. It can be caused by stimulus too powerful or too sudden and unexpected to be assimilated or processed in a normal way by our body and brain. This painful experience overwhelms our ability to cope.

Hold on, wait a minute, you might be thinking, I'm not sure what trauma has to do with me. I'm depressed and not sure what to do with my life, but I don't think I've been traumatized. Or you might wonder, Well, I struggle with getting close to my husband, but I think that has more to do with him than anything in my past. Or another thought: Yeah, I got into drugs as a teenager, just like all my friends, but I am the one who made choices along the way, and that had nothing to do with trauma.

These thoughts are common. Many of us aren't aware of what trauma actually is, so contending with the possibility that we may have experienced trauma at some point can come with some skepticism. I ask you to be open to learning about traumatic stress, because so often it is the biggest influencer of our self-destructive thinking and behavior, and at the root of many of our problems.

"Big T" Traumas

Also known as blatant and acute trauma, a "big T" trauma is typically what we think of happening in our psyches following something that makes the news, like experiencing severe flooding, a community shooting, or a car wreck. While many of these traumas may be a one-time experience, others are repeated, and some are ongoing. Here are a few examples of big T trauma events:

- War or invasion
- Act of terrorism
- Natural disaster

- Sexual assault
- Car, plane, or train accident
- Serious illness or injury
- Witnessing violence
- Unexpected death of someone close
- Forced relocation
- Witnessing or experiencing a life-threatening situation
- Physical abuse
- Incest
- Violence in the home
- Neglect

"Little t" Traumas

Don't let the moniker "little t" mislead you. In no way are little t traumas less significant than big T traumas. It is not about size. Little t traumas are the result of a string of unavoidable painful events and experiences, repeated over and over. A typical example is the experience of growing up in a family impacted by addictions, mental health issues, rigidity, neglect, or emotional abandonment. While little t traumas may be more subtle, they are chronic and far more common than big T traumas. In fact, they can be so common that we may not recognize their effects on us until years—even decades—later. Here are some examples:

- Harsh, unfair, or extreme criticism
- Being bullied
- Being shamed or demeaned
- Being ignored, disrespected, or discounted
- Control or manipulation by someone you trust
- Discovering or witnessing infidelity of a partner or your parent
- Acrimonious divorce
- Enmeshment (thoughts and feelings are merged with those of another person's)
- Unrealistic expectations
- Inconsistent or contradictory responses from a parent or partner

- Loss of important relationships or friendships
- Loss of goals or dreams

Some of these events may not be traumatic if they occur only once or just a few times. But they may create trauma when they are repeated enough times.

The reality is no one can move through life without experiencing some type of trauma. It seems to be a part of the human condition, whether it takes the form of losing a child in childbirth, losing your home in a tornado, living with severe criticism, growing up with addiction and violence, being raised with physical or sexual abuse, growing up in a highly rigid and controlling family, being a person of color in a racist society, being LGBTQIA+ in a homophobic and gender-phobic community—the list goes on.

The Adverse Childhood Experiences Study

The Adverse Childhood Experiences (ACEs) Study is the largest survey of the impact of childhood abuse and neglect on adult health and well-being. The original study was conducted in 1995 and strongly validated that ACEs—or painful, chaotic, and/or hurtful childhood experiences—set the foundation for mental health, relational, and addiction problems later in life. ACEs consist of a range of adverse events, from physical and sexual abuse to neglect to having parents who were divorced, mentally ill, addicted, or in prison. The study concluded that the more ACEs we have, the far greater likelihood of struggling with depression, anxiety, substance use disorder, or multiple health issues.

In addition, researchers found that ACEs are interrelated, meaning that people typically don't experience a standalone adverse experience but rather multiple, related ones.

The presenting problem—difficulty with intimacy, substance abuse, behavioral addiction, depression, eating disorders, and more—is often only the marker for the real problem, which lies buried in time and concealed by shame, secrecy, rationalizing, and denying. The Centers for Disease Control and Prevention (CDC) continues to study ACEs and provides current data at www.cdc.gov.aces.

Key Aspects of Trauma

Here is what we know to be true about trauma:

- **Most traumas occur in the context of a relationship.** In these situations, people are hurt repeatedly or unexpectedly by someone they trust or care about.

- **Trauma doesn't exclude.** It isn't like a virus only striking the most vulnerable. Any person regardless of their age, state of health, or emotional maturity can experience trauma.

- **Trauma is common, not rare.** Almost all of us hold trauma in our bodies. Many of these traumas are small, and people create ways to work around them. They don't seriously diminish our lives. But many other traumas run quite deep and can cause serious pain.

- **Trauma isn't just an individual response.** It can be collective and historical. Examples of *collective trauma* would be when great numbers of people experience a school shooting, an act of terrorism, or a natural disaster. An instance of *historical trauma* is the hundreds of thousands of people of different racial and ethnic backgrounds who have been geographically displaced or subject to racism and control by a more powerful group.

- **The younger the person, the greater the impact.** Those who experience a relational trauma at an early age can expect a greater impact on their life. The trauma impinges on the still developing body and brain.

- **Trauma has a compounding effect.** If you have had previous traumas, trauma upon trauma can impact you cumulatively.

- **Unhealed trauma gets in the way of happiness.** It can negatively impact nearly every facet of your life, preventing you from living the life you deserve.

- **The sooner the help, the quicker the recovery.** The help that others provide or fail to provide after a traumatic event can have a profound effect on how well and quickly you recover. Support from family, friends, and community can blunt the effects of trauma or make it less likely to occur in the first place.

Living with Trauma

Traumatic experiences put us at risk for not being able to feel safe in the world, setting us up for hypervigilance. When we have been traumatized, we operate from a place of fear and seek to garner control in reaction to having felt powerlessness or defeat at some point in time. Over time, we may lose faith in others, whether a particular person or group, or all people in general. We feel a disconnect from others, unable to feel close. We keep emotional or physical distance from others in an attempt to avoid being hurt again. Or we may do the opposite, actively seeking to be rescued and not developing our own strong sense of self.

We may question what is true or real in the world. If we have lost our innocence, we may no longer see the world from a place of wonder, faith, or hope. Any spark or joy or curiosity is squelched, and our profound need to protect ourselves diminishes our creativity, our adventuresome spirit. Trauma may make us feel as if we don't have much influence in the world. We might no longer trust that the universe is benevolent or in good hands or that a power greater than us is looking after us. We no longer recognize ourself or no longer are clear about who we are or what we value. Any sense of calmness is long gone; we are generally tense, worried, or afraid. Just being who we are, or simply being alive feels painful or risky.

REFLECTION ACTIVITY

This is an opportune moment to pause and reflect on what you have read so far. Whether it is you or someone you care about who experienced trauma, consider the following questions. You may answer them quietly to yourself, or grab a notebook and write down your answers.

- What are you thinking right now? What are you feeling?
- Was there a storm in your family of origin? Things that made it feel chaotic, unsafe, unpredictable, cold, frightening, or demanding?
- Were there big losses in either your growing up or adult years that changed your world view?
- Have you been subject to any of the big T or little t traumas noted above? Which ones?
- Have you been subject to historical trauma?

For the moment, simply be with this knowledge. As you continue to read, you will discover insights about what you did to cope with your experiences and strategies that will be helpful in your process of healing.

You also need to take care of yourself. Do you need to do anything to offer yourself greater comfort? It could be a five-minute break, or to put on music in the background. It may be getting yourself some water or changing to a different chair or room. As you continue, periodically ask yourself what would make you more comfortable in the moment.

What Happens in Our Bodies

Whenever we have a frightening encounter, our *autonomic nervous system*—which regulates many bodily functions automatically, such as our heart rate—goes on alert. It pumps out stress chemicals designed to do one of two things: flee for safety or stay and fight. For instance, we may fight off an attacker or run to a safe place. If there is no perceived opportunity to do either, then the body's automatic response is to move into a freeze or collapse state. Depending on the situation, this may mean standing very still in place, or crawling into bed and refusing to respond to others, and/or going numb on the inside. These are natural survival reflexes. We are hardwired for this.

Let's say a burglar is trying to break into a home. Some people will go for their gun or knife (fight response) in an attempt to protect their home and self, others will run out the back door (flight response), and some will stand frozen in place (freeze response), unable to move. Now imagine being threatened as a child. You are small and your father is two inches from your face. His expression is contorted, he is screaming at you, telling you that you're stupid and worthless, and you're terrified he is going to hurt you next. You can't fight, he is stronger than you; you can't flee, he will find you; so you stand in a frozen state. That is absolutely understandable.

When we have an experience that exceeds our brain and body's ability to cope, we experience trauma. That painful moment becomes frozen in time and imprints powerful thoughts, emotions, and physical sensations related to the event in certain areas of our body and brain. These sensations remain embedded, potentially for years or decades, until the trauma is addressed and healed.

If the trauma is not addressed, then we are at risk for our fight, flight, and freeze responses to misfire as we go through life. In this case, we also often have an altered perception of risk and safety. The limited or missing capacity to evaluate relative danger and safety in one's environment results in what is called *faulty neuroception*. This means that we may have a hard time feeling calm or safe. In addition, we may rarely feel in control of our emotions because trauma also impacts the *limbic system*, which is responsible for regulating our emotions and behaviors, particularly when we feel unsafe. The defenses we used when we were young and scared may have once insured our survival. But over time, they interfere with our ability to be present, be rational, feel secure, maintain calm, or experience a range of emotions. They keep us from being able to be genuinely intimate in relationships, fuel overreactiveness in personal and work situations, increase anxiety, and impede our ability to trust others.

Our toxic stress response leads us to make impulsive decisions. Or we find rigid defenses to help us cope with an internal uneasiness. Or we engage in certain behaviors compulsively, such as gaming, gambling, sex, eating, exercise, and so on to calm us down, or to connect with others when we can't otherwise. For many, alcohol and use of other drugs is a great medicator. It may be the only way in which to feel any sense of control or power over our lives. These false solutions keep us from realizing all of our potential.

Reconciling the Trauma

With skilled therapists and proven modalities, our lives *can* change in ways we never thought possible. The search to understand trauma has led clinicians to think differently not only about the structure of the mind but also the processes by which it heals. Coupled with the growing body of knowledge of the neuroscience of traumatic stress, important changes in treatment modalities have begun to take shape. The biggest change was that *cognitive behavioral therapy* (CBT) is no longer recognized as the only treatment option. CBT is most effective at enhancing a person's ability to problem-solve, reason, and make informed decisions—when they have a regulated nervous system and a calm limbic system.

For the traumatized individual, who doesn't have a regulated nervous system or a calm limbic system, a different approach is needed, because in order for the mind, body, and brain to heal, a person first needs to feel safe. Calming the brain stem is the doorway to successfully working with the emotional and cognitive parts of the brain. Healing needs to occur from both a sensory and cognitive capacity. In order to heal, we need inner stability. A treatment approach that emphasizes emotional regulation will help you develop an internal capacity to feel safe and calm.

Neurofeedback and *Somatic Experiencing (SE)*, as well as mindfulness practices, breathwork, yoga, and music are a few of the therapy and healing modalities that help to activate social engagement and calm physical tensions in the body. These interventions are now seen as imperative to healing trauma. Together they help shift people out of the fight-or-flight states, reorganize their perception of danger, and increase their capacity to manage relationships.

Also important to healing is addressing any profound beliefs in your lack of value, in your unrelenting shame. In essence, healing involves learning to deactivate the defensive maneuvers that once insured your survival.

Mental health and addiction problems frequently have a *co-occurring diagnosis* that requires treating both it and the traumatic stress and its many symptoms simultaneously. Thanks to advances in our understanding of neurobiology, we can treat current presenting symptoms (often the primary diagnosis) while addressing a significant underlying contributor (trauma). By attending to the dual issues, recovery is even more possible.

The twenty-one stories in this book hold a promise of how you can find your way out of your self-defeating thinking and behavior—irrespective of how complicated your life has become. As you read, look for the similarities and parallels in your life. As these storytellers confronted their own barriers, you can as well. The education and explanation in the commentary can lead to insight that will give you direction and validation. You will find that getting honest, with proper support, can cultivate an authentic sense of self-worth that leads to healing and recovery.

CHAPTER TWO

Unwittingly Brave
RECOVERY FROM TRAUMA

I'm still here, living the best I can, so what's the big deal, I got through it.
That was a long time ago, so what does that have to do with now?
I don't want to blame my parents, they had it tough too.

Nearly every one of us, at some point in our life, will experience an extraordinarily distressing event. It may be sudden and unexpected, or painfully consistent over months or years. This event is so powerful that it can overwhelm our body's ability to process it and cope in a helpful way. Among a number of side effects is an impaired sense of safety in the world. This response—our emotional and physical reaction to the terrible event—is called *trauma.*

Trauma exists on a broad spectrum, showing up in nearly as many ways as there are types of events that cause it. For some of us, our trauma has become so commonplace that we may not even recognize its presence. For others, the humiliation and intense fear is so unfathomable that we have no words to describe it.

All we know is that we become so angry at times that we can't keep a relationship, or we feel unhappy and dull, despite our outward success. We may be so fearful of change that we avoid taking risks in our career. We may drink because we can't find peace any other way, or we insist on pleasing others or being in control to quell a fear that something bad is going to happen otherwise. We may have panic attacks, display obsessive-compulsive symptoms, experience flashbacks, dissociate, be hypervigilant, or have nightmares. These are some of numerous common trauma responses.

You don't have to be a combat veteran, the victim of a sexual assault, or caught in an act of terrorism to encounter trauma. You may have trauma as a consequence of listening to parents argue nightly for years; bearing ongoing, severe criticism by a caregiver; losing a parent to abandonment or suicide; or being consistently bullied in your growing-up years. Or you may not even remember the event. Your physical and emotional response that is playing out today is what's important to address. Your life can get better.

Everyone is deserving of healing. The impact of trauma on our brain, our nervous system, our emotions, and our body is worth healing. Our constant impulse to fight, flee, or freeze can be healed. If you or someone you care about is experiencing trauma, know that everyone—especially you—are worthy of healing.

While trauma is an underlying factor in most of the stories in this book, trauma brought the following two people to treatment, and it would be their primary diagnosis. Their narratives capture the pain of traumatic experiences and speak to the resiliency that everyone has—and the gifts of recovery once engaged in a healing process.

Don't Expect Me to Cry   BY JANET

From the time I was four years old, I was responsible for taking care of my seven younger siblings. I learned to change diapers, do the laundry, cook, and babysit at an age when I should have been doing the things four-year-olds do: play, explore, be curious, be comforted.

Waiting for the Axe to Fall
My dad grew up rejected by his dad, abused by his stepdad, and in and out of foster homes. He was homeless and living under the pier at Venice Beach, California by the time he was fifteen. Involved in criminal activities, he was ultimately told by the courts that it was prison or the Navy. So he went into the Navy but was discharged for drug abuse.

When my dad drank, he was violent. One minute things would be calm, the next my parents would be arguing about something, and he would start beating my mom and at least one of us kids. Sometimes she cowered, and other times she fought back, which always made it worse. The chance that my mother would be killed in front of me was beyond terrifying. The constant waiting for the axe to fall took its toll on us. I have no memories of any period in my childhood when there was not raging, name calling, and yelling.

And yet, my dad was the most important man in the world to me. I wanted so much for him to love me.

My mom was a different type of drunk; she was moody when she drank and became an expert at guilt trips. Her mother had been an alcoholic too and died from cirrhosis of the liver. A hard part of growing up was that I could never tell when my mom would lash out at us for the smallest thing. She could make me feel loved and cared about one moment and then as if I were not good enough the next moment.

When I was about five, I woke up one morning to a lot of blood in the kitchen and living room. My mother and father were nowhere to be found. I gathered up my younger siblings and we hid in the bedroom all day; I could barely move except to change diapers and get food. That was my father's first suicide attempt that I remember; he had several more. My mom's suicide attempts usually involved the supply of pills that were readily available throughout the house.

I was angry and scared after her attempts, because how could she leave me alone with a monster such as my dad? I would also feel inadequate because I was not able to help her feel better. I required her love and approval to function. The problem was that I could never please her enough. I depended on her for my own happiness.

A Shattered Sense of Safety

The sexual abuse started when I was four. The first time, my mom was in the hospital having another baby. My dad came into my room and told me that I was special to him and that I would have to help him while Mom was gone.

The next night he came home, and he was not so comforting. He was in a rage. All of the other kids were crying, and I was scrambling to give them comfort. I started crying and then he screamed, "Stop crying or I'll give you something to cry about!" and that's when he ripped my clothes off and said it was time for me to take care of things. Before I could even begin to think about what was happening, he had his penis in my mouth. He kept jabbing it deeper, and the next thing I knew I was gagging and I threw up. Tears were streaming down my face, and he told me I needed to clean up the mess. I didn't sleep much that night for fear he'd come into my room again. It shattered my sense of safety. I never felt safe again.

After that first incident, he came into my room regularly. Sometimes he was angry and drinking, and other times he would act normal and caring. He made me touch him and did horrible, painful things to me. When my mom was home, he would still visit my room. My dad told me it was our special secret. I didn't want him to get angry and knew somebody would get hurt if he got angry. It was also the only way that I thought he would ever love me.

We moved multiple times, as either my dad was in trouble with other drug dealers or the authorities, or he would lose his job. I dreaded the change of schools. I had become extremely shy by grade school and was an expert at blending into the background. I had these horrible secrets that ate away inside of me. I couldn't tell anyone because of my fear of what would happen if I did.

I was constantly criticized for being too sensitive. My father always told me I was crazy, and as I got older my brothers and sisters and mother also called me crazy. I kept thinking, If I were good enough, my dad would start to love me.

My sadness and loneliness enveloped me like a black cloud. I was powerless to escape. I spent much of my childhood in my room alone, crying and feeling as if there was nobody to help me. So many times I wanted to die, but thankfully I was so petrified of death that fear kept me from making any serious suicide attempts.

The White Numb Place

I was nine years old when I was awakened to the loud voices of my dad and another guy that my dad owed money to for drugs. Suddenly the arguing subsided, and my dad was pulling me out of the bed. He looked at me with that drug look and said he needed me to pay a debt. I started sobbing, and the other man slapped me across the face, telling me to shut up. I begged my dad to intervene, but the man dragged me to the living room, ripped my clothes off, and raped me.

Where was my mom? Why didn't anyone help?

Afterward, lying back in bed in the same room as my brothers and sisters, I made a conscious decision that I would stop crying. I would pretend like I was not there. It was like when my dad molested me—I would go to places in my mind. This time, though, it was more intense. I was able to shut down the hurt and pain and feel nothing. My mind went white while there; I didn't have to exist in the present. I would wake up the next morning wishing I could die and be in that white numb place all the time.

Turning Eleven

I didn't feel comfortable with my body as it developed from a child into a woman. I didn't want my breasts to develop. I wanted to remain a child. Becoming a woman felt wrong and disgusting. To leave the house I had to walk by the dining table where my mom and dad sat chain smoking. It became a terrifying walk of shame. It was where the drug deals happened and where my dad's friends would whistle, grab at me, and make sexual comments. This affected my intimacy toleration forever.

Fortunately, two wonderful things happened when I was eleven. I started menstruating, which caused my dad to stay away from me, and a new family moved into our neighborhood. One of the girls became my first real friend. She invited me with her family to church. It was like a miracle to go to a place where people were welcoming and kind, where I could escape the drugging and drinking and fighting. I was embarrassed because my clothes were too small and very tattered, but they did not seem to notice.

Soon I discovered that there were a lot of rules. Girls could not cut their hair, sleeves had to be below the elbow, dresses below the knees, no jewelry, no listening to anything but church music. I started to feel uneasy, but I followed the rules the best I could; I was trying to please God.

When I was twelve, I went to a church revival. One day a boy who I thought was my friend approached me saying that he wanted to be my boyfriend. He was acting really nice and said he wanted me to meet me in his room, which I did. Then he violently raped me. Once again, I found myself from above and was thoroughly disgusted by who I was. I told myself I deserved it; I should not have gone to his room. But I so wanted him to like me. I thought I had found somebody safe for the first time in my life. After that he totally ignored me. That led to my first abortion. Yet, I continued at the church.

My Ticket Out

I actually found high school very exciting; I liked all the different subjects. I was starting to enjoy some independence from my family, taking the bus on my own, and then I took a job while in school. We had been poor my entire life, and with the job came my ticket out of the house, out of that nightmare, and, most importantly, away from my dad. I finished high school with a 4.0 grade point average and a full ride scholarship to four years of college. My parents never knew about this. But I passed on the scholarship because making money seemed more practical than going to college.

I left home when I was seventeen, took out a small loan, and bought my first car. I gave my parents no warning; I just left.

We Functioned as a Good Family

Jack was the first man I had had an interest in. When he returned that interest, I clung to him for dear life. I felt like I was a virgin when I met him, though technically monsters had stolen that part of me. It was as if all my sexual feelings came out with him, and most of them felt okay.

I immersed myself in him and developed an extreme dependence on him for my happiness. Well, Jack made it clear that he did not want to be tied down in a relationship. That triggered my insecurity and made it difficult for me to have difficult conversations such as about birth control, so within two months of dating I was pregnant. I had my second abortion.

After two years of dating, we moved in together. We started to have problems arising from my smothering Jack with my clinginess and my insecurities about his commitment to the relationship. We began to argue more often. Our sexual life was up and down. I went through periods when I didn't want to be sexual; I only tolerated the act and would employ the same mechanisms I used when I was being abused.

Then I became pregnant and had my daughter. The pregnancy reinforced that sex is for creation of life, and I was okay with that. After her birth I would find excuses to avoid sex. We argued, and he made me promise to see a therapist. I couldn't imagine talking to a stranger about this problem, but I wanted another baby. We'd gone a whole two years without having sex. I had become petrified of it. But I calculated the optimum day in my cycle, and we had sex. Afterward, I felt as if I would die.

I wondered if I was crazy. I couldn't shake the feelings of shame and disgust. I wondered if I had fallen out of love with him, but when I thought of life without him it was unbearable. I was totally confused.

Much to my relief, that one episode resulted in a pregnancy. Over the next several years, we functioned as a good family. We had family outings. There was no sexual intimacy, and with that tension and broken promises things finally blew up. On our eleventh wedding anniversary, we'd had seven years of a sexless marriage. He was tired of my not seeking out a therapist. He gave me an ultimatum: I had to find a therapist or we were over.

I made an appointment, but I was scared about opening up to somebody. Many things I thought were buried safely inside me came bubbling up to the surface, just as I had feared. It became an emotional rollercoaster. I began to have nightmares. Images would flash in my mind at various times. I had nausea, headaches, and insomnia, and I was always irritable and on the verge of tears. Every time I tolerated any closeness with my husband, it was as if I were reliving my abuse. I wanted so badly to go back to when I remembered only what I chose to remember. So, I began Prozac, the first of many pills I would take in large doses—not to die but to shut down.

"If You Are Going through Hell, Keep Going"

After fifteen years of marriage, Jack and I filed for a divorce. I was thirty-four years old. Within the next year I met another man, and after a period of time living together, Simon and I were married.

In the years that followed, I struggled with numerous issues. First, I developed premenstrual dysphoric disorder, which caused me to have close to ten days a month feeling very irritable, negative, and extremely defensive; ultimately I would need a hysterectomy. I also had a malignancy in my colon.

Second, I got involved in an unhealthy long-distance relationship, which brought a cycle of deception, guilt, and frustration. Again, I was going back and forth between feeling so dependent on a relationship that it was life or death, and feeling suffocated by it.

I was also missing outings with my kids; I had no energy. I was taking more anxiety medications than I was supposed to, to escape all of my pain. My depression became even worse. I was seriously thinking about ending my life.

The only good thing about the lowest point is there's only one direction to go. And as Winston Churchill said, "If you're going through hell, keep going."

Gifts of Recovery

Shortly after my fifty-fifth birthday, I began treatment. It's been both a painful and joyous journey. I went to The Meadow's forty-five-day inpatient treatment program, then their intensive outpatient program, and today I remain in therapy. It sounds like a lot, but I have needed it all.

The inpatient program gave me three wonderful gifts: First, I learned about how my childhood sexual abuse dominated my emotional development and caused my brain to learn dysfunctional ways of coping. I learned that the way I am was my brain's natural reaction to what happened. I learned about the concept of *emotional immaturity* and that, if I wanted to live a functional life as an adult, I needed to take charge and protect my inner child, the girl who was still suffering the effects of the abuse. I would need to teach her how to establish good boundaries.

During the survivors' workshop, using experiential techniques, I was able to confront the very deepest trauma memories and face my abusers as an adult. I realized that I had grown up as a chameleon, on hyperalert to whatever I perceived people wanted me to be. That was how I got out of my childhood alive. That week was the most exhausting and emotional I've ever spent, yet it was incredibly healing.

Second, I was given tools to start functioning as a healthy adult, such as setting boundaries, communicating, and learning to retrain my brain through repeating healthy steps. With enough practice and repetition, you can retrain your brain to react differently to triggers; being more emotionally regulated can begin to show within ninety days, and that gave me hope.

Third, I got to feel a kinship with friends that I've never felt before. We had to do an exercise documenting our personal histories and identifying all of the abuse and traumas, and then present that to a group, making it visible to everyone. I was consumed with fear and shame, yet all these wonderful people accepted me. I learned to trust them. It was and remains the most powerful experience I have ever had.

More Triggering Memories

I was very delicate after treatment, so I enrolled in the intensive outpatient program (IOP). But without the structure of the inpatient program, I found myself triggered during weekend trips with my family. Memories of my childhood came flooding back.

Then I went to a weekend reunion of sorts with a small group of people whom I had met during treatment. There, I fell into a deep shame spiral. I felt like I wasn't good enough to be with these people. I felt like that poor, damaged little girl I had been growing up. The first night, I called my husband and sobbed for almost two hours. I couldn't escape the thought that I wished I didn't exist.

As the next few weeks passed, I was feeling increasingly overwhelmed, and I wasn't sleeping. My psychiatrist (outside of the Meadows system) put me back on Xanax, which had been taken away from me during treatment. When the Xanax did not help me sleep, I was switched to Klonopin. Both are benzodiazepines for which I would have an adverse reaction: suicidal ideations. During one family outing I took close to a bottle of Klonopin. In a stupor, I called my doctor, and that resulted in spending seven days in detox withdrawing from this overdose.

One of the conditions for being able to continue my work at the IOP was that I had to live in a structured sober living environment. While I wasn't happy about it, it was truly the right thing to do. I attended the IOP every day, I went to every group I could and was introduced to twelve-step meetings where I found Pills Anonymous, Codependency Anonymous, and Adult Children of Alcoholics. I was feeling much more stable.

After three months, I started writing a book about my journey. I was excited to do it, but I was triggered all over again. I started to drink again. I had stopped once I was in treatment. Mike, a Meadows-trained therapist, referred me to AA. I didn't want to go. I had this horrible vision of AA, because my dad would go to those meetings, then drink and molest me. I didn't want to say that I was an alcoholic because I thought that it made me like my dad. Mike said, "You don't have to say you're an alcoholic. All you have to say is that you have a desire to not drink." So I went, with a desire not to drink.

Today I have no doubt I am alcoholic—and it does not make me like my dad. AA has helped me take responsibility for my recovery and given me a spiritual program. Because of the religious abuse I had been subjected to, I found great comfort in a spiritual program that was not religious. It's giving me so much peace.

I've not had a drink in four and a half years.

I Deserve Good

I identify as being sexually anorexic; in the way that a food anorexic starves themself, I struggle being sexual. I used to be plagued with guilt and feel as failure as a wife. But letting go of false beliefs and using tools that have taught me that I have value, that I can express my needs and wants, and how to know what is safe, gives me hope and intimacy that I have never had before.

In the past couple of years, I have felt strong enough to face my intimacy fears. Facing intimacy and sex in a loving relationship without alcohol is so difficult. Alcohol was the only way for me to be relaxed enough to have sex and not experience the flashbacks, which made me feel like I was being abused.

My husband and I have been married now for twenty-six years. We have done a lot of work on codependence, rescuing, and boundaries. I was so scared to set a boundary. It felt so dangerous. I thought that if I set any type of boundary or expressed any kind of need or want, I would be abandoned.

Once I started setting boundaries, although awkward and imperfect most times, I started to trust myself. I could see that I could take care of myself. Knowing that allowed me to trust my husband and feel safer expressing myself. I needed to learn to say no so that I could say yes.

I still have shame spirals. There are moments when I want to lie down, crawl under the covers, and make myself small again. When I catch myself feeling undeserving of good things, I catch my breath and remind myself that I am as worthy as any other human being. I am no longer paralyzed by the triggers when they occur.

At times the urge to give up on things has been strong, and I want to push others away. But instead I reach out to my sponsor, my support group, my therapist. I don't isolate. I'm also actively involved in nonprofit work on behalf of sexual abuse and assault survivors. In this process, my book, *Don't Expect Me to Cry*, was published, which has been a lovely part of my recovery. Today I feel feelings versus medicating them with alcohol, pills, suicidal thoughts, or isolation. I put one foot in front of the other. I move toward connection, toward life.

Today, I know in my heart and soul that I deserve good.

◆ ◆ ◆

What Is Dissociation?

From Peter Levine, PhD, Sr. Fellow (Developer of Somatic Experiencing)

Dissociation is the experience of disconnecting from reality. We all disconnect at times—such as when we're in a flow state and focusing, or when we're daydreaming—but dissociation describes a more intense experience, often as a result of trauma, whereby we lose awareness of what's happening in the moment, as if we have detached completely. Dissociation is one of the most classic and subtle symptoms in trauma. It is a favored means of enabling a person to endure experiences that, at the moment, are beyond endurance. When the trauma has been chronic, dissociation is a preferred mode of being in the world. We can dissociate readily and habitually without being aware of it.

From Deirdre Stewart, MS
(VP of Trauma Resolution Services)

When a parent violates a child's sexual boundary and uses the child for their sexual gratification, it sets up the child for internalized shame. They grow up to believe there is something wrong with them. They carry that shame into adulthood, with it affecting all areas of their life. When a traumatized person organizes their internal experience around a shame-based identification, they run away from themselves—they use their history against themselves.

The neglect, abuse, and trauma Janet experienced led to *arrested psychological development*—meaning that some of Janet's emotional and mental abilities stayed stuck at the age she was when she endured the trauma. Pia Mellody, who developed the original model of trauma work at The Meadows and all MBH programs, says that learning to protect, honor, love, care for, and moderate oneself fails to happen when there is arrested psychological development. To begin to remedy this, for example, when Janet was overwhelmed with an emotion in a given situation, we asked her, "What does your ten-year-old need right now?" We assisted Janet in recognizing that she was feeling the vulnerability she felt as a child, and that she has a functional, healthy part of herself that can speak to the vulnerable part. That functional part of herself will affirm and remind her that she is okay, she is not bad, not in trouble.

When there is sexual abuse, sexual intimacy can get equated with fear and terror; compulsive avoidance of sex can result. Dissociation allowed Janet to bear the unbearable, and while it was lifesaving at the time of the abuse, it became life diminishing when she was attempting to be intimate, to share vulnerably with another.

If someone grows up in a family or cultural system like the church Janet attended, where sex is deemed bad and dirty, it may result in a propensity to either act it *out*—such as objectifying yourself or being sexually promiscuous—or act it *in* and against yourself—such as by avoiding all things sexual.

Janet talks about how her lack of boundaries impacted her life and how implementing them has been important to her recovery. Indeed, healthy boundaries protect a person from victimization and also offer containment so that we don't violate other people's boundaries. They allow us to honor and respect ourselves and others. A *physical boundary* informs that "I have a right to determine how close someone gets to me and whether they get to touch me. I have the right to say to someone, you are in my space and I need you to please back up." The other person has that same right. A *sexual boundary* informs that "I have a right to determine with whom and when and where I am going to be sexual, and the same is true for others."

We also teach a communication skill called boundaries for talking and listening. The *talking boundary* allows us to share our reality with another in the interest of speaking to and being known, not to control or manipulate. The *listening boundary* allows us to take in what is real and true for us and discard what is not. This entails recognizing that when people are talking to us, they are telling us who *they* are, not who *we* are. This is imperative to protect our reality and not live in reaction to others and the world around us. Our sense of feeling okay is to be generated internally regardless of what others are or are not doing.

I liken the listening boundary to a wetsuit. You can zip it up and can keep out what is not true or real for you, and you can choose when to unzip and let the external data into your reality. With healthy boundaries, you develop a sense of self and have the opportunity to be genuinely intimate with another.

From Jean Collins, LCSW
(Clinical Consultant)

Janet credited a lot of her healing to the experiential work during what is called Survivors Week. It is an extremely empowering group process that heals old wounds and corrects deeply entrenched messages that drive so many self-defeating behaviors. It entails a variety of techniques, such as guided imagery, letter writing, artwork, gestalt, role play, and psychodrama. And, as Janet experienced, it can be an emotional week— but we methodically pace the work so that clients feel safe, so they can become vulnerable, can be present with their emotions, and can let go of certain feelings they have carried with them as a result of childhood relational trauma. We work with them to access and strengthen skills that help them have success in daily life, as well as to affirm, nurture, and protect their still-tender aspects of themselves, while setting limits.

From Peter Levine, PhD, Sr. Fellow
(Developer of Somatic Experiencing)

I was deeply affected by Janet's honesty about her situation, and about her authentic needs and her need for an extended recovery. Her extensive history of abuse and of living with her trauma led her to develop some protective features. Her ability to dissociate (see sidebar "What Is Dissociation?") became, in a sense, her safety valve. This valve let off just enough pressure to keep her system running. Another symptom Janet developed was *hypervigilance*, or a heightened state of alert. Janet's protective hypervigilance can be viewed with a sense of appreciation and even gratitude, particularly if we consider what might happen if her system did not have this safety valve.

While it would take Janet many years before she found the help she needed, she demonstrates that you can begin to heal at any age. I suspect that many people feel shame about having ongoing needs. But recognizing your needs is essential for lasting recovery. So, speaking for many, I thank Janet for her honesty, courage, and persistence on her healing journey.

Boots on the Ground

BY CARLOS

I was in the military ROTC when 9/11 occurred. A guy called and said, "Get your ass over here. We don't know where the hell we're going, but we're going somewhere." That was the beginning of being assigned to mostly combat or intel units that oversaw airstrikes over the next eighteen years.

My initial mission was taking money to people for rebuilding projects and to get their economy going again. One day, when we were flying in the Chinook helicopter back to Baghdad, somebody shot at us and hit the gunner. He fell out of the way, and because I was sitting next to him, I grabbed the machinery and started firing at anything that moved.

In that moment I felt pure rage and hatred. I didn't know I was even capable of those feelings. I didn't recognize myself. I thought, Who am I, this monster? Of course, I had trained for something like this, but you never really expect it. It's quite different to pull the trigger at a firing range when you're practicing compared to actually seeing people run and duck from your bullets.

That was probably the incident that started my post-traumatic stress disorder (PTSD).

Over the next few years, I was in similar situations. I actually sabotaged my career because I chose to stay at my current rank. I wanted to stay in the fight; I wanted to be the boots on the ground.

By the time I came back from the desert, even the first time, I wasn't the same guy who left. My marriage wasn't good, as I wasn't communicating; I was just boxed up. My mother told me that my light had gone out. At one point, when I knew I was drinking too much, I decided to go into recruiting so I'd have a better lifestyle. But I was still so full of rage; the only thing that allowed me to get it out was to blow up things. Sure enough, I was allowed to go back to Qatar.

In the last couple of years in the service, another guy and I started calling ourselves the Bad News Bears, because we were dealing with death and destruction on a daily basis. We handled all of the reporting and coordinating of help when there was a suicide, accident, domestic violence, or natural disaster. By then my drinking had seriously increased.

Then one of my best friends at the Pentagon committed suicide. It really crushed me. He and I had just talked, and I knew he was having trouble. But in the field when you ask, "Hey man, how you doing?" And they say, "I'm good," that's the answer. I told myself I should have seen the signs. But I was caught up in my own stuff.

A Hot Mess

Then Covid-19 hit. I was no longer seeing anybody face to face. It was all telework. My PTSD was full-blown. I felt like I was going crazy. I had this record playing in my head about how we were supposed to accept the maiming and killing as just an act of war, and those who died as the enemy instead of people. If civilians were lost, we were told we couldn't help it. But to me, so many of those killed in villages were innocent. While I didn't allow myself to think about it, deep down I knew what it was to be that innocent.

As I was getting ready to retire, I was handling things to make sure my family was financially secure, and then I decided that I was going to disappear. I was just going to crawl into a foxhole. I was toxic to my family. I was drinking. I was distant. I was in my head all the time, hearing and seeing things about what I had witnessed, what I had done. Looking back, it seems as if my entire career was about dealing with death.

Then one day I drove a young woman in my troop to the airport. She was flying to attend a young adult treatment program at the Meadows' young adult program. She was twenty-four, had been in the military four years, and was having a lot of psychiatric problems.

Forty-five days later, when I picked her up, I thought I had a different person in my car. I couldn't believe what I saw and heard. I asked her what happened there, and she told me all about herself and what the treatment program was like. To my surprise, I found myself telling her about my problems, and she told me I needed to go to treatment. Inspired by what I saw in her, I went to the mental health department that week and said I needed to go to treatment too.

By that time, I went to bed every night worried my suburban California house was going to get bombed. I looked at my wife and kids, and all I could hear and see were scenes from Iraq. I drank to quiet the images. I had been having panic attacks for years. I was surviving on water and alcohol, eating only enough to mask the smell of alcohol. Truth be told, I was a hot mess.

On a Mission

I knew I needed help, but I was scared. I didn't know what to expect. So I went to treatment with the attitude that I was on a mission, and the mission was to get fixed. And if I didn't get fixed, I was going to find that foxhole and never come out.

The first assignment I had was to talk about my life up to the age of seventeen. I had decided my problems started after I joined the military, so I was angry they wanted me to talk about my childhood. I had told myself that I had already come to grips with it. The truth was, I hadn't done anything other than to put it in a box, shove it in the closet, and leave it there.

As I started working on my timeline, the tears began. I grew up in El Salvador, where I was the rich kid on the block. We were upper middle class, with a two-story, three-bedroom house, and I had remote control cars and lots of toys, whatever I wanted.

But this was during the civil war, so as a young boy, I was trained on how to detect tripwires and recognize mail bombs. Going to school, I would sit near the back door of the bus because you never knew when somebody was going to bomb the bus, throw a Molotov cocktail, or set it on fire. This was just a fact of life.

I saw lots of killings. One day when I was eight, a bunch of us kids were walking up a stairwell heading to school when the seven-year-old girl next to me was blown to pieces, the bottom half of her suddenly gone. I freaked out. I turned and ran. I told myself, "Get it together, don't freak out, don't cry." I was shaking when I got home. But I was also quiet and stoic, as if nothing happened. Yet I saw the whole thing. It's still vivid in my mind. I saw the body, I saw people rushing, crying, everybody freaking out.

Border Crossing

When I was nine, we immigrated to the United States because the rebels were starting to kidnap kids and make them into soldiers. My dad went a few months ahead of us. A few months later my mom, sister, and I fled in secrecy. We didn't know what to expect, so we dressed up in our Sunday best. We flew to a city next to the border, stayed in somebody's house, and then were driven for a while and ended up in an alley.

We did what we were told to do. We had to hop a wall, get over some dumpsters, and make our way through some fencing. Then we reached a field that took us to a bridge that would take us into the United States. At one point we were spotted by some officials who shined their lights on us. Maybe the way we were dressed confused them, but they left us alone. We made it across the bridge, crossed the border, and ultimately made it to where my dad lived in Southern California.

When I got to the United States, I didn't know how to speak English, but after three months of watching TV and reading books only in

English, I was speaking it fluently. We were living in somebody's garage with a sheet for walls, and we didn't have any toys. I went from getting anything I wanted to having nothing. I went from having grandparents who loved me to being alone.

Part of my survival was not acknowledging that I missed people. I wired myself to not get close to people. I wanted friends, but I didn't know how to keep them. I hated living like that.

I joined ROTC when I was in high school because I wanted to be one of the good guys. I wanted to protect people. I didn't want people to live in fear like I did.

I started college, but I also had to work because being illegal meant that I couldn't get any scholarships. I soon met my future wife, and she got pregnant shortly after we met. I had a pretty decent job, but we didn't have health benefits.

By this time in my life, I had only lived in garages. Throughout high school each move was into a slightly bigger garage. We also lived in inner-city communities with lots of drug dealers and drive-by shootings. I was working hard for a new life, and I couldn't accept that the future mother of my child would be relegated to deprivation. When 9/11 occurred, I had my green card which allowed me to enlist in the military.

I Didn't Want to Be That Monster

Doing the timeline exercise made me realize that I was not okay with everything that happened in my childhood. That led me to work extensively with a trauma therapist and do a lot of EMDR. The first session was tough. I was sitting there following a light with my eyes, which is a part of the process. I could feel the gun in my hands. I felt the trigger. I felt the recoil. Then I started going back to that scared kid in El Salvador. There was this monster, and I left that monster behind when I came to the United States. When 9/11 happened, that monster came after me, so then I became that monster and I went after others. But I didn't want to be that monster. I just wanted to live in peace.

The biggest moment for me in treatment was realizing how scared I was as a little boy and how traumatic everything had been in my childhood—and that the kid inside me was still afraid. My inner child didn't want to be a monster, and he didn't want to play with monsters. I cried a lot during treatment. I took my tears to my therapist, who reminded me that everyone was there for me, that I wasn't going to walk through the pain of my memories alone.

There are things about my story I couldn't share, details regarding my work, but at treatment they taught me how to talk about my feelings, my thoughts, and how to talk about the present. My past influences my present, so it's acknowledged.

It was a relief to talk about my drinking and validating to hear other guys talk about their alcoholism too. Alcohol was tearing up my body; I felt like an old man. I'm forty years old, and I was getting winded when I walked. I felt physical pain. Turns out it was all alcohol. While in treatment, I started to go to the gym twice a day and did five miles on the elliptical most days.

Finding Peace

Today, two years after I left treatment, I'm at peace with a lot of things. My memories are very manageable. I don't have panic attacks or nightmares. I'm on medication for anxiety and depression. I don't put myself in triggering situations. I see a trauma-trained therapist. I continue to use the CES (*Cranial Electrical Stimulation*) machine regularly, which helps to regulate my brain waves to lessen anxiety.

After everything I have survived, I don't want to die, and I certainly don't want the bottle taking me out. That would be pretty embarrassing. I try to do everything I can to not go back to feeling fear and then acting out in rage, which at this point is directed only at myself.

I shared so much of myself and my dark place with others in treatment that I feel safe with that group. For now, they are my main support system. A small group of us do virtual check-ins or have twelve-step meetings during the week. We also reach out independently if we want to chat more. I can be honest with them.

My kids are now twenty-three and seventeen, and I want to be a good parent to both of them. My wife is working on some of her issues, and we are working on our relationship. But first I had to work on myself. Since retirement and feeling like I have a basis to my recovery, I've just started back to college studying psychology. This continues to be a time to think through what I want to do. I need time to learn how to be Carlos.

◆ ◆ ◆

Fight or Flight
By Peter Levine, PhD, Sr. Fellow

On a biological level, success doesn't mean winning, it means surviving, and it doesn't matter how you get there. All species of animals develop mechanisms that are well-suited to keeping them safe. To avoid attack and detection, the zebra uses camouflage; the turtle hides in its shell; the mole burrows; dogs roll over in submissive posture. Universal and primitive defense behaviors are called the *fight or flight strategies*. If the threatened animal is likely to lose the fight, it will run if it can. These choices are not thought out, they are instinctually orchestrated by certain parts of our brain. When neither fight or flight will ensure safety, we may resort to *freezing*, or immobility, which is just as universal, basic, and viable in a threatening situation.

The objective of all of these protective mechanisms is to stay alive until the danger has passed. However, humans can inadvertently get stuck in the stress response. Trauma occurs as a result of the initiation of the instinctual cycle that is not allowed to finish. Yet there are many effective strategies for becoming unstuck, for releasing ourselves from the terrible grip of trauma, for good.

COMMENTARY

From Peter Levine, PhD, Sr. Fellow

As a child, Carlos could not fight, but he could flee (see sidebar "Fight or Flight"); as a young child he physically fled the El Salvadoran military, and later, as a family they fled their country. As a young adult, he took on a fight response; wanting to be one of the good guys, he joined the ROTC to protect people so they wouldn't have to live in fear like he did. Then when he was in that first threatening situation in the military, having the resources as a soldier, he fought for real.

It is gut-wrenching when Carlos describes his first experience of killing civilians, and how it opened him to "pure rage and hatred," another trauma response. This is sometimes called *moral injury*. Moral injury is when one feels they have violated their conscience or moral compass when they take part in, witness, or fail to prevent an act that disobeys their own values or personal principles. But I think that applying this term in Carlos's case misses the point, because his rage is more a trauma response, not just a violation of his morals. In Iraq, he randomly killed anyone on the ground from his helicopter. This was his rage, which was a trauma response going back to childhood. In his therapy, he was able to recall an episode from when he was eight and was walking up a stairwell at school when a seven-year-old girl was blown to pieces in front of his eyes. He recalled shaking when he returned home, and how he then told himself: "Get it together, don't freak out, don't cry."

In treatment, Carlos's tears started to flow as he began to recover and re-own his hurt inner child. He had the chance to own and put to rest his childhood fears, pain, and helplessness. He found other ways to cope when his vulnerability was triggered. He no longer needed to disappear, rage, or medicate his pain with alcohol in an attempt to function.

Regardless of the particular war, it is our responsibility as healers to offer healing for these warriors.

From Deirdre Stewart, MS

Being exposed to war as a child, and being a soldier in active duty naturally led Carlos to feel fear when there was no true imminent danger. The parts of his brain that monitor for danger remained overactivated. This can happen to anyone who experiences a traumatic event. Even the slightest sign of danger—real or imagined—can trigger a stress response. We may overreact, lack patience, be unable to relax or focus, to a name a few. When trauma is left untreated, this excess energy in the nervous system becomes so chronic that we can resort to certain behaviors (such as social isolation) or substances (such as alcohol) that help to calm the excess activation, albeit temporarily.

Carlos embraced every aspect of treatment, and was particularly helped by the *CES machine*, one of many tools used in the Brain Center. The CES machine recalibrates the nervous system so that someone with PTSD can get unstuck from hypervigilance and the fight-or-flight response and experience a state of relaxation and inner calm. The machine supported Carlos's recovery from addiction to alcohol, helped him to not overreact and move into rage, and made it easier for him to socially connect. The "wiring" that was keeping Carlos from getting close to people was created by his trauma. Developing an inner calmness on a regular basis rewires the brain and creates a lot of possibilities he was not able to previously experience, one of them genuine friendship.

Carlos also had a lot of success with *EMDR*, which stands for *Eye Movement Desensitization and Reprocessing*. EMDR focuses on following a thread of subconscious thought and reprocessing the traumatic memory so it can be stored in a more organized and coherent way. How someone adapted to a traumatic event and how they currently relate to that experience is what creates the suffering. EMDR heals by changing the nature of memory so that it is no longer disturbing or distressing and triggers dissipate.

From Jean Collins, LCSW

As with Carlos, many of our clients find working with their *inner child* extremely important in their recovery process. In the various Meadows' programs, we introduce Pia Mellody's "inner child" work, which includes working with the "wounded child" and "adapted child" ego states. The inner child is the part of us that is inherently valuable, vulnerable, imperfect, dependent, and spontaneous. The wounded child is the part of self that results from not being nurtured adequately in our early childhood. It is a part that represents the preciousness of being a young child, in our innocence, that was hurt by the actions of others. It holds the feelings that most often were not able to be acknowledged or expressed.

Carlos said, "I was realizing how scared I was as a little boy, and that kid inside me was still afraid. My inner child didn't want to be a monster like those soldiers, and I didn't want to play with monsters." The adapted child portrays how that wounded child morphs into their survival state, often creating a false sense of self. Its role is to protect the wounded child. Carlos was taught how to show compassion and listen to both the wounded and adapted parts. This was significant in his healing process.

Undaunted Hope

We all have our own complicated stories, and most of us can identify times of trauma in our life. As painful as the experience may have been, it has not robbed you of your beauty. You are not your trauma; it is something that happened to you. You don't have to live with the residual negative effects. It begins with a willingness to show up for yourself. This may happen in baby steps: by reading a book about trauma, hearing another's story that has some semblance to yours, or sharing with someone a few of the struggles you have kept hidden. You don't have to shout from a rooftop what has happened to you, but allow others to shine the light that is hard for you to see and provide the safety to venture down the path of self-discovery.

CHAPTER THREE

Holding Out for Hope
RECOVERY FROM DEPRESSION

I thought this is just the way it was, I had no idea
I was looking at the world through a dark lens.

I hated my life and just didn't see how it could get any better.

It was as if I lived in this hole, full of self-hate,
feeling different from everyone else.

Abraham Lincoln, the sixteenth president of the United States, wrote most eloquently about his struggles with depression: "I am now the most miserable man living. If what I feel were equally distributed to the whole human family, there would be not one cheerful face on the earth. To remain as I am is impossible; I must die or be better, it appears to me."

For those of us struggling with *major depressive disorder*, his description speaks to the dark hole we often feel sucked into. In this classic form of depression, we don't see any light; we can't imagine how life can get better. It can be a debilitating way of living. We don't want to leave our house, don't want to talk to other people. If we do manage get out, we count every hour we are at work or school, just wanting to be somewhere else. We hate everyone around us, including ourself. We assume no one can understand how we feel or why, because we don't really understand it.

There's also a less conspicuous but nonetheless a serious form of depression, called *dysthymia*, that deprives us of inner joy in spite of outer appearances. We smile while everyone laughs at a funny joke, but we don't feel the humor in it. We feel lost, flailing without direction. We may have people around us and may even have incredible social skills, but we feel emotionally disconnected. We can be highly functioning, managing a household of kids, performing well at work or school, and yet have thoughts of suicide.

If we are depressed, we experience life as if we are wearing sunglasses with a dark tint, everything shaded by negative thoughts. We see all of the possible painful things that could happen, we make assumptions about failing or not being accepted. We find fault with the positive things that happen to or surround us. Our thoughts and emotions are dominated by our *inner critic*, that inner voice that is incessantly judging and criticizing us. We may have obvious outward signs of struggle, or we may be skilled at compartmentalizing our pain—either way, we are unnecessarily hard on ourselves.

Bipolar disorder is a type of depression where people experience significant fluctuations in mood, going from despondent to periods marked by extremely high energy or activity. Some women struggle with depression that is specific to hormonal changes that occur during or after pregnancy, called *perinatal depression*. And there are other types of depression with varying symptoms. Depression does not show up in everyone exactly the same. Also know that males and females frequently present symptoms differently.

To mask the depression, we sometimes turn to addictive substances or behaviors. Of course, this only worsens our symptoms and makes it harder for us to find peace.

But why do we become depressed in the first place? And how come we can't just snap out of it?

Like all mental illness, depression is complicated. Some of us are genetically predisposed, giving us a greater likelihood to experience depression, particularly if there is psychological injury. Depression can be attributed to incomplete sorrow, meaning that we can become stuck in a grief process. Depression is also strongly fueled by distorted thinking, when we engage in an exaggerated thought process not based in fact or reality, only see the negative in situations, catastrophize, or have similar distressing thoughts. Current research correlates rising depression and increased use of social media; young people are particularly vulnerable to internalizing toxic media messages, causing them to have thoughts like, "I'm not good enough" or "I don't have enough."

But possibly the biggest contributor to depression is growing up with adverse childhood experiences, which we discussed in Chapter One. These include various forms of neglect, abuse, or abandonment. Whether or not we are in that debilitating dark hole or joylessly going through the motions of life, the message our society gives us is that we are not supposed to feel like this. After all, "we have so much in our life to be happy about, to be grateful for," which simply reinforces our self-loathing.

The bottom line is this: if you are depressed, you likely hate not just your life but also yourself. As impossible as it may sound, there is a way out. Everyone deserves happiness, and it's possible for you, just as it was possible for the individuals in this chapter. The following narratives describe the complexity of life that can create depression, but also offer hope that you can live your life differently.

Hiding Within Myself   BY BRE

I think I have always been depressed. In some ways, always scared and not trusting that things were going to be okay, too. I got disconnected from my feelings pretty young. I started my life in foster care. When I was five, I was adopted into a family who seemed to care about me. I don't remember much about those first five years. My biological mom gave up her parental rights in the hospital, and no dad was ever identified.

When I first came to my new home, I had my own room. I had never had my own room before. It was scary, and my parents would often find me cuddled up in a corner of the bedroom in the morning. I don't remember doing that; they told me this story later. I didn't know that adoption meant I wouldn't be given back. So it took me a few years to trust they wanted to keep me.

I had a brother and sister, and they were in many ways my best friends. But being Black adopted into a white family, I always stood out in our basically white community. While shy, I did like school. I always felt like

I was the class pet, though. In some ways kids wanted to be my friend because I was different—and there was no pretending I wasn't. But my siblings didn't treat me like I was their pet. We did a lot of the normal kid stuff: played, had secrets from our parents, laughed, even got mad at each other. I was fortunate in many ways.

Then my dad got cancer. He looked really bad, and I was sure he was going to die. I was in high school, and I didn't want to leave the house to go to school or to see friends. I just wanted to stay at home and help if I could. While my parents reassured the three of us kids that he would be okay in time, I didn't trust it.

In the next few years, my dad got better, then worse. Since education was pushed on us, the plan was to go to college. I was really good in science and thought I might pursue that. I chose a college in the same state as my family so I could return home a lot. My brother and sister did the same thing.

Quietly on the Outside

College was much more culturally diverse, and I was intrigued with being around so many people who looked like me. I excelled in the sciences, I think because it is such a logical subject that I found it safe for me. I had an interest in guys, but that was a strange world to traverse. In some ways I was more comfortable being around white guys, but it was the Black guys who showed an interest in me. I felt as if I lived my life in two worlds that didn't really reconcile.

Then I met a guy who was a Black History major and encouraged me to take some classes. This is when my low-level depression got stronger. I started to question myself. I started to really look at my body and wonder what my mother may have looked like. I didn't want to think about my mom because she didn't want me. Then I began to wonder "Where was that biological dad of mine? Did he know I existed? Did my mom have other kids? Did she raise them? Why didn't some grandparents or aunts and uncles show up?" These thoughts flitted through my brain periodically. I had never been too interested in my original family history, and no one ever talked to me about it either. It was as if the stork had delivered me into the white world, and I just navigated in it.

The more I got into Black History classes, the more I found myself confused, sad, and angry. But I knew I had a better life than my first mom could have ever given me. My family loved me, and I loved them. Yet I felt as if I was trying to move away from them, betraying them, by thinking about my original family. So I just stayed busy and tried not to question things so much.

My World Coming Undone

My dad was better by the time I graduated, so I made plans for medical school. I was really busy, very stressed, and yet liking it. Then one day I got a call from a woman who said she was my sister. I didn't know what to do. I didn't know if I was happy or terrified. What did she want? What did I want? I felt as if my world had just come undone.

Well, she wanted to get together. I put her off for several weeks, but she kept calling. Her upbringing wasn't nearly as good as mine. She was in foster care until she aged out. She was struggling to support herself. She was dependent on a lot of guys. I didn't know how to relate to her, as she seemed so different from me. Then after a couple months of talking she started to ask me for money. She started telling me how much better my life was than hers and that I owed her. We didn't have anything in common other than we were my mother's rejects. And that our mom had died a few years earlier. I was keeping all of this a secret from my family.

Then the depression started to escalate. I was having a hard time concentrating on my academics. I was distracted when I was on the floor in my internship. I didn't understand what was happening. I felt like I traversed the day in a hazy fog; it was slow, but it was persistent. I started to have nightmares. I was out in a lake, a long way from shore, and I was drowning and no one was coming for me. I was hollering to my dad, who was on the shore, and then he evaporated into thin air. The dream ended only to return nights later. This went on for months.

In the next year and a half, I gained forty-five pounds, and for being five foot four that was a lot. I didn't know how to tell my family about this sister of mine and what all of it meant to me. Then again, I wasn't sure what it meant. It meant I did have family, yet I had the one that raised me. Could I have both? Did I even want my sister in my life? After all, it didn't take her long to start to take advantage of me. Would other siblings show up, and did I want that? By then, I had both white and Black women friends, but I only told one white friend about this sister. And I felt guilty talking to my Black friends for some reason I didn't understand.

I didn't feel like I had the right to be distraught over this. I told myself to be grateful that I was given the beautiful family that embraced me, loved me, and wanted the best for me. I told myself the color of family did not matter. I thought my Black friends would not be accepting of me if I shared my conflicting feelings with them, and I was afraid I would lose my adopted family if I told them. So rather than get honest with people, I just kept faking life. But as I was getting close to finishing med school and having to choose a residency, I began to wonder, do I even want to be a doctor?

One night, when I was driving home for the holidays, I was listening to a podcast about a Black woman who had committed suicide. She had been Miss USA, and they called her a "high-functioning" depressed person. The experts talked about people hiding depression. That's when I began to think about whether I needed help.

I decided to go to counseling. After about five sessions, the therapist suggested I go to treatment. She told me she thought I could address these issues over time, but that I would jump start my healing with a more intensive experience. I was willing to trust her judgment and I was tired of hiding, so I went to treatment.

Reconciliation

One more time I was in the racial minority, but there were other people of color among the staff and patients, which I appreciated. I had a lot of feelings—especially conflicted feelings of being raised in a white home. I knew I had to talk about that, but I also had a lot of guilt for even wanting to question what my family had given me.

One of the most valuable pieces of being in treatment was trying to reconcile these different parts of me that I felt were operating against each other. I had the Black me, the white me, the scared me, the achiever, the chameleon. I even had an angry me that I needed to explore, as I had nearly extinguished all my anger.

I also did symbolic work around my two biological parents. I wrote letters to them that I read to the group. I told them about my life and thanked them for allowing me to be adopted, but I also let them know I wished their lives had been different, that they missed out on being able to raise some beautiful children. It was hard, but I felt like something was lifted from me that had been holding me down. It was all a part of reclaiming my color, my beauty, my value.

I realized I had a lot of fear of loss, as I was the product of loss. My dad's illness triggered feelings of my not being safe in the world, and of being abandoned physically (one more time). I explored the walls I put up in friendships that got in the way of being genuinely close to others. Rather than risk anyone leaving me, I convinced myself that I wasn't important and that it was easier to keep a distance. This may have been obvious to others, but I thought of myself as just introverted.

I was put on a fairly low dose of medication for depression that helped get me to a place where I could engage in the psychotherapy. The staff was really good at not letting me be invisible in my quietness, my pleasantness. They frequently held the feeling list up to me and asked me what was under that quietness.

Family week was huge. My parents shared their concerns they had over the years about how potential original family members could reach out to me and what that would mean for me. They owned that they didn't know how to help me embrace my Blackness. They were vulnerable.

I told them how grateful I was for the life they had given me, and the love they showed. That I did love them and still needed to own my Blackness—and didn't want that ownership to build a wall. They assured me it would not. They expressed regret about not broaching the whole issue of my being Black openly. We all cried, every one of us. Then we talked about my dad's illness and how it impacted us individually. We cried some more there too. But a lot of our tears were ones of being happy we could all be so honest with each other.

No Longer Hiding

Since treatment, I finished my residency and ended up in child psychiatry. I love it. I work in a major hospital in a highly culturally diverse community, where we see a lot of children who are like I once was. They have been abandoned, transient, and a part of the community's social systems. I have become connected to the African American medical community. My social circle is ethnically mixed, and I am able to enjoy both without conflicted feelings.

I found out I had two biological brothers I didn't know about; one has died, the other and I share letters, and time will tell whether or not we will see each other.

I have never felt closer to my family and siblings. I feel so much more real with them. And with my parents, in particular, there is a new feeling of being more relaxed with each other. I find myself able to share things I had tried not to think about. It's a whole new beginning.

I am dating and am hopeful I will find the right relationship. I am only thirty-two. I am glad I have gone through all of this before I commit to someone.

As far as depression, it's really not there. My eating is healthy. I exercise. Mostly my issue was about hiding within myself, and I am no longer willing to do that.

◆ ◆ ◆

Adoption

By Claudia Black, PhD, Sr. Fellow (Pioneer in Addictive Family Systems, Clinical Architect of Claudia Black Young Adult Center)

When people come to treatment, rarely is adoption a presenting issue; most often it is simply a fact on a form. Yet when it comes to depression, anxiety, oppositional defiant behaviors, and relationship problems, having been adopted is often a contributing factor.

The following are some of the variables that can influence psychological development in an adoptee:

- Age at time of adoption

- Family environment prior to relinquishment

- Reason for relinquishment

- Reason for adopting
- Time and setting between relinquishment and adoption
- Open or closed adoption
- Manner in which child discovers they were adopted
- Awareness of siblings in original family
- Strength and health of adoptive family

More likely than not, adoption results in greater happiness for everyone involved. Nonetheless, adoption-related issues that bring clients to treatment include

- Loss, often an ambiguous unknown but felt sense
- Sense of Rejection, whereby an adoptee personalizes the need for adoption and wonders what was wrong with them that their biological parents did not keep them
- Fear of Abandonment, a fear that others will reject and consequently abandon them
- Guilt, a felt sense of not being good enough to have been kept, or for leaving other siblings behind
- Toxic Shame, internalized belief they lack value, often harboring the belief they don't have the right to exist (see sidebar "Toxic Shame")
- Inability to trust in others
- Identity Issues, which lead to the all-important question, "Who am I?" which then goes unanswered

Addressing these issues does not lessen the love experienced in the adoptee's family. Rather, it allows the adoptee to resolve problems that are getting in the way of healthy relationships with others, as well as themselves. It creates a better foundation for overall personal growth, with great potential to offer them an inner peace they have not previously felt.

COMMENTARY

From Whitney Howzell, PhD, MPH
(Executive Director, Claudia Black Young Adult Center)

Unfortunately, lack of emotional connection can be common among Black women, often influencing misleading stereotypes, like being intimidating, or tropes, such as the "strong Black woman." As Bre found out, when you do not acknowledge your past or try to heal from your trauma, you may develop other mental health problems, such as depression, anxiety, PTSD, hypertension, and substance use disorders. In fact, eight out ten Black women will experience trauma in their lifetime. Historically, Black women have suffered in silence, using their pain to reinforce a shield of resilience.

Disconnecting from your emotions in predominantly white institutions (PWIs) can be both a conscious and unconscious protective factor. From my own experiences, in these environments, it's lonely, and you can feel like a token or "class pet" (like Bre cited). Nonetheless, you try to be invisible, dawn a mask of "pleasantness," succeed and even excel, or just try and blend in. It's truly a daily practice of assimilation to fit in, protect yourself from rejection, and survive. The psychological trauma incurred by Black people during the process of assimilation can be acute. And this type of trauma may be more complex when Black children are adopted into white families, particularly as the adopted child becomes curious about their biological family and ethnic culture.

It is normal for young adults to have questions about who they are or who they would like to become. While not all adoption circumstances are the same, if one is adopted, this question is often more confusing and troublesome. As well, this question is still relevant and being sorted through when entering college or leaving home. You may be exposed to different people and cultures for the first time. In Bre's case, the experience of being around "people who looked like me," was intriguing yet uncomfortable. Of course, Black people are not all the same, but often there is an underlying connection of culture via oppression and similar lived experiences among Black Americans. Bre, having grown up in a white household may have only been able to relate superficially to other

Black people. I would think this experience dredged up complicated emotions that served as a catalyst for her individuation process.

Using the Black Racial Identity Model originally developed by Cross in the early nineties, we can conceptualize the process of Bre forming her identity. The pre-encounter stage is characterized by the dominant white world lens and a passive denigration of one's own racial group. The encounter stage describes an experience or series of events that forces an individual to acknowledge the impact of the white world view of their life, such as encountering racism, discrimination, or different cultures. In Bre's situation, it occurred as she left her home and entered a college community that was much more racially diverse than she had been exposed to, and in meeting her biological sister. Bre's curiosity and immersion into Black history is an example of the immersion/emersion stage. Here an individual seeks opportunities to learn about aspects of Black culture and history and socialize more with people of the same racial background. The internalization stage is marked by a sense security in oneself racial identity, a nuanced definition of "Blackness" based on their personal lived experiences and values.

Racial identity is an important aspect of self-concept and may safeguard against the psychological effects of racism and other forms of discrimination. Bre's shaky self-concept was linked to fear of not being accepted by her Black friends and the fear of losing her adopted family. This seemed to trigger old wounds of abandonment, ultimately resulting in compulsive overeating, extreme busyness, and relational reactions such as avoidance, trouble trusting others, and feelings of detachment. The work Bre did in treatment strengthened her self-concept.

From Resmaa Menakem, SEP, LICSW, Sr. Fellow
(Chaperone of Abolitionism Philosophy and Practice)

Bre is a Black body born from another Black body that has been impacted by 500 years of *white-body supremacy*. She has inherited those hundreds of years, producing high levels of cortisol, epinephrine, and adrenaline in the nervous system that influences the body to recoil from something or lean into something. Bre is a soup of cortisol, carrying an energy load that shows up with feelings of vibrations but no context for it, a load that the people who are caring for her have not had to contend with. As loving and as kind as Bre's adopted family were, as white bodies they were inadequate to deal with the day-to-day ravages of historical racism.

While addressing childhood issues is important, the historical, intergenerational, persistent, and institutional racism creates an internal constriction that white bodies can't contextualize for the Black body. And the Black body picks up on this as something they need to be protected from. Bre says, "I felt as if I live in two worlds that did not reconcile. And mostly my issue was about hiding within myself." Reconciling does not contend with the charge in our bodies. And that charge can show up as confusion, anger, or in her case, annihilation. For *bodies of culture*, the charge she carries happened to whole communities. Developing an individual response to the charge of communal horror is inadequate. The protective response is to go inside because she couldn't contend with 500 years of charge. She needs a container in which to hold and navigate that charge, and it begins with community. And if you don't have other bodies that look like yours to hold that charge, it's going to be really hard to manage. Nonetheless, building a container doesn't just happen by surrounding yourself with people who look like you.

Dealing with historical racism must be done from an embodied place, not a cognitive place. Trauma does not live in our brains or emotions but in our bodies. Healing from racialized trauma needs to begin in our bodies. The charge in our bodies needs to be metabolized. We need to slow down the charge and discern pieces of it.

As generations of racialized trauma have been held in the body, allowing yourself to pause and recognize the vibrations, the sensations, the feelings, meaning, and behavior will be essential in addressing the experiences of feeling unsettledness and the constricted energetic load.

From Dick Schwartz, PhD, Sr. Fellow
(Developer of Internal Family Systems)

Bre emerged from her adoption experience with a plethora of vulnerable feelings: being abandoned by her mother, guilt that her adopted family was loving and so much better off than her siblings, afraid to upset her family by talking about her racial identity confusion, disconnected from them, and alone because she couldn't talk about it.

To survive, she had to lock all of that away. She distracted herself from all the inner chaos and polarization by striving in school and trying to please everyone around her and telling herself she should feel lucky. As is true for so many, that strategy works until it doesn't. Bre's encounters with her biological sister triggered feelings of abandonment and guilt. Her experiences with new Black friends triggered feelings of loneliness and difference.

While at The Meadows, Bre was able to identify the parts of her that felt hurt and examine how they relate to one another. She was also able to listen to each of them with acceptance, to help them listen to and reconcile with each other. She was able to get past the parts of her that were chameleon-like and bent on achieving and listen to the part of her that was angry at her family for ignoring that she was Black. The *Internal Family Systems* model of therapy was very helpful in this situation. This set the stage for family sessions that were moving. Her family was able to get past their fears and their feelings of inadequacy to help her with her identity struggles. Whenever family members are able to drop the defenses they used for protection and speak their truth, healing happens. During family week, Bre didn't have to hide who she was any longer and instead felt accepted and loved. The healing started when she was honest with her feelings and had the courage to share them.

Childhood with Secrets   BY RICH

I have come to believe there are no secrets so bad that you don't deserve a better life. I had to learn that the hard way. I also had to learn that other people out there really do care about me. And that I deserve that. Wow, even saying that now—that I deserve to have caring people in my life—that's a big one for me.

I grew up with my single mom and younger brother, never knowing who my dad was. My mom presented herself in the community as this kind, caring woman with the woes of raising two boys by herself. But at home she was physically abusive toward me—for some reason not toward my brother. I often got hit on the side of my head as I walked through the door coming home from school. She might be upset that I hadn't made my bed that morning, or because I left my breakfast plate on the kitchen table, or because I wore a dirty shirt to school—really slight things that I guess made her look like a bad mother. I never knew what I did to deserve the abuse, but whatever the offense, she sometimes made me stay in my room for hours, days in a row, with no electronics. She brought me some food, thank heaven.

School was a good escape for me. I was liked and did well academically. By the seventh grade, I was the token gay kid. None of us talked about it, but it seemed like people accepted me for who I was. In high school, I had one really good friend, Katie. She and I did a lot of leadership at school together. She even campaigned for me when I ran against a popular jock for Student Body President. I won. She and I also created a youth center for teens. We located the premises, garnered fundraising, and opened it up. We were a good team.

But I had this secret life the last couple of years in school. I would hitchhike to a neighboring community and connect with guys I found online. My sexual behavior certainly wasn't safe. Then I'd return home and try not to displease my mom.

By my senior year of high school, I was secretly using drugs that I was getting from my weekend escapades. In spite of my use, I was still doing well in my classes. Then prior to graduation, I won first prize in a national speech contest. This was a prestigious event in that there were only one thousand high school students across the United States and Canada to win. The prize was to meet up with other winners and go to the United Nations in New York City and then to the Capitol in Washington DC. But on graduation night, I got so loaded on drugs and went so crazy at this party that the cops were called. As a consequence, I lost the opportunity to go on the trip.

Life Just Not Working Out

Hoping to attend medical school, I went on to college. Unfortunately, with all of the freedom I now had, my use of drugs and my secretive sexual behaviors escalated. I amassed a record that prevented me from applying to med school. By the time I received the rejection, I had already significantly tapered my behaviors and ended up pursuing a degree in microbiology.

Over the years, I was successful professionally in medical research, but my relationships were suffering. I always got into relationships with guys who I wound up taking care of. My partners were often younger than me. I usually supported them financially, bought them nice things, took them on great trips. I didn't want them to leave me. But I didn't like me, so why should they? There was this feeling of not having enough of me that was likeable, so I tried to buy their love and my security.

In between relationships were lonely times for me. On weekends I would find myself not changing my clothes, spacing out on movies all day, and not leaving the house. I had all this negative self-talk going on about not deserving people's love. It was torturous. But after a while, I would get back online and then be in another selfless relationship that would ultimately end, with the cycle repeating itself.

All of that time, I kept a sick relationship going with my mom where I was taking care of her financially and trying to make her life better, while she continued to be verbally abusive. She would say derogatory things about my being gay and tell me I would never find a boyfriend who really loved me. Then she would tell me how wonderful my brother as. I felt like a small, abused child just wanting her love. So I never llenged her.

en I suffered a significant financial setback when a friend I used ndle my financial investments stole huge sums of money from my nts. I was totally stressed out when the pandemic hit. The tipping vas I discovered that my then-partner was seeing other guys and me about it. I found myself driving to some dangerous places in nd just sitting, hoping I would get beat up, or, better yet, killed. ay to commit suicide, but that was my fantasy.

Entrance to a New Life

is dark place for about six months when one day my brother rough the front door and simply told me he was taking me ment program. He said that he had gone to a program for m, which I didn't know, and that they could work with my n and trauma. I was surprised because I had always dismissed ot caring about me. As a kid I had taken care of him, protected asn't sure what to make of this role reversal.

Initially I resisted and denied I was depressed. And what trauma? I didn't know what my brother was talking about. But he said when he was in treatment he found himself talking about our childhood and how strict and punitive our mother was. He shared how guilty he felt for me taking the abuse, and often for things he did. My brother had flown across the country, and he said he wasn't leaving without me. So I agreed to go on the condition that if I didn't like being there I would leave. I purchased an open ticket back home as my assurance.

In my mind I pictured a big brick psychiatric institution from the 1950s. My brother assured me it wasn't so. He said there was green grass and mountains in the background, and lots of cactus. Being from the East Coast, it was hard to picture.

Giving Up the Fight

When I got to The Meadows, I saw other people who looked normal. I realized how tired I was—tired of the pretense that I am fine. Tired of looking good for other people. Tired of taking care of others. Tired of wondering whether I am liked. I was emotionally spent. It was as if the ride across the country took any strength I had out of me.

The people there took care of me. They helped me to sleep; they fed me. They also put me on antidepressant medication. While I wouldn't have considered that before, once I was in there it made sense. The doctors talked to me like I was a human, not a patient to be condescended to. I met others who, like me, had successful professions and similar problems. And lo and behold, I even met a few other gay guys. But that didn't matter—what mattered was I was done hiding.

I realized that I was depressed, and that I had hated myself for most of my life. And that I had trauma. I knew what my mom did was wrong, but I was good at rationalizing her tough life as a single mom with two boys, one of them gay.

What really resonated with me was the Meadows Model, where the talked about our worth and value, and how, due to life circumstanc such as abuse, we think of ourselves as less than, not of value. They talk about how I had become needless, meaning I had denied my needs of them not being met when I was young. I identified with spend much of my life in the adapted state, not functional state, which me I was not operating from a place of esteem, not operating with g boundaries, but allowing others to take from me. I was giving too much of myself away while not taking care of myself. I came to realize that my relationships were like an addiction; I used them to anesthetize my pain. I was taking a hard look at my self-abuse over the years, and how I set myself up to be used.

In the trauma work, I was able to address the anger and shame I had from my mother. I also did work around not having a second parent to protect me, to nurture me, to model healthy behaviors for me. I liked the neurofeedback component and learning about nervous system regulation. I could actually see how my negative thinking increased my stress level. Better yet, it confirmed I had the ability to change my mood with my thinking.

My brother came to family week, where we talked about each other's experiences growing up. He also shared about his alcoholism. Life wasn't as good for him as I thought it was. I don't know how my life would've turned out if my brother hadn't come to my house that day.

A Work in Progress

I left treatment eighteen months ago, and since then I see the world differently. I asked my then-partner to leave; it wasn't a good relationship for me, though he certainly had been happy with me meeting all of his needs. For the time being, I have chosen not to be in a relationship or even chat online. I continue to work on myself and want some confidence in my newly found self before seeking a partner.

Recovery is a work in progress. Today I know the signs of when I am slipping, not active in my recovery practice. I know my negative self-talk. I know my behaviors. I work once a week with a Meadows-trained therapist. I also belong to a men's therapy and support group, and we meet weekly. I also downsized my practice so I don't have some of the work stress I had.

I set some boundaries with my mother. First, I sent her a letter and told her I wouldn't be in contact for a while because I was working on myself. I told her to not write back or call, as I would not answer, and that in time I would be in touch. Just a month ago, I wrote and said if she wanted, I would fly out for a short visit. I don't have any need to share with her the intricacies of my treatment or therapy, or even my life. I don't think she is healthy enough for me to have that conversation.

But out of the belief that she did try to raise the two of us boys and it had to be hard, I still value her, and seeing her says that. I'm confident I won't lose myself in her presence. I will need to continue to look at my boundaries with her and sort out my motives in financially helping and reassess how much I continue to do so.

One of the other things treatment triggered was realizing that there were and are people who have cared about me and who I lost touch with. So I located that woman from high school, Katie, and we are now corresponding. I need to pay attention to the positives in my life.

I have never been good at asking for help. But I have learned that I am worth asking for help. Because of my group therapy, I feel more connection to others. I have even attended social gatherings with a few of them. I also have pursued martial arts; it's something I have always had an interest in but never followed through with. It's been empowering and given me another place for social connection. I think life can only get better.

• • •

Toxic Shame

By Claudia Black, PhD, Sr. Fellow (Pioneer in Addictive Family Systems, Clinical Architect of Claudia Black Young Adult Center)

The primary consequence of living with abandonment is *toxic shame*, the painful feeling associated with the belief that who we are is not good enough, not okay, that we are inadequate, not worthy, or not of value. In time, toxic shame is not so much a feeling as it is a belief that becomes an emotional block.

People often confuse guilt and shame. Yet there is a fundamental difference between the two. Guilt is synonymous with remorse. It is what we feel when we realize we have made a mistake. Toxic shame is the feeling we have when we believe we are the mistake.

When we experience this shame, we feel as if there is something inherently wrong with who we are as opposed to what we have done or not done. Toxic shame makes us feel alienated, defeated, and not quite good enough to belong to our family, our community, to the human race. In short, toxic shame is a deep internal darkness, a psychological and emotional prison. Worse, it's a prison you believe you deserve to be in, believing you are inherently flawed.

Many trauma responses are manifestations of toxic shame. Perfectionism, rage, and controlling behavior are attempts to garner power over shame. Substance and behavioral addictions are a way of medicating the painful feeling. Depression and victimization are often ways we succumb to it.

None of us are born with the belief that we lack value. But hearing messages that tell us we need to be different than who and what we are is unavoidable since they're so prevalent in advertising, serial entertainment, and social media. Many of us can move on from this type of subtle but insidious bullying. But those who struggle with toxic shame most likely internalized these messages from the most important people in our lives: family. Be it blatant traumas such as physical abuse, or more subtle traumas, such as being subject to criticism, the messages internalized due to an unhealthy *family system* remain long after the traumatic events have ceased, often in the form of self-deprecating inner dialogue.

COMMENTARY

From Tian Dayton, PhD, Sr. Fellow
(Developer of Relational Trauma Repair/Sociometrics)

While Rich had secrets that had seriously undermined his ability to succeed, he also demonstrated powerful qualities of resilience. Some of these qualities are grit, initiative, intelligence, sociability, and his ability to mobilize supports in his environment both on his own behalf and on behalf of others. Rich's "grit" cut both ways, it gave him the ability to work hard and actualize his plans while at the same time endure some heart-wrenching behaviors. Long, painful isolation in his bedroom, coming home not knowing how he would be treated and not thinking he could do anything to stop his mother's abuse, took grit to endure. There are few more painful wounds than a parent's chronic disapproval, which can lead a child to depression, despair, and a feeling of deserving abuse. Virtually all children want to please their parents, such is the parents' evolutionary power over the child. Rich's not knowing his father and the pain he was forced to hide of his mother's abuse likely fueled his sexual acting out, which may have allowed him to feel wanted and valued.

Once Rich felt permission to open up in therapy, he could feel his real longing.

Equally important as calling out his abuse—so that Rich can identify a path out of his guilt, negative self-image, and shame and reframe his belief system so he no longer blames himself for his mother's abuse—is identifying and mobilizing the resilient qualities that he used in order to get through his childhood. He can now put those attributes to work in his own recovery.

From Claudia Black, PhD, Sr. Fellow
(Pioneer in Addictive Family Systems, Clinical Architect
of Claudia Black Young Adult Center)

Rich grew up with his father's absence, his mother's physical abuse, and hefty *emotional abandonment*. Emotional abandonment is when you are not valued for who you are, when your needs and feelings are not attended to on a consistent basis. It happens when parents are not willing to take responsibility for their thoughts and behaviors but want another to be responsible to them.

Due to his mother's abuse and his father's abandonment, Rich internalized the message that "I am not wanted," "I am bad." He was also subject to extreme homophobia on the part of his mother and systemic homophobia everywhere else, which reinforced his thinking there was something wrong with him. He would internalize these beliefs at a young age and then act out throughout his adult life.

Rich was also very skilled in *compartmentalizing*, a defense he learned as a child. Everyone learns to compartmentalize; as humans we need to do that to have daily order in our lives. For example, "I set aside my concerns at work as I re-enter the family home each eve." When you are raised in an environment that is not safe or secure, the need to compartmentalize what you are thinking and feeling is even greater. In addition, not conforming to a heterosexual identity only reinforced a stronger need to present one way at home and be and feel another way elsewhere. No one knew how insecure and afraid he was.

This is a set up for many mental health issues, and in Rich's case, depression.

Having his needs discounted in his family life, he continued that pattern in his relationships. His job was to make the other person happy, while his needs were not acknowledged or valued by himself or those he invited into his life. His self-talk was about not deserving other people's love, and it was torturous. Relationships, performing, and achieving would become Rich's addiction.

As vulnerable as people are when they seek or accept help, when they have been subject to various traumatizing experiences, there is always a resiliency that can be tapped into. His resiliency showed itself quickly in his recovery. For example, he ended a bad relationship; he sought out his high school friend, Katie, who represented something positive from his childhood; he was able to make a sincere commitment to therapy; he pushed himself to engage socially. Irrespective of our history, we can all find points of resilience in our selves.

From Jack Register, LCSW
(Claudia Black Young Adult Center)

Rich's story has elements of the toxic masculinity and hyper-independence that many queer men possess. It is as if the ways in which we lose the queer is to become more successful than others. The consequences of consistently comparing the "inside world" to the outside world and knowing we are not in alignment with it can be daunting. LGBTQIA+ folk grow up with a consistent sense that we are at odds with the world. We are surrounded by a culture that says what gender and sexuality should look like. We don't have the fairy tales or first crushes or presence in mainstream media that cisgender heterosexual people do. We don't have supportive legislation. Couple that with growing up with one parent that totally abandons you and then the other who physically taunts and abuses you, and it is a potent prescription for depression and many other life problems, such as choosing abusive partners. Rich's self-worth and his ability to achieve were in a constant contest.

Rich's examples of wanting to go and get beat up or even killed by strangers—as if there is no hope left for him—is an example of feeling so isolated that it becomes hard to breathe. In treatment, learning about the unconditional support of others in recovery—truly being accepted, even with the scars and pain of depression and shame—Rich was able to find a new path.

The move to unconditional acceptance and being seen by those around you as not only valuable but lovable goes a long way toward easing the isolation.

Rich's capacity to grow through this pain and find the community within recovery is a clear example of his resiliency in recovery.

Leaning into the Pain BY LAINEY

I was twenty-two when I drove myself to the emergency room suicidal. The people there didn't do much but ask me a lot of questions and then suggest I go to a traditional psychiatric program in my rural state. I didn't think I was psychotic or crazy, just severely despondent. I didn't want to live with wanting to die. I knew I would take my life at some point if I didn't get help. So I googled "treatment centers" and found the Claudia Black Young Adult Center (CBC). I came to treatment really wanting help. And the treatment saved my life.

The White Picket Fence

I came from the white picket fence home. I was groomed to be the consummate achiever. I had perfect grades and was a four-sport high school athlete credited as the hardest working player on the court or field. I learned to look people in the eyes, shake their hands, and have the appropriate greeting. I was constantly chasing down another project or accomplishing another big goal. My parents noticed my efforts and attended every event, game, or awards ceremony, but they only talked about games that did not go well, or the award that I had not won.

Throughout my childhood, my dad had been my primary role model. He'd had a perfect ACT score and started a multimillion-dollar engineering firm at the age of twenty-one—all the things I was striving for. I never got to be a little girl; I was always the little adult.

When I was eighteen, I dove into being a small business owner by starting an LLC and obtaining my personal training online certification, then started training clients. I went on to invest in a rental property that formulated a second LLC.

Achieve was the unspoken rule. This rule seems to have passed through the generations in my family. Feelings didn't exist in our family; looking good was what was important.

My white picket fence house was really a façade. My insides broke when I was sixteen, the year I accidentally discovered my dad was having an affair. I became angry and confused because I felt that I should have known sooner. I was also angry about having to tell my mom, if it was even my place to do so. I had such respect for my dad as a leader and business owner that I wondered why my mom couldn't make him happy and be what he wanted. I realize now my reasons for resenting my mom were just projections from my dad. But I didn't have any way to express all that; I couldn't talk about it.

I told my mom and brother, only to find out my mom had known about it for seven years. But the discovery blew up the family anyway. It led to an acrimonious divorce that took over four years, with nothing but fighting about money and business. I became the middleman.

Just Do More
All I knew to do was keep performing and achieving. "Just do more," I said to myself, "you will get there."

I was running as fast as I could, patting myself on the back and getting pats from everyone else. But there was always this hollowness. I reasoned that if I just did more, I would feel better. If I was not happy with what I was doing, then I just needed to try the next thing.

But eventually striving to always be the best, to exceed all expectations, had taken its toll. I was left feeling empty and in despair. I was close to finishing college with an industrial and management engineering degree, and I was three weeks away from my sixth national bodybuilding competition, when I hit a wall.

The wall was "I won't have anything to chase anymore" after the competition. Preparing for the competition takes a lot of self-discipline, grit, and energy from all aspects of well-being. I was chasing a perfect body image that I, quite frankly, was never going to have, and I knew that.

I had had suicidal thoughts before, thoughts about crossing the lane while I was driving and crashing head on into oncoming traffic. But with the looming competition ahead and the wall in front of me, I just couldn't do it anymore. I couldn't do life and I just wanted to die.

My Mask

When I went to my first therapy session at CBC, the therapist looked at my totally put-together mask and said, "Lainey, you have got to lean in to the pain."

As we talked, he kept confronting me about my mask and kept asking what was beneath that face. I didn't know what to do, but I knew I didn't want to die. So I went with the pain, and I got totally open with him.

I would also be diagnosed as bipolar. I had no idea; I knew I had high energy, but I thought I was just very motivated and driven. In hindsight, I was always juggling multiple projects and goals—and then I would suddenly snap. This was followed by bouts of keeping family and friends at a distance for long periods, allowing them to see the side of me I wanted them to see. I would stay home and be angry, and everyone knew it. I had a lot of really negative internal dialogue I carried in my head.

I was put on medication for my bipolar depression. The medication alleviated my moods that used to leave others walking on eggshells. Taking medication is a non-negotiable for me; it is the basis of my mental health.

I also had disordered eating related to my bodybuilding regimen. I followed my restrictive diet to the microgram of food. But I also had binge periods, and I would lose my menstrual cycle. I accrued a number of food intolerances. Plus, with my energy drinks I was also caffeine dependent.

I had never thought to identify with trauma, as I always saw it as the "big T" traumas, something very blatant like being in a car crash, or a hurricane, or domestic violence. But I came to understand "little t" traumas—and I had enough of those. A little t trauma can be anything that takes away your ability to know and feel your inherent value, your worth. I could identify with that, and seeing this was crucial for me. My biggest little t was not enough acceptance for being who I am. I didn't allow myself to be a child, experience pure joy, or be vulnerable when needed. My parents allowed me to do any activity, event, or program. I was involved in so much, yet was never able to establish my identity. I wore a million different hats and rotated them to reflect who I needed to be in that environment. Even behind closed doors, I was holding up an image that hindered me from getting to know who I really was. I have had to discover my worth and value for *being*, not just doing. It's harder than you think.

I had to grieve the loss of my family as I had wanted it to be. I had to learn to set healthier boundaries and not try to take care of other people. In treatment, it's easy to want to get into other people's lives and drama, but I kept getting redirected to step out and let others handle themselves.

I had to take my dad off his pedestal. I had to realize how much my fantasy of who he is crushed my spirit when I realized he had an affair. In time, I needed to tell my dad how his behavior impacted me. He was not capable of hearing it when I was in treatment, but when I left treatment, I was able to share it with him, and he heard me. I needed him to accept some accountability for how his behavior impacted both myself and my brother. Because of treatment I have learned to pick my battles.

Embracing Imperfection

Since treatment ended three years ago, I completed my undergraduate degree in industrial and management engineering and decided not to complete a master's in business administration, but have since completed a master's degree program in counseling. I would like to help others with depression and addiction. Addiction was not a part of my story, but I met a lot of young people with addiction, good people who were just struggling.

I also got married. He knows my story and is loving and respectful. We have mutual goals about what we want in a relationship and as a family. And we have a baby!

Throughout my pregnancy and postpartum, I was very communicative with my psychiatrist and OBGYN to monitor moods and symptoms, while remaining on my dosage of medication. Today I feel my emotions, which I appreciate. I also know that throwing a medication prescription at me without the therapy work I did, and what I continued to do after I left treatment, would have gotten me nowhere near where I am today.

Today I know what healthy eating is, but I had to get there slowly. I was messed up hormonally from bodybuilding and disordered eating habits, but I learned in treatment how to get better. I knew I could relapse if I ever wanted to bodybuild again. Even the gym is a trigger. Today I do one good workout a week and take my baby on a lot of walks. I continue to abstain from energy drinks. I drink coffee, however, I limit myself to one cup a day. I am confident I will be able to stay healthy and fit.

What helps during my recovery is that I stay connected to some of the young adults I went through treatment with. We understand each other and can talk freely, with a vulnerability that's hard to find in anyone except a lifelong friend. Probably with my tendency to be intellectual, I still love reading self-help books. They have helped me a lot. They give me a way to understand myself and then talk about it. I also still do journaling.

Today I embrace imperfection. Having the baby, I have to accept imperfection. It's okay for me to have a messy house, to not get all the household chores done. I recognize that I have only so much time, and so I don't try to do everything. I don't set unrealistic goals, and I don't chase false images.

I want others to know that they don't need to run from their pain, and they don't need to mask it. As I was told, *lean into it.*

Today I am free and very alive.

◆ ◆ ◆

Medication and Depression

By Madelyn Rousku, MD (Chief of Psychiatry at Claudia Black Young Adult Center)

Current guidelines continue to recommend both medication management and therapy as the gold standard treatment for most depression and anxiety disorders, based on ongoing evidence that the combination of both is more effective than either one alone. It is important to recognize the type of depression we are dealing with and other disorders that may be accompanying it, anxiety being the most common, so that we can formulate the appropriate prescription recommendation.

Through their therapeutic work, patients often realize the extent to which these disorders have had a negative impact on their lives. They begin to understand that to change a pattern requires insight, effort, and commitment. Medications often help this process by reducing the severity of symptoms and allowing the patient to engage more earnestly in the work. As the fog of depression begins to lift and the restlessness of anxiety starts to settle, one can think more clearly, feel less held back, and start to make better choices.

If depression or anxiety are longstanding or recurrent, an effort should be made to uncover the individual's deeper underlying issues. Today, there are plenty of interventions available, and most patients are likely to respond to one, or more often, a combination of them. We encourage those who come to Meadows' programs to use every tool at their disposal to achieve the highest level of remission possible.

COMMENTARY

From Whitney Howzell, PhD, MPH

Perfectionism seems to be an overarching theme throughout Lainey's story. Love from her parents was conditional on her achievements, so Lainey unconsciously equated her achievements to her worthiness. She exhibited the classic characteristics of the hero child, who perpetuates the family's façade that everything is fine, despite an underlying dysfunctional system. The hero appears to be high functioning and driven, with an ability to be disciplined and achieve success. Lainey was able to excel scholastically and in extracurricular activities, while harboring family secrets and acting as a family peacemaker throughout her parent's divorce.

As with most overachievers, Lainey inevitably hit a wall. She struggled with finding purpose beyond her agenda or next competition, left feeling empty after each new achievement. As is common with hero children, Lainey struggled with perfectionism, severe anxiety, mood swings, fear of making mistakes, and codependency.

Like many young adults, Lainey didn't consider her struggle with disordered eating and caffeine dependency an "addiction" in the traditional sense. While her disordered eating and caffeine dependency were directly related to her bodybuilding, they were also unhealthy ways of coping with unresolved trauma and lessening anxiety. Behavioral addictions are very common among young adults. Developmentally, young adults are more vulnerable to engaging in risky behaviors and experimentation; this is normal for this age group.

From Kristin Kirkpatrick, MS, RDN, Sr. Fellow
(Wellness and Nutrition Specialist)

While psychotherapy for Lainey's depression and bipolar disorder is key to her recovery, nutrition will remain a critical factor in her long-term recovery as well. How often and how much she eats is important when treating disordered eating. What's also important is limiting foods believed to make anxiety and depression worse, such as sugar, ultra-processed foods such as fast food, and nutrient-lacking snacks, which are often cheap, quick, and full of ingredients that prolong shelf life.

Lainey needed to learn that she had value and worth absent the perfect physique, the perfect degree, and the perfect family.

Undaunted Hope

One of the most effective things you can do to stay in recovery from depression is to be vigilant about your recovery practices. This means taking an active role in your tasks: "This morning I will read my meditation book." "Today I take stock of what I have to be grateful for." "After lunch I will make a point to reach out and connect with someone." It's *not* about monitoring your mood throughout the day. Doing so will only cause anxiety and fear, since your mood changes in any twenty-four-hour cycle. Everyone's mood fluctuates; it's a normal, natural part of being human. When you check in with your recovery practices rather than your mood, you're acknowledging and validating yourself for taking action. Action is what keeps you in recovery.

CHAPTER FOUR

Standing Tall
RECOVERY FROM SUBSTANCE USE DISORDERS

I know I am in trouble; does that mean I am addicted?

Do I need to stop every drug if I am only in trouble with one?

If I stop, how will I ever be able to socialize with others?

No one has ever thought, I want to drink or use to the point I lose my family, my health, my job, my friends. Yet, how many times have some of us tried to stop drinking or using but couldn't sustain it? Or we stopped one drug only to pick up another? We know it's hurting us and our relationships with our children or partner. For some, our only friends are using or partying buddies, not really people we can rely on. We lie, fabricate stories, manipulate people or situations, and may even hate ourself for it. And yet we can't seem to stop.

We all think we have the power to stop our drinking or using. We reason that if it becomes a problem—which we think it never will—we will just not use so much or simply stop when the time comes. But then we realize that our plan didn't work. Why? Because once we enter an addictive phase, it has the power to override willpower, moral code, and value systems. We lose control over the ability to say no to the drug. Becoming addicted has nothing to do with morality, willpower, or strength of character. It has everything to do with the neurochemistry of the brain.

Repeated use of alcohol or drugs changes how our brain circuits function when it comes to feeling pleasure (the high), and our ability to learn, make decisions, and control our impulses. One effect is that we need more of the substance to feel good, as our brain adjusts to repeated and higher concentrations. Because these same circuits control our ability to experience pleasure from everyday experiences, the rest of life can feel less and less enjoyable in the absence of the substance.

Initially our using feels good, or at least lessens any anxiety or emotional pain with few or no negative consequences. But after a while, with repeated use, we spend more and more time searching, planning, arranging, and engaging in the use. Now more and more of the substance is needed to create the same good feelings and to get relief. This begins a downward spiral that affects every area of life. Lastly, the use becomes about just getting through the day; the primary motivation is now to escape from the pain one feels in the *absence* of the substance, plus the pain it's causing others and the chronic mess that life has become.

Why some people become addicted and others do not is complex. Some people are genetically vulnerable, which means there is a higher probability that addiction may activate under the right, or more accurately wrong, circumstances. Family modeling (we tend to do what our family members do) and peer influences (we tend to do what our peers do) can set people up so that using an intoxicant seems normal. A mental health condition, particularly depression or anxiety, is often a precursor to addiction, as this person seeks out a medicator to assuage uncomfortable feelings. But childhood trauma is the greatest contributor to becoming addicted. Substances can give traumatized people who feel powerless or fearful a sense of power and courage. Granted, this may be false power or false courage, but for the defeated and scared, false may be their best hope in the moment.

Addiction is said to be an equal opportunity illness. Substance use disorders affect twenty-three million people in America alone, regardless of economic status, political views, gender, sexual orientation, intellectual abilities, schooling, worldly achievements, religion, race, ethnicity, or beliefs. Every day, people die from illnesses and behaviors connected to their addiction.

Fortunately, there is hope. Today, hundreds of thousands of addicted people are living a life of recovery and the promises that come with that.

The following narratives are shared by people who knew they were in trouble. Their addiction had strong-armed their lives long enough. They reached their tipping point and needed a way out—and were open to help. Some had doubts about whether recovery was even possible. But for these individuals, as they took actions to reset their brain circuitry, began to heal, and boosted their desire for a different life, they realized that yes, recovery is possible.

Always Chasing Something   BY LIZ

By the time I got to The Meadows in 2018, my use of drugs was out of control. I was thirty-one years old, and I was using everything I could get my hands on. It had all began so innocently. I started smoking after school with girlfriends when I was thirteen. I didn't think it was a big deal, but I did feel rebellious, and I liked that feeling. That quickly led to alcohol.

My parents are really good people. They taught the four of us kids to value education and be respectful of others. To be nice and to avoid conflict. They wanted us in sports so I played soccer in high school, took music lessons, and did well academically. I didn't talk back to my parents or anyone and was good at being respectful—except when it came to lying or stealing. My lying was mostly what I didn't tell them. I would tell them I was at a friend's house, but I didn't tell them we snuck out after her parents were in bed, met up with others, and drank ourselves silly.

Because I did well in the things they valued, they didn't take a hard look at me. My brother who got into a lot of trouble got a lot of attention. Plus, there were my two younger sisters, so I think they felt I gave them a break.

Just Having a Good Time

I had a good drinking history behind me by the time I left home for college. Always having a high tolerance, I could drink longer and more than most without getting sick like they did. Not wanting my parents looking over my shoulder, I deliberately moved out of state to go to school. We didn't have much money, so I didn't go home except for the major holidays. And I always managed to have a reason not to go home in the summertime, such as doing an internship.

I took a communications major because it was easy and didn't put pressure on me to study. That gave me more time to party, and I found others who partied like me. "I'm just having a good time," I told myself.

Constantly on the Move

I began to have the sense that I was always chasing something. I would try different drugs, from Adderall to Xanax to cocaine, all while using alcohol. Then I would try different locations: I grew up in Virginia, went to college in the Midwest, and then moved to the West Coast. Alcohol cured my boredom and lessened my performance anxiety. It got to the point that I was so busy partying that I never got bored. And I thought I was so smart I didn't have anxiety about performance.

By the time I got my first job, I was blatantly lying. Lying on my resume, lying to my parents. I was shoplifting for the fun of it; I enjoyed the risk of getting caught. I was blowing through relationships with guys. At first, they thought I was fun, but then I outdrank them and used more than they did, and they disappeared from my life. But I didn't care. I still thought I was having a good time.

I was at my job in restaurant management about a year when my boss took me aside and told me that I needed to cool down some of my partying at work events; he said he was hearing rumors about me. A few months later, I had a different boss and she told me I might be better suited for another company. At twenty-three, I lost my first job due to my drinking.

Thinking I Was Still in Control

I was good at getting jobs but just as good at losing them. Over the next couple of years, I started to lose friends. I had become high maintenance. They told me my behavior embarrassed them. They often had to drive me home. They would intervene when they saw me leaving a bar with a stranger. My solution to all of this was to move to another community in the Southern California area.

The last time I had been home to see my family, one of my sisters questioned why I was so thin and appeared anxious. I told her I had a lot going on and that I had joined a cycling gym and probably took it a little bit too seriously.

Then one day my parents surprised me with a visit and caught me at home with a hangover and missing work. I told them I had the flu. It was easier for them to believe me than create any conflict.

Another day I ended up in an emergency room, not remembering how I got there. It wasn't my first blackout but the first one that scared me. I had laughed off the others. When I was discharged with both of my arms bandaged up from some horrible fall, I told myself I better really cool things. I decided to go clean, and life got much better. I cleaned my apartment. I realized my coworkers could be nice people. I took the time to communicate more with my family back east.

Then I won a trip through my work to this great island in Central America. I decided I could drink on vacation, and I was loaded the whole time I was there. I don't even remember coming home. That's when my employer stepped in and told me I needed to get some help or I would lose my job.

Continuing to Fool Myself

My answer to that was to go to a therapist for my supposed depression. I told her I drank too much at times but was able to control it with the exception of this last trip. So, we worked on my depression that I connected to not finding the right man to settle down with. After four months in therapy, I quit. I did okay the following few months, but then I fell down truly by accident and broke my leg. That is when I was exposed to OxyContin. This was a drug I had not tried. Somehow my leg didn't heal like it should, and I kept rationalizing my continued use of the pills. I started to miss work. I didn't keep up on my bills. One day I was stopped for driving through a red light and caught with an expired registration for my car. My boss found out, as my driving was essential for my work, and this time he told me, "No excuses, you need drug treatment." In my mind I was not a druggie or alcoholic; I just hadn't handled things well and overused at times.

Not having much of a choice, I went to treatment. I let my parents know it was for stress and depression. Though concerned, they didn't ask much. I didn't think I was as bad as the other residents there. I went to the therapy groups but didn't talk much. Being in sales, I thought I was presenting a good game, that "I had just made some mistakes." I left the program two weeks before I was scheduled to leave. Then I lost my job because I didn't complete treatment. It wasn't a total surprise. My employer had told me they would support any treatment suggestions, but if I did not follow through then I would be terminated from my job. I just didn't know they really meant what they said.

I didn't care. I wanted a different life anyway. Eighteen months later, I was bartending and still trying to control what I was using when I had a really bad experience in a blackout. I was scared. So, at thirty-one, I took myself back to treatment, and this time I went to The Meadows.

Did I Really Want to Stop?

This time I listened. I didn't compare myself to how different I was to others; I paid attention to what was similar. We did an exercise—a timeline of my use of alcohol and drugs—and I was blown away. I had at least fifteen years of using heavily, and my consequences were a mile long. It was all on paper before me.

But did I really want to stop? I knew I was addicted; I was done explaining my behavior and rationalizing. But did I want to say out loud I was an alcoholic and an addict? That was hard. At first, in twelve-step meetings and in group, I introduced myself with the claim, "I don't want to drink or use drugs." But eventually I found myself saying, "I am an alcoholic and an addict." That was huge—and I felt such relief. I found that by admitting it out loud, I was reinforcing the fact that as long as I used or drank, my life would keep getting worse.

I wasn't sure how I could do recovery. I wasn't sure what my family would think. I had no real friends to count on, just using and partying buddies. But I knew I no longer wanted my old life.

It took me about five weeks to realize it would be good for me to come clean with my family about my use. I had distanced myself from them for years. But with the help of the staff, I invited them to Family Week, and I shared my history going back all of those years. They were shocked, but they also realized that being nice all the time, rather than being honest and handling conflict had hurt us as a family. They ultimately owned how the family system hadn't kept eyes on me as a teenager. I verbally made amends, knowing behavioral amends would only come by staying honest with them. Today both my parents go to Al-Anon. At first, I didn't see that they needed to. After all, I was the one with the problem. But the meetings have led to a lot of really good, important conversations between us.

Getting Sober

The smartest thing I did was to go straight into a sober living home, and I chose a place in a different area than where I lived. I started a new job. It wasn't going to be a career, but the discipline of showing up and being accountable was good. I went to at least one Narcotics or Alcoholics Anonymous meeting a day for ninety days. After the ninety days, I went five to six times a week. I listened to everyone, but particularly women. I found a woman sponsor right away. She happened to be five years younger than me but was five years sober.

It's been four years now, and I still go to at least three meetings a week. I continue to use a sponsor. Addiction was destroying my life, and I just couldn't see it. That's the nature of addiction. I never thought about my life making a difference in someone else's, but today I sponsor other women and it makes me feel good about myself.

I can't believe the friends I have. At first I was wary. I thought, how am I going to I figure out how to have fun without using? But I stay close to a group of other clean and sober people, and we have a great time. We laugh a lot. We go to movies, we attend sporting events, we find clean places to dance.

When I go out, I no longer embarrass anyone or myself. I'm not losing jobs. I went back to school and got a job in technology, which I love. I stayed away from relationships for about two years. Now, I have a boyfriend—my first relationship that doesn't center around using. I am taking it slow. Recovery has given me more than I could have ever imagined.

• • •

Boundaries: A Part of Recovery
From Jerry Law, D. Ministry, (Executive Director of The Meadows)

While in active addiction, people are boundaryless. This is commonly referred to as *lacking containment,* meaning their need to use overrides their respect for others. The impaired thinking that accompanies an addiction leads to questionable and often bizarre behaviors. Once in that cycle of denial, the individual will frequently violate the boundaries of others as well as their own. They will lie, steal, and manipulate without regard. Boundaries transform from *concrete* to *relative* as the addiction takes over the life of the individual.

Good treatment and solid recovery must include skills in setting and maintaining both external and internal healthy boundaries. An example of an external boundary designed to protect themself could be identifying trigger situations and avoiding or limiting exposure to specific people, places, and things. An internal boundary could be utilizing the *Serenity Prayer* or reaching out to a sponsor or therapist when the urge to engage in ineffective reactive behaviors rises.

COMMENTARY

From Kevin McCauley, MD, MPH, Sr. Fellow
(Expert on neuroscience of addiction and recovery management)

Liz describes how she always had a high tolerance for alcohol. In fact, she reported that she could outdrink everyone. It's possible that Liz inherited genes that meant she had to consume more alcohol to get the same degree of intoxication as those around her. Her genetic vulnerability *plus* her early exposure to alcohol may be why she developed alcoholism.

There are also genes that can determine how it *feels* when we drink alcohol or use drugs—with this gene, we love it more than the next person. There are also people with genes that lead to a "reward-deficiency syndrome." They tend to overconsume alcohol, food, sugar, and drugs to get the same level of reward that most people get from normal consumption.

But here's what's important: genes are not the cause of addiction because they only describe our vulnerability to addiction. While genes are fixed, they do interact with our environment. And if our environment is filled with poverty, prejudice, stress, trauma, easy access to alcohol, etc., it can cause *epigenetic* changes that can increase risk of diseases such as diabetes, cancer, and alcoholism. Most epigenetic changes are short-lived; they only last a few weeks or months. But some epigenetic changes last long enough to be passed on from one generation to the next. There is growing evidence that trauma may be heritable.

But resilience (see sidebar "Resilience") may be heritable too! Getting sober may erase bad epigenetic changes and create beneficial epigenetic changes that result in resilience to trauma, stress, addiction, and disease. This is an acquired resilience that may make up for (or even surpass) the genetic vulnerability that we were born with. Those benefits may even extend beyond just us to our other family members, or to our own children. Alcoholism runs in families, but so does recovery. However far back alcoholism goes in our family history, it may end with us when we recover.

From Jennifer Angier, MS
(Vice President of Addiction Services)

I am moved by the way Liz follows the story of her unraveling and the attempts to stop. The inevitable story is one that defines the brutality of the disease of addiction—convincing herself that she doesn't need to really stop, quickly followed by a deep loss of clarity of what matters the most.

But never underestimate the love of others during treatment and recovery in helping us regain that clarity. Because that love helps the hard truths land on us in ways that offer us a belief that we are finally finding our way out. Liz found those a life-saving message while in treatment and in twelve-step meetings: What happened to you isn't the whole story. It is only a part of who you have been, and it isn't the end of the story. Now we work to bring it all together. Bring the pain and hope to this place and fight for the person you want to be. Every time we return to a meeting, we're reminded we aren't meant to do this alone, none of us are.

Liz speaks for many when she describes what it is like to be scared in a way you have never known and yet have the courage to be propelled by that fear into a relationship with truth and love.

Last Stop on the Train BY CHASE

I can remember thinking, If I don't stop this, what is next? If I go back to using, will I hurt somebody else? Hurt myself? I was scared, my friends were scared, my parents were scared. It was time to get help.

It All Seemed Normal

I started smoking weed when I was twelve and drinking at thirteen. The first time I smoked, I loved it. I was super giggly, felt like I was floating. I wasn't in my head, and my head was always so full of energy. It was a relief to be outside of it. For the next few years, it all seemed normal in that I was doing it with friends and we still did things like surf, play soccer, and just hang.

But looking back, I always got more drunk than my friends, and I usually ended up being the entertainment. Like the time I was so drunk they stripped me to my boxers, zip tied me to a pole outside, poured honey on me, then put feathers on me. A part of me was ashamed when I woke up that next morning, but the other part of me thought it was funny.

By fifteen I was taking alcohol to school and drinking throughout the day, and then I started to use other drugs. I dabbled in psychedelics and got codeine from a friend's dad who prescribed it for me.

I left Hawaii for the mainland to go to college, and by then I was drinking daily. By the time others were starting to get ready for a party, I was already hammered. Wanting to be able to socialize and not be too drunk, I started to do cocaine. In the beginning, I only did it on weekends, then it became an everyday thing.

After a year at college I was heavily into methamphetamines. I knew what meth could do to people; I just didn't know it could happen so fast. After doing it every day for about four months, I went into full-blown psychosis to the point of having hallucinations. I'd be in a store or alongside of the road, fighting the air. I was convinced mold was flying into me, hitting my skin, attacking me. When I was in my apartment, I would not move for hours because I was too scared of the flying mold.

Maybe I was always an addict; anything I did, I was fully into it. Plus, both grandparents on both sides of my family were severe alcoholics, and others in the family too. For me there was never any middle ground.

Prior Attempts for Help

I went back to Hawaii to try to get my act together, and after days of sleeping I was able to stop the meth on my own. But it didn't last long. I would see my friends and go to parties, and I couldn't drink just a little. I tried, though. I would plan to stop for a month, and for four or five days I would show up at work, work hard, surf every day, not drink or drug. But it never lasted longer than six days. While I had escalating guilt and shame about my failure to follow through, the quitting would not stick. The next thing I knew I'd be at a party with a plate of cocaine and a bottle of vodka in my hand.

When I was twenty-six, my grandmother died. I was so miserable and very high. I had suicidal thoughts and actually went to my mom—who had been pretty emotionally abusive my whole childhood—and told her I had a cocaine addiction.

I said, "I have a problem and I need to figure this out. Can you help me?"

She started yelling, "No, no, no! What are you talking about?"

And then she fainted right in front of me. We ended up taking her to the hospital. The next day it was like the whole scene never happened. A couple of years later, when I told my dad I had issues, he didn't want to hear it either. Even when I was in treatment and I told my dad about the meth, he didn't believe it. He had always been on the sidelines while I was growing up. I lied a lot so maybe he didn't know what to believe.

Desperate to Stop

My actions were getting violent. I would go crazy tearing things up, wanting to fight, throwing things. Clearly I was dangerous. I had to have the whole fifth and down it in minutes along with Xanax and cocaine. My friends wanted nothing to do with me anymore.

Then I had this huge breakdown. After days of not sleeping, I collapsed at my parents' home. When I finally woke up, I started to destroy the kitchen when they wouldn't give me the money I was demanding. I broke things, threw stuff around, shoved my dad. I grabbed a knife and threatened to stab myself. Then the cops came; I had a weapon in my hands, and they were close to drawing theirs. I don't remember much else other than waking up the next day in a hospital.

When I was in the hospital, a guy who worked there came into my room and told me we had a friend in common. I immediately wondered who he knew from my small hometown when he said "vodka."

We sat together for over an hour. He told me about how he was living his recovery and how his life was. I had this preconceived notion that recovery was like living in a cult. I thought it was like one ongoing church meeting. I had no idea recovery was living a normal life, that people had jobs, friends, fun, and they liked themselves—just without drugs. Then he told me that other hospital staff, people I had been looking up to, were in recovery too. At the end of our conversation, I finally admitted that I needed to get help. I like to think of it as my first AA meeting.

If This Is Like a Cult, I Am Out of Here

I went to treatment at CBC desperate. Homelessness, jail, or death were my only other options. At the same time, I was telling myself, No way am I going to be reading any bible. If this is like a cult, I am out of there.

After that first week I was in a group about spirituality. I told the group leader that I couldn't force myself to believe in God. He told me I didn't have to believe or know what my higher power was, just know the distinction between religion and spirituality. He said my spiritual path was up to me. I decided right then, Okay, I can do this.

I wasn't sure how to go about building a relationship with my higher power, but I started to look for connections with people who had a mystery to them. For example, I saw a guy in the cafeteria wearing a Hawaiian shirt, something that I was willing to believe was saying I was in the right place. I started noticing things like that and just kept saying that it was my higher power. I had to believe in something.

One day we were doing a ropes course and I was halfway up hanging there and I thought, There is no way I can do this. I literally can't move. There is nothing left in me. I told the guy who handles the rope to let me down. But then out of nowhere I felt like someone shot me with adrenaline. When I got to the top, I felt like my friend—a using buddy who had died in a skateboarding accident—was there watching me, that he had lifted me up. It was the anniversary of his death. I felt really emotional and was taking it all in when two feet above my head, a great horned owl flew right over me. Holy crap! That was the moment I realized, Okay, I have my higher power.

Once I got past the God thing, it made sense. In some ways when it came to the steps, I was lucky; I had number one down. "We admitted we were powerless over alcohol—that our lives had become unmanageable." I knew drugs had more power over me than me over them.

While I wanted recovery, I had no confidence in my ability to do it. I had no confidence in myself. My therapist saw that, and we worked on it a lot. I trusted her and was able to be vulnerable with her. I cried a lot. She gave me a clicker and told me I had to tell myself affirmations daily and click the clicker when I did. It was hard to believe these affirmations: *I am lovable. I deserve recovery. I am a good person. I have value. I deserve respect.* I only had twelve clicks the first week. But after three weeks, I was believing in myself more. These affirmations somehow were just what they were supposed to be: affirming.

Family week, which was on Zoom due to being in the middle of the pandemic, was really helpful too. In these structured meetings, my parents and I talked and listened. I said things I could never have said on my own. I said them in ways they could be heard, and the staff worked with my parents to be able to listen and respond in a way that wasn't defensive. I had a lot of things that had festered in me since I was a child. And I wanted to be heard.

There are still things I need to sort out with my parents that I didn't get around to in treatment, but I now have the skills and the confidence to know I will do that in time.

Hope, Love, and Friendship

After treatment I would go to an aftercare program for several months, then lived in a sober living house with some counseling. Most of my therapy work is twelve-step work. Doing the Fourth and Fifth Steps is heavy stuff; it's emotional, it's where you don't leave anything in the closet, but you are sharing with a sponsor, someone who will not hurt you, will not be judgmental, who understands. No stone is unturned about your past; you face it head on.

In the meetings, I realize I am not alone. Being in a room where people are struggling as much as you are, or have, and some even more, gives you hope. And a lot of love. And friendship. I get to put down on paper all the things I regret, all the things I resent. Get them off my chest. Lift the weight off my shoulders. I feel free. While doing it, I feel things I may not want to feel, but when it's over it is all worth it.

The Twelve Steps are something that everyone should do. They are so healing. They help you find peace, self-love, and teach you responsibility for yourself. It's not an "I" program, it is a "we" program. I have to let people in for me to do the work. I can't do it on my own.

I am an active person, and today I actually do the things that I tell myself I am going to do—and it feels fantastic. I follow direction. I am open to what I don't know. I listen to others and to what is inside of me, and then take action. I can go out and have genuine fun—and I can remember it all. Of course, it was awkward at first. Trying to socialize without having the crutch of drinking and drugs forced me out of my comfort zone, and I became okay with being uncomfortable. Drinking and using is really overrated.

Making Genuine Connections

Following through with things, being trustworthy with yourself and others is what it is about. And on top of this you make genuine connections with others. Today I can meet somebody for the first time, and they will actually care about me and I will care about them, and we show each other that. I receive the feeling of unconditional love that I have not known my whole life.

I know not everyone has the desperation I had when I went to treatment, but I can say that not drinking gives me clarity and the tools to figure out who I am, to figure out what makes me happy. Some people spend their whole life trying to figure that out; thanks to giving up my crutches, I am figuring that out now. And one of the things that makes me happy is helping others. I have just moved into my own place and have taken a job as a behavioral tech in the addictions field.

♦ ♦ ♦

Addiction Is a Learning and Memory Disorder

By Kevin McCauley, MD, MPH, Sr. Fellow (Expert on neuroscience of addiction and recovery management)

Many family members ask me a perfectly reasonable question, "Why don't they just stop?" The answer is that something has gone terribly wrong in the brain of the person with addiction. The intoxicant—alcohol, drugs, and certain behaviors—wins out, even when they don't want to drink or use, and even despite promises not to, and even when drinking and drug use get dangerously out of control. It's irrational, it's hurtful, there's no excuse—but there is a reason for it. It lies in the learning and memory function of the brain.

We've all heard of the brain chemical *dopamine*, which is released whenever we engage in pleasurable behaviors. In a nutshell, dopamine grabs our attention and directs it toward the thing that released it. In the brain of person with addiction, the drugs, alcohol, or intoxicating behaviors are flagged as important for survival.

The brain chemical that works with dopamine is the neurotransmitter *glutamate*. Glutamate plays a key role in brain development and helps with learning and memory. Essentially, the job of glutamate is to lay down a memory of a thing, freezing it and everything that went along with it into memory. Dopamine says, "Hey, this is important!" Glutamate says, "Okay, I'll remember it!"

That's the way the brain's normal reward-learning system works. It's how the brain recognizes things in the environment that are good for survival, learns them, and can then anticipate them. Intoxicants overdrive this system by releasing too much dopamine, which overvalues the drug, and too much glutamate, which doesn't just freeze the drug into memory, it burns the drug into memory, like a cattle-brand.

So all the things that go along with drug use—the people they were with, the places they did them, the sights and smells in those moments, and even the time of day when they did them—are now drug cues that can trigger *relapse.* Fortunately, with treatment and what we know about how the brain, relapse can be avoided.

COMMENTARY

From Jennifer Angier , MS

One night when it mattered, Chase was told by a stranger exactly what he could hear. It was there he found his desperation and his way to treatment. Chase was no stranger to stopping, and he was almost drowning in the escalating guilt and shame about his failure to follow through; the quitting would not stick. It is easy to assume that it takes a room of people sitting in a circle telling stories of the way they love you and miss you in their life as the perfect sendoff into the unknown that treatment offers. Yet Chase is a beautiful example of someone meant to make those circles for others.

With honesty, Chase found recovery using a process one click at a time—that's really how it happens. He was able to find connection in the formula of the Twelve Steps, to others and in the seeking of spirituality. He reminds us to never forget to sit and listen to the ones who are put on our path; it may be our heart that guides them off the train tracks into the color of life.

From Kevin McCauley, PhD, MPH, Sr. Fellow

Chase, like the other three individuals in this chapter, had a very hard time stopping his drug use. While he was able to stop using for short periods, Chase couldn't stay stopped, which eventually led to severe *psychostimulant psychosis.*

His addiction followed a nearly universal component of addiction called *progression*:

- Drinking alcohol and using other drugs for longer periods than they intend
- Continuing to drink and use despite social and interpersonal problems, physical and psychological consequences
- Attempting to lessen or stop their drinking or use but unable
- Difficulty meeting their obligations at work, home, and school; losing relationships, jobs, or schooling
- Giving up social and recreational activities in favor of drinking or drug use

- Combining drugs or alcohol to counter unpleasant side effects of one or the other
- Change in tolerance, needing to use more to get the desired effect
- Symptoms of withdrawal

Another component of addiction is impairment in the frontal cortex. This is the part of the brain that handles what is known as "executive functions": our ability to make decisions and predict consequences of future actions, our ability to regulate our emotions and therefore negotiate complex social and family relationships, and our ability to monitor our own behavior and be self-aware of how our behavior impacts others.

If the systems of brain processing are faulty (see sidebar "Addiction Is a Learning and Memory Disorder"), this will compromise the various areas of the frontal cortex that we need to make good decisions and manage our relationships. As our addiction progresses, we become impaired—and this impairment is obvious to everyone except, sometimes, ourselves. We can't see it.

Running from Myself   BY SUSAN

By the time I got to treatment, I almost didn't recognize who I was. I've had an alcohol use disorder my entire life. From my first taste of alcohol, around age eight, I loved it. I was shy and introverted, and it took away my anxiety. I began social drinking when I was sixteen. I consumed huge amounts from the beginning and would have blackouts, starting from that first time, even though I knew it was a problem and felt ashamed.

Start. Stop. Start. Stop.
Over the decades of my drinking, I could go weeks, months, and sometimes a few years without drinking. I had a great ability to compartmentalize. For example, I was a really good athlete and competitive runner in high school and college, so I didn't drink on a continuous basis then. When I had my son, I threw everything I had into raising him, and drinking was not a part of that. And then I threw myself into my career as a way to keep me from drinking.

But when I wasn't drinking, I was white knuckling it. I craved the next drink, so I had to be obsessive about whatever my distraction would be to keep me from it.

I loved tequila and a good Manhattan. In the later years, I drank straight vodka, and often directly out of the bottle. I was predominantly a closet drinker, very secretive about the amount I drank. If I drank with others, I would be drunk before I even went out with them. Initially, I was good at hiding it. People didn't see all of the drinking because I'd sneak outside or into another room. I didn't drink while working, but after I would land a big contract or after a big work trip, I would be drunk the whole time. I hid bottles and drank myself into oblivion.

I didn't know the concept of stopping at one drink, and I would get progressively sloppy. I would black out, not remember what I had done or where I had been. Often in later years, after a full day of drinking, I'd pass out—at family meals, at the table in restaurants, at holiday meals.

In the last ten years, after many binges, my husband would explode and tell me that I needed to stop. I would stop for months, let things settle down, and then start back up. I would tell myself that I could drink normally, knowing that I couldn't. By this time, I think my husband felt like he was my babysitter when we went out.

I once saw a movie from the 1940s with a character who was stereotypically alcoholic. He was a hobo, continuously shaking until somebody would compassionately give him a bottle of whiskey. I remember thinking, My god that's me. There were times my shakiness was so bad I couldn't sign my name on a piece of paper.

Over the years I would read memoirs of women who identified as alcoholics and who were embracing recovery. I was secretly reading those books thinking, Oh my God there are people who drink like me. How could they stop and never drink again? I could never do that.

In the Closet

I hated myself for the way I drank, but I also hated my life. There was this other big secret part of me: being gay. I was out of the closet as a teenager, and in college my friends and family knew. They were all okay with my being gay, as I also have siblings who are gay. But I went deep into the closet after my first year in the business world. Back in the early

1980s, it was a male-dominated field with misogyny, sexism, racism, homophobia. I was so anxious of being exposed.

By the time I met my husband, I was dating men. He knew I had been in gay relationships because past partners were acknowledged in conversations at times with family and friends. But he didn't ask me about this, and unless I was drunk, I never talked about it. Hiding from being gay, no way I was happily married. But I was on the road working, and that kept me sober. As the years went by, I would talk to my husband about my past with women, usually when I had been drinking a lot, then I would sober up and it was like the conversation never happened. Then he and I would go back to our routine, working like crazy during the week and then the good times on the weekends and vacations. As a family, my husband, son, and I did have a lot of fun with each other. We traveled the world, golfed, skied, went to games, visited with friends and family. But I was always drinking. Secretly.

So add the shame about being gay and then the shame about being an alcoholic, and I was running from myself as fast as I could.

The Final Binge

It was the pandemic that helped get me to treatment. I was totally off the road, at home, isolated with my husband of thirty-five years. I was looking out the window from inside my beautiful house, thinking about the life I had lived and the one I hadn't. I was living a lie. I didn't have the courage to live my truth.

I didn't want to drink. Then again, I did. And after another binge that lasted for days, my husband threatened to leave me. I stopped drinking for several weeks, and then on our anniversary weekend over Memorial Day I just couldn't *not* drink. I felt as if I were coming out of my skin. I knew I was heading into what could be one of my worse episodes, and I was praying to God "please help me because I'm going to drink and I know it's going to happen." Then at dinner, when I took that first drink, I saw the look on my husband's face, and I thought he was going to die.

He left me at the resort. He knew the next binge had just started. He was just so angry; he saw his life imploding, and he didn't know what to do. I actually thought I was going to die from my drinking in those next few nights. Then my son called me and begged me to go to treatment. He told me that my family was losing me, and he said, "We are not going to let you die." My husband and my siblings were all busy texting and calling each other in their despair over me. My son reminded me of how important my grandsons and his wife were to me. He said, "You are drinking yourself to death." And I knew he was right.

Telling the Truth

By the time I went to treatment, I didn't think there was anyone like me. But I went with a glimmer of hope from that first telephone call saying, "I need help."

From the moment I arrived, I started to tell the truth. I immediately told them that I was gay and had been living a secret life. They said that was okay, they were going to help me. On the first day, I was sitting with some women down by the pool, and they were laughing as they talked. I thought, How would I ever laugh again? I just blew up my life, I've left work, I've left my family, and I'm coming out of the closet. Then I realized that my life was never going to be the same—and that was a good thing.

They have a lot of therapies that were very helpful, but the most impactful experience was knowing in my heart I was not alone, and I felt that the moment I stepped on campus. I met people from all walks of life all there for different reasons, and some for the exact same reason, and all of a sudden that shame started to be lifted. I cannot even begin to express the love and support that I have felt from that first moment.

We would certainly do a lot of our sharing in groups, but much of it took place in the dining halls during meals, in the afternoons, and early evenings before or after groups. I met people from all walks of life, and it was such a powerful experience to be with so many other people who also wanted their recovery. Knowing in my heart I was not alone was an incredibly impactful experience.

I took treatment seriously. My life depended on it, so I was all in. The twelve-step meetings were really important to me. I looked forward to every meeting. When I left, I completed ninety meetings in ninety days, all on Zoom. Today, the twelve-step meetings are vital to my recovery.

Reentry and Revitalization

I used The Meadows case management services for several months, too. I received individual support for my health and reentry to work. I had gained over sixty pounds from drinking, so I started to exercise with a stationary bike, and that got me to running. The healthy eating began while in treatment. I also stopped smoking. And over the last two and a half years, my level of anxiety has almost totally dissipated.

In treatment, I learned about boundaries, so I talked to my manager about boundaries at work. At first, I didn't know how I was ever going to do my job as well as I did when I was a full-blown alcoholic because I worked addictively and had increased the bottom line for my company by 500 percent. But without the stress of working twenty-four/seven, I was sleeping for the first time through the night, and I was no longer anxious. Funny how it works, but I've never been better at my job than I am right now. It didn't matter how many hours I worked, I had been working with one arm behind my back, and now I've got both arms. I am not the one who loses her credit card, her notebook, her phone anymore. My work doesn't define me today. My work is something that I do; it is not who I am every day.

I start each day with prayer and gratitude. Previously prayer had never been a part of my life—other than being on my knees in front of a toilet and praying "God, please help me" after a terrible binge. Today I pray for God's will, and I also journal.

No More Lies

I didn't have to come out to my sons and husband as gay; they knew from the family stories or when I was drunk and talked about it, but now I was reaffirming being gay. No more lies or living a lie. My husband and I live independently and in separate homes now, but we have remained best friends.

Six months into my recovery, my twenty-eight-year-old stepson died of an accidental overdose. He had been clean from heroin five years and after a surgery was given opiates. He took too many and died. This has been tough and maybe always will be, but I kept practicing my program and staying true to who I want to be.

People get sick of me saying one day at a time, but I say it all the time because it works. I need to stay present in recovery. Putting myself first and being loved and accepted by the people that matter the most is so liberating. I don't take my sobriety for granted. I know I have to continue to do the work. My sobriety has to come first and stay first.

Before I left treatment, I had to write a letter to myself that would be mailed to me in six months. It was a letter to my future. I was to write about what I thought I could have in recovery. That letter came right on schedule, and I periodically read it and cry. I am living what I had hoped for. I am living what I dared to envision. I was living the promise of the Big Book of AA. I love the promises. This letter had hope all over it, and I am living that today. I am actually living even better than that.

◆ ◆ ◆

COMMENTARY

From Jerry Law, D. Ministry
(Executive Director of The Meadows)

Susan's story highlights several hallmarks of addiction. In her opening, she mentions having blackouts. In a blackout, the individual continues to function, at least on some level, and generally has no recollection of the events that transpired while in the blackout state. It is not the same as passing out, or losing consciousness, rather it is as if the person's memory bank goes offline while he or she carries on with life.

Two more strong addiction indicators were her ability to compartmentalize coupled with a preoccupation about "the next use." Susan had a powerful ability to keep secrets about her addiction and sexual identity, which further exacerbated her obsession with chasing the high. For the addict, thinking about using can be as stimulating as actually engaging in the substance or behavior.

Addicts often become masters of two (or more) lives and are astonishingly believable in each role. When addicted, one will go to any length to protect themself from the inevitable day of reckoning when faced with the choice of getting help or possibly dying. The shame of carrying the burdens of hidden identities clearly kept her in her disease. A famous saying heard in twelve-step meetings is, "We are as sick as our secrets."

Susan's belief that "no one will ever understand me" reinforces a terminal uniqueness that keeps millions from receiving the help they need and that is readily available. In recovery, we discover that we are all much more similar than we are different.

It is said that addiction thrives in isolation and heals in community. Susan's shame and fear kept her isolated for many years. Fortunately, in recovery, she discovered the power of community. While in recovery, Susan experienced the death of her child, due to the very disease from which she is recovering. Yet, in community, she has been able to grieve this loss and remain true to herself. What a gift.

From Kevin McCauley, PhD, MPH, Sr. Fellow

Susan describes the worst symptom of addiction, which is directly related to problems in the brain's frontal cortex: craving. When she wasn't drinking, she was craving alcohol, white knuckling it, coming out of her skin, praying not to drink but helplessly knowing that she would.

Craving is hard to describe, especially to people who have never experienced it before. It represents a brain state that, when it comes on, really represents the suffering of addiction. It is an emotional, obsessive, repetitive, seemingly unending, and most importantly involuntary thought process about drugs.

If the consequences of drinking or using drugs were severe enough, a person may be able to choose not to drink or use. But they likely couldn't choose not to crave. That's what a lot of people don't understand about addiction: at some point you don't have to be drinking or using drugs anymore to have the suffering of addiction.

The neurotransmitter glutamate is important in impulse control. When the brain's reward areas (the *child* part of the brain) come up with the great idea of doing something new and risky, the frontal cortex (the *adult* part of the brain) says, "That's a terrible idea," and vetoes the impulse.

This glutamate-driven inhibition fails in addiction. You see people with addiction drink when they don't want to, drink even though it makes their problems with family and friends or depression and anxiety worse, and drink in hazardous situations leading to accidents, injuries, and sometimes death. What goes wrong here explains much of why people drink or use when they don't want to and the phenomenon of relapse, which is common in addiction (See sidebar "Addiction Is a Learning and Memory Disorder").

From Kristen Kirkpatrick, MS, RDN, Sr. Fellow
(Wellness and Nutrition Specialist)

Susan made significant advances in her treatment, one of which she discussed was the beginning of healthy dietary habits from our Fuel Well program. Alongside exercise, these habits most definitely contributed to her admission of seeing her anxiety dissipate. Studies show that nutritional measure may significantly contribute to treatment outcomes associated with depression and anxiety. Susan's dietary change most likely included more attention to nutrient dense foods such as fruits, vegetables, whole grains, and healthy fats. These nutritional components may have worked toward better gut health and reduced inflammation but have also been shown to improve depression and anxiety. Her continued success will rely on making dietary modifications a way of life. Susan can continue her everyday dietary journey by keeping color in her diet; we recommend getting at least five plant-based colors daily. She can also focus on good mood foods, shown in the data to significantly impact mental health, such as omega three fatty acids found in fatty wild fish, walnuts, and flax seed and folate found in beans and legumes and leafy greens.

Nutrition will remain a factor in her recovery. She will also need to work on limiting foods shown in studies to make anxiety and depression worse, such as sugar, ultra-processed foods, and nutrient lacking snacks that are often cheap, quick, and full of ingredients that prolong shelf life. Good nutrition is a way for Susan to continue to respect her body. This does not mean she can never have food from her previous life. It's not the cookie we have once in a while or the pizza on Friday nights, it's when these habits become the norm and healthier habits become once in a while. Like her treatment for alcoholism, Susan will need to look at her diet day by day.

It Was Time for Help
BY JASON

I grew up in a wealthy household. We were always traveling and doing things when I was young, and I had some great times. Yet, I really wasn't close with my dad or my siblings; in those years it was my mother who I felt the closest to. So when my parents separated and then divorced, two of my siblings and I lived with mom, and my oldest sister lived with my dad. The three of us kids were all home the day that would change my life.

That was the day I found my mom hanging in my sister's bedroom closet, still alive. I had no idea she was suicidal, or even depressed, or in any despair at all. But I was only twelve. It was shocking. I didn't know what to make of it.

My mom was in the hospital for a long time. After she came home from the hospital, I started to see how much of a mess she was. At that point I was taking care of my siblings a lot and making sure she got out of bed in the morning. If I didn't go into her room, she wouldn't get out of bed until one or two o'clock in the afternoon.

My mom also denied what she had done, which made it crazymaking for me, but I knew what I had seen. I found out later that she had attempted suicide before, by taking a bunch of pills. My dad had taken her to the hospital, but once she was physically stable, she had refused any sort of treatment.

Then my mom started to date someone that I was skeptical of. I felt like he did a lot to make my mother feel like she wasn't able to handle things on her own. I began to spend more time with my dad, and I ended up moving in with him. I wasn't living with my dad too long when my mom began leaving me nasty voicemails. She would say that the divorce and her wanting to die were all my fault. I didn't know what to do, so I said nothing. I was fourteen.

Then one day she left another voicemail accusing me of not answering her phone calls and not taking any time to talk to her. Two days later, and less than six months after I had moved in with my dad, she parked her car on the train tracks across the street from my high school and took her own life.

Into the Darkness

After my mom died, and all of us kids were living with my dad, he quit work and became a full-time parent.

Within months I started using marijuana and drinking. I couldn't put myself out there to talk with people. My palms were sweaty all of the time, and I had a hard time sitting still. I stopped doing the things I enjoyed. My life centered around when I was going to smoke pot or get my next drink. That was my whole universe from the time I was fifteen.

In college, I was using Xanax on top of the marijuana and alcohol. I was loaded every day. When I got a job and started having a little bit of money, I began doing cocaine on the weekends. But the next thing I knew, it was all week, every day. I was spending a fortune on that stuff.

Then the pandemic hit. I was supposed to be home working remotely, but it just escalated my situation. I was drinking and drugging the entire day. I could get *anything* delivered right to my door. Whatever I wanted, all day, every day.

I was also having two different recurring, never-changing nightmares about my mom that no one knew about. In one nightmare, there was a long hallway that led to an attic. And as I opened the attic door, I could see this dark image of her hanging there. In the other traumatic dream, I was in a car with her. From the passenger seat, I could see a train coming. I would beg her to move the car, but she wouldn't look at me. She wouldn't say anything, just kept looking straight ahead. I would wake up just as the train was hitting the car.

I was totally isolated and alone. I went from 200 pounds to 140. I began having panic attacks nearly daily. I lost my job. I was pretty much out of money. I was even having a lot of suicidal ideations; I didn't see myself going on for another year. I was twenty-five, and my life was a mess.

Then my dad came to my apartment to check on me. He and my siblings were aware I was in bad shape. So, my dad, this basically non-emotional guy, suddenly got emotional with me about the things I was doing. When he told me how concerned he was and suggested I go to treatment, I knew I needed to make some sort of change.

Breaking the Rules

There was no denying it for me, I needed help. I was willing to go to treatment. I wanted to feel better. I was in trouble. My intention was to get the depression and anxiety under control. Those conditions were what I saw as my real problem, then I could get back to partying. That was my plan.

I was a true problem child at CBC, yet I clearly needed to be there. I was rude, angry, and I used my leadership ability to get other guys to rebel against the rules. I didn't want to go to group, or at least arrive on time. I didn't want to have to eat at a certain time. I didn't want to have to do anything on a schedule. I was going out of my way to break the rules. I got mad about everything and made a big deal about it.

Things quickly escalated, and the clinical director, Ryan, told me I was leaving. He had already called my dad, which made me very upset. Ryan said they would be discharging me, but then he said I had one last chance. I had to turn things around immediately, or I would be going home. Until that point, I really thought the staff there would break, that they'd bend to me. But they held onto their boundaries. They knew what I needed, and they were right.

I didn't really want to get kicked out. I knew that I had an opportunity to fix a lot of my issues from the past and leave there a better person. So from that point on, I took full advantage of everything there.

Connecting the Dots

There were times when I felt very distraught—not about being there or the rules, but about the things I was working through. Ryan was confident that if I applied myself, I wouldn't continue to feel that way. I didn't think it was possible, but slowly, slowly the feeling did fall away.

Talking to Ryan was the turning point. My whole perspective changed after that conversation with him.

When I told my story during treatment, the staff reminded me I was only fourteen when my mom suicided. I had kept my mom's last voice message for a very long time after she killed herself. I really thought that a lot of what she said was my fault, and that if I had done something different, I could have stopped her. But I learned that it was not my job to save her. That I was not the source of her despair, her suicide. My job was just to be a kid. That's when I began connecting the dots and realized there was nothing I could have done differently, as my mom had been extremely sick and needed help.

Maybe if I could have opened up about this stuff earlier, I wouldn't have gone down the path I did. I had been keeping so much to myself and not talking to anyone about it. I came to realize that my mother's suicide doesn't define me. It's sad and painful, but it doesn't have to impact my future nor control how I go about my life.

Doing a timeline of my life events and then overlaying it with my use of alcohol and drugs was a game changer for me. I threw myself into the assignment and wrote pages and pages. It was a shock for me to see it documented that way, how the drugs and alcohol were controlling so much of my life.

By the time I was scheduled to leave, I was excited about my life but still feeling rocky. After all, I had missed a couple of weeks of treatment in my rebellion. So, I enrolled in an additional program. The extra time solidified the change I was trying to make. By the time I went home, I had enrolled in a third program, purely outpatient. I wanted to know that if I needed to talk about something, I had someone available. They also would drug test, and I thought that would be good for when I first got home. Just a few months before, I had been rebelling against rules, and there I was welcoming structure.

Nothing Is the End of the World
Prior to going to CBC I thought that depression and anxiety was just something I had to deal with. But after treatment I realized those conditions were influenced by the trauma in my life, and that using substances made them a lot worse. Today, I don't have anxiety, I don't have panic attacks, and I am not depressed. My trauma was the source of it, and I faced it directly. That first treatment set the foundation, giving me tools to handle anything that could be stressful and to keep me levelheaded.

I'm thankful I went down the road I did because of where I'm at today. I wouldn't trade who I am now for anything in the world. I'm a two and half years clean. I have a job, and my relationships with family members are incredibly close, which is very important to me. They were supportive of me through my whole recovery process. I am getting serious about a woman. I have been totally transparent with her about my history, and we are good.

Today, I am not as active in twelve-step meetings as I used to be, but I still use a sponsor. I have a different group of friends who aren't into drinking and drugs. We do some rock climbing and spend time out in nature. I also have a great group of friends in video game playing. We meet in person too, sit down, talk about things. I gave up all of my using buddies; they were just people to use with, and there is no reason to have them in my life now.

While life isn't perfect, I no longer freak out when things don't go the way I want or think they should. Nothing is the end of the world. Before treatment, every slight issue was game over. I didn't think it was possible to have a life that's simple. I enjoy it. It's not filled with all the excess noise.

I am so glad I got the help I did young. I know a lot of guys feel as if they are going to miss out on things being in recovery in their twenties. But the truth is, you will avoid years of going crazy, making bad decisions, and hurting other people. You can get a handle on it early and live the rest of your life actually being happy. In a great way, life is more colorful.

◆ ◆ ◆

Resilience

By Resmaa Menakem, SEP, LICSW, MSW, Sr. Fellow (Chaperone of the Somatic Abolitionism Philosophy and Practice)

While traumatic energetic loads can spread from one body to another through families and communities, and from generation to generation, resilience is built into the cells of our bodies. It can also ripple outward, changing the lives of people, families, and communities in positive ways. And like trauma, resilience can be passed down from generation to generation. One of the best things we can do for ourselves and our descendants is to metabolize our pain and heal our trauma.

COMMENTARY

From Claudia Black, PhD, Sr. Fellow
*(Pioneer in Addictive Family Systems and Clinical Architect
of Claudia Black Young Adult Center)*

The depression and anxiety Jason experienced were symptoms of his trauma related to his mom's suicide attempts, her final act, and her blaming him for her despair. Seeking drugs and alcohol was an obvious solution when he couldn't talk about his feelings. It's possible he could have found abstinence from his addiction, but to fully experience recovery, his trauma had to be addressed. In some programs, it is common to hear that trauma can be addressed later. But later may be too late. The unaddressed trauma, and any accompanying mental health conditions, are setups for a relapse. Jason was fortunate he had a family member that intervened when he did.

From Jennifer Angier, MA

First came the voice of Jason's father saying he was concerned, then the clinical director saying he saw more in Jason. Both men knew Jason was sitting on the edge of his own destruction, and they took the time to say they saw him and a path for him. Having people confront you while believing in you is often the pivotal act for change.

Undaunted Hope

Recovery is neither rare nor random. It happens all the time. There are millions of people around the world in recovery from substance use disorders at this very moment. With a willingness to genuinely surrender to the fact that your drug of choice has power over you, and that you would like your life to be different, recovery is within your reach.

One of the many gifts of recovery is it offers a plan in which we learn to live life on life's terms. Liz, Susan, Jason, and Chase found their pathways into recovery, and you can too. You deserve to let go of the shame and pain you carry. It's time to quit beating yourself up and to forgive yourself. That comes with a genuine willingness to let go.

CHAPTER FIVE

Discovering Myself
RECOVERY FROM
INTIMACY DISORDERS

What's wrong with me that I can't seem to settle for one guy?

Isn't there one man out there I can trust?

If people knew all of my sexual secrets, they would be shocked.

Intimacy is cultivated in our private, most personal spaces, and it can often—or at least early on—feel murky or elusive. We may wonder if we're doing it "right" or question what it means to love or be loved, unsure of our desires, needs, or ability to give. We may desperately cling to another or run in the opposite direction. No matter where our ability to relate intimately to another lies, being able to form close bonds is a basic need for everyone. We are hardwired to make deep connections. And bottom line, we all want and deserve to be loved.

The ability to be intimate with another and find the person who reciprocates with respect does not come readily for many people. Having healthy interpersonal behaviors, as well as choice of partners, is strongly influenced by what was modeled to us at a young age. Sadly, for so many of us, the portrayal of intimacy we witnessed and then internalized was a hodgepodge of truths, lies, and distortions. Even if our parents had the skills for healthy, loving connection, an addiction or mental health issue would readily interfere with those skills. If our family or cultural environments were also toxic, we may have developed untrue beliefs about ourselves and others that set us up as adults to repeat the dynamics we were exposed to: show affection or withdraw, be honest or deceptive, express tenderness or violence, be self-reliant or rely on others.

Interestingly, those of us from impaired families don't necessarily have difficulty getting into relationships; the challenges are more apt to arise once in one. We adapt, tolerate, intimidate, or control. Both men and women can struggle with intimacy to the point that we sabotage monogamous relationships with outside emotional or physical affairs or compulsive pornography. Many ultimately experience a diagnosable depression, succumb to substance addictions to bathe their pain, or engage in self-harm, or illegal sexual activities.

We do not willfully spend our life in self-sabotage; we simply do not know how to do it differently. We don't have the insight or skills. All we know is our fear and shame, often covered up with other behaviors. The impact of *developmental trauma*—trauma that occurred in our growing up years as we were developing our belief system—is likely what set us up to have our own chaotic and painful relationship styles. A few types of trauma that impact intimacy include domestic violence; abandonment; neglect; and sexual, physical, or emotional abuse. These can lead us to having a fear of intimacy or an inability be intimate in a healthy way even if the desire is there.

However the intimacy disorder is acted out, whether or not it is about attempting to gain power and control or a passive attempt to garner love, we can find healthy ways to be in a relationship with ourselves first, then another.

The following stories are from women who found they needed an intensive therapy experience to help them understand what was happening in their relationships to cause repetitive self-defeating behaviors. Addressing their family of origin history, learning to recognize boundary distortions and faulty thinking, then developing the skills for healthy external and internal boundaries would be critical in their recovery. In this process, they were able to stop their behaviors, heal from their pasts, and repair their bonds with others and themselves.

Finding Stillness   BY COURTNEY

Since I was a little kid, I have been in constant motion. I was the dancer, the musician, the straight-A student. I performed in whatever way I could. I was always seeking attention. *Look at me! Look at me!* This is how my flirting and getting involved with men started—and it became like a drug.

Other people might start with a little bit of crack, but a little bit of crack only lasts for so long. Then they need a little more to get the same effect, and then before they know it, they're sniffing a whole lot of the stuff, because it takes so much more to get the feeling they want. Well, it wasn't crack for me—it was attention. It got so it had to be more and more and more.

I am a talker, so the flirting would start with just talking, and then more talking, and then hanging out, and then one thing would lead to another. Never intercourse though. I think that helped me rationalize that what I was doing was okay.

Prior to getting married at twenty-two, I always had a boyfriend. I would start to mess around with another guy and then break up with the boyfriend; there was always this overlapping pattern. Even weeks before my wedding, I was having an affair with a college classmate. I rationalized that I was not married yet, so it was no big deal, it didn't count.

The Devil's Playground

My son was born after five years of marriage. By then, my husband started law school, and then my daughter was born, four years after my son. She had medical issues and needed a lot of attention. That seriously drained our relationship. She needed constant protection, attention, and treatment. I distanced myself emotionally from my daughter, I think both out of fear of losing her and because my husband was paying all of his attention to her. This isn't to blame him or excuse me, but my desire to be seen, heard, and validated wasn't being met.

When Facebook came into being, I began messaging with guys. Usually there were at least three of them at the same time who I was giving attention to and hoping to get attention from. Facebook was the devil's playground for me. As more and more people started using social media, I began hearing from guys from my college days—and I was off and running. Sometimes it was only virtual: texts, messages, videos, pictures. Other times I saw them in person, and there was kissing, heavy petting, but never intercourse.

I became increasingly distracted by my phone and laptop. I was always checking to see if anyone was reaching out to me, and to be sure no one saw something I didn't want them to see. The best place for privacy was the bathroom. I would take a long bath every night, at least an hour, easily longer. If I heard someone coming, I would delete whatever I was on or put the phone on the side of the bathtub where nobody would see it. It was an obsession. I took care of my responsibilities, but I certainly was not prioritizing my relationship with my kids or my husband.

In 2012, the same classmate I had an affair with before my marriage showed back up. I had been watching a popular reality show and a man on the show started thanking his brother, who happened to be the guy from before my wedding. So I picked up my phone, found him on Facebook, and messaged him. Like all my communication, it began with what sounded like an innocent message, "Hey, I saw your brother on TV," and then the conversation just continued. But when I couldn't physically get to him, I started flirting with a young guy in our neighborhood, and after a few months, my husband intercepted some very descriptive and incriminating text messages. We went to counseling then, and my husband took ownership for being absent a lot because he worked an hour away and spent long days there. We made up and kept going. My behavior lessened for a while, then I started up the long-distance emotional affair again with the guy from college. And again, when I couldn't get my needs met by him, then entered yet another college friend who was much more accessible. I was so obsessed with my original affair partner, and so delusional, that this new guy was really just a convenient substitute.

He was just one of my many emotional affairs.

My husband again sensed something was up and began investigating. This led to him confronting me in public in a parking lot while I was waiting for our daughter to finish dance class. Afterward, he went home and began packing his things, and I was unpacking them as fast as he was packing. I was a wreck. Thank heaven it resulted in our going back to therapy. This time the two therapists we were seeing suggested a ten-day intensive to focus on my stuff and us as a couple. After that, I stayed in individual therapy for a year, then I decided I didn't need it anymore. I was feeling close to my husband and on my best behavior.

Then we moved into the home where I grew up and eventually built a large addition. There were contractors coming and going; some were younger and cute, and one in particular fueled the flame of my addiction sparking my need for attention and validation. I would find any excuse for him to come back around, even breaking things for him to fix. There was never any physical contact with him, but he filled that desire for attention. My love addiction was in full swing. I was like a needy cat, going *pet me, pet me, see me, talk to me.* I had to have that fix of validation and interest constantly. With it came my eating disorder, mainly because I was too busy juggling my hectic life, and the anxiety from all the multitasking kept my stomach in knots. I even went to a GI doctor thinking I had a serious problem. But when your main foods are peanut butter and vanilla wafers, it can really mess with your body. I wanted people to notice how skinny I was getting, even women, which I see now was really a cry for help.

Fessing Up

I got so caught up in my addictive behavior that I didn't think anyone was noticing. How I thought I could get away with it—living in this small community I've lived in my whole life—made no sense. But people noticed; they weren't stupid. My boss and people at work had their suspicions and called me out for always checking my phone. My brother and my father saw my sneaking around, being distracted by my cell, getting caught in places I was not supposed to be. They asked my sister-in-law to talk to me.

After reminding me that she loved me, my sister-in-law said, "I'm noticing some stuff going on with you, and I need you to fess up to it. Like, right now. I need you to spill it. What's going on?"

While I didn't tell her everything, I did tell her a lot of it.

"Okay, when are you telling your husband?" she asked.

Two weeks before Christmas, I told my husband I was having an emotional affair with a new neighbor who had an interesting career that

I had become fascinated with. I can say I never had intercourse with him; whatever ever else you can imagine probably happened, but not that.

My husband said, "Go to treatment or the marriage is over."

I thought, No way could I go, I have two kids and it's the holidays. But I didn't want our marriage to end either. I didn't want to lose my family. I wanted to make my husband happy, so I decided to think of treatment as a vacation.

Then the therapist told me it was for four weeks. I threw a fit like a toddler. I thought, I can't leave my job, as a retailer in the holiday season. I can't leave my house. My family can't survive without me. No way am I going for a month! I cried hysterically. But it only got worse when they told me it was a six-week stay. I flipped my lid.

I said, "I can't do it."

My husband said, "If you don't do it. You are gone. And not just me, your daddy will tell you to get your shit and get out. You will be out of this house, and your family will live here without you."

I resigned myself to going. We negotiated, and I was able to stay home through Christmas day.

Pretty Little Bow

I entered treatment at Willow House (WH) on December 26, 2020, along with a wonderful group of ten women. I came to recognize that much of how I valued myself came from the outside. I had put a lot of energy into my outer appearance, and I didn't let anyone in. I have my box with a pretty little bow. But inside this box, when you open it, it's full of all kinds of shit. That's how I grew up; keep the outside together, and don't show the inside.

My family were big rug sweepers. We didn't talk about things that happened because if nobody talked about the elephant in the room, it didn't exist and it's not a problem. I grew up with rigid rules and had no experience trusting it to be different.

When I was fourteen there was this "incident in the woods." I had always called it that. My boyfriend raped me. I only told one friend and that was because I was scared I was pregnant; her mom brought a cup for me to pee in and then took it to a clinic to have it tested. I remember punching myself in the stomach so much, trying to undo what I thought

I might have done. I blamed myself for being out there in the woods and putting myself in a position to be taken advantage of. My parents didn't notice or ask anything; I would come to find out later that my mother was having an affair at that time, so she was preoccupied, and my father was always busy at work.

In treatment, I came to realize what happened in the woods was not my fault; what he did was against my will. I let go of the thought that it was my fault, I asked for it, I let it happen, or I should not have been where I was. Instead, I realized I told him no, and he did it anyway. It was a breakthrough moment for me to talk about it and say it wasn't my fault.

While I had not consciously made the connection previously, in all of my emotional affairs the one boundary I had was no intercourse. That boundary had been crossed in the rape. As much as I wanted the attention an affair was giving me, that was a boundary I would not cross.

The other trauma I experienced was my grandmother dying suddenly when I was ten. She was one of my caretakers and my best friend. It left a huge void in our close-knit family; my mom and dad went into survival and caretaking mode for my grandfather, who was lost and heartbroken. The message we all got was that we had to be strong and not upset him because he had a weak heart, but he died two years later. I think that is where my codependency started—managing people's emotions, people pleasing, and not allowing myself to feel my feelings.

The Value of Trust
Once home from Willow House, I took the advice of engaging in ninety meetings in ninety days, therapy, and twelve-step meetings. My main group is an all-female SLAA (Sex and Love Addicts Anonymous) on Zoom for moms, and I also do a Zoom codependency group weekly. My husband and I did couples counseling with a husband-and-wife duo for about eighteen months, which was so beneficial. I still do a weekly book study group and individual therapy weekly.

Intimacy was my problem, and now I know how to be intimate. It starts with being present with myself, so stillness, as silly as it sounds, was big. In treatment I learned both the value of being still and how to be still, how to stop the perpetual need to be in motion, to make something happen. This is in part why I did not return to work full-time. I needed to be more still, but also needed to not be in a job that required "selling myself" to get people to buy something. That's not a good way for me to find my value.

I am happy to say today my husband and I have no secrets, and we don't minimize things. I used to be a big minimizer by sugarcoating and telling half-truths to make things seem okay. I could also be passive aggressive, but now I try to express my feelings instead of stuffing them. We are brutally honest, and if that means we disagree, we disagree. Conversations are much easier when you aren't trying to hide things.

I know what I need and what I don't need. I no longer search for attention. If I notice another guy, I don't give him the sign that I am "open for business." Now I attach far more value to having trust in a relationship than to the high of the dopamine.

◆ ◆ ◆

What Is Love Addiction?

By Pia Mellody, RN, Sr. Fellow (developer of original Meadows Model of treatment)

There are six criteria for *love addiction*:

- Falling in love with the fantasy of a relationship
- Assigning a disproportionate amount of time, attention, and value to the other person in the relationship above yourself
- Neglecting or devaluing yourself while in a relationship
- Perceiving yourself as one-down (thinking and acting as if you have less value than the other person)
- Fear of being able to take care of self
- Perceiving any distancing as a threat to your survival

Those with a love addiction may also have underlying codependence, trouble loving themself, trouble containing or protecting boundaries, trouble being authentic in a relationship, or trouble living in moderation versus in extremes.

* While there is not yet a formal clinical diagnosis of love addiction, the pioneering work on love addiction, first outlined by Stanton Peele and Archie Brodsky in the late 1970s, was expanded upon by Pia Mellody over the decades.

COMMENTARY

From Havi Kang, LPC
(Willow House)

When women come to Willow House for treatment, they carry with them various types of trauma that have impacted their ability to have healthy intimacy (see sidebar "What Is Intimacy?"). For Courtney, it was rape, the death of a caretaker, and an insecure attachment to her parents. The traumas will vary from person to person. But no matter the trauma, for these women, their intimacy compass is skewed.

The first step in healing intimacy issues is understanding and identifying the beliefs, feelings, and behaviors that are driving the inability to be an intimate human being. Once you can see the behaviors that perpetuate this, you can begin to explore where these behaviors began. It's important to look at the messages you received throughout your life that are rooted in these behaviors, as well as have the willingness to start changing the behaviors.

Typically, these behaviors are serving us in some way—perhaps they're protecting us from being hurt. For instance, it may feel safer to be alone, or to be in some semblance of a relationship but emotionally disconnected. You might think of this relationship as two people walking down a railroad track together, parallel to each other, heading in the same direction. They have mutual goals—a family, a house, participating in community—but each is on their own track. Should they reach their arms out to each other, they won't connect, as there's too much distance between those rails. They cannot connect emotionally. Courtney and her husband outwardly appeared to have the relationship people aspire to, but that could not happen with Courtney's unhealthy drive for attention by other men, her fear of genuine intimacy, and her unresolved trauma.

Her behavior gave her temporary validation, what is called *outer esteem*, a moment of esteem that she had not learned to develop internally. A part of her treatment is learning how to validate herself and to embrace her inherent value.

Another big step in the healing process is learning and practicing boundaries, which include external and internal boundaries. Oftentimes, during traumatic events when boundaries are not in place, their absence may increase the intensity of the trauma symptoms. For example, Courtney's response to her accumulated trauma was acted out in extreme compartmentalization and secrecy, coupled with an attraction to dangerous and high-risk situations.

From Jean Collins, LCSW
(Clinical Consultant)

All intimacy disorders are born out of a fear of intimacy. Courtney's overlapping-relationship pattern tells me she was never fully present in her primary relationship—she was afraid of getting too close. She sought intimacy outside of her primary relationship but would only take it so far, mostly to the stage of getting attention. Courtney's intimacy disorder merged as sexual intrigue, attention-seeking using her sexuality, exhibitionism, and sexual compulsivity.

Her sexual acting out was what Sr. Fellow Patrick Carnes calls a "trauma repetition." In part, *trauma repetition* is an effort by the victim to bring resolution to the traumatic memory—in Courtney's case, her rape, when she felt powerless. Later she would use her sexuality to get the attention she desired while having control over the situation. By repeating the experience, the victim tries anew to figure out a way to respond in order to eliminate the fear. Instead, the victim simply deepens the trauma wound.

Courtney is accurate in describing her behavior as an addiction—and like any addiction, it helped her to escape unwanted feelings, assume power and control, and fill an emptiness inside. She was aware of her behaviors, as she talked about how she learned to stuff feelings, about the control she assumed by allowing anything but intercourse in her encounters, and about her tenacity to be noticed, filling a void.

In addition to growing up in a family that was rule-heavy, Courtney's family also contained an element of hypocrisy. Her mother modeled living a double life outside of the family values, deceit within her marriage, and poor sexual boundaries. Both parents were preoccupied, neglecting Courtney's needs, which likely fueled her need for attention.

Courtney also exhibited many of the characteristics of someone who is *love avoidant*, which is the other side of the *love addiction* coin. *Love avoidance* is a compulsive relationship cycle that appears to be intimate but avoids vulnerability (intimacy), because the love avoidant is walled in. Someone who is love avoidant may have sufficient social skills to reflect an interest in another, but they will not share intimately their thoughts and feelings. Like Courtney, love avoidants will evade intensity within a relationship by creating intensity outside of it. They will avoid being known in order to protect themself from engulfment and control the other person.

While Courtney benefited from her initial and follow-up therapy after her ten-day intensive, she did not have the foundation to sustain her in recovery. She was in need of more long-term treatment that offered her a milieu of other women working on similar issues and doing more in-depth trauma work. Completing long-term treatment gave her the foundation she needed to fully understand the root cause of her acting out and the ability to be intimate in her primary relationship.

Down the Rabbit Hole Again   BY MEGAN

"I'm never going to find another healthy man," "I am never going to be attractive again," "I am not smart," "I can't take care of myself," "I ruined my kids' lives." Down the rabbit hole I went. I wasn't getting out of bed until late in the day. I was consuming movies. I was constantly worried and anxious about anything and everything.

Just Looking for a Good Time

I wasn't always depressed. I always had a lot of friends in school. The things I liked most about school were the other kids, and I was athletic and played sports a lot. I didn't have any real goals as much as I was just trying to have a good time and avoid what was happening at home. Getting a boyfriend was never a problem. I was fun and attractive. After high school, I moved fifty miles away and shared an apartment with a girlfriend. I went to a local community college and worked in restaurants. That's where I met my first husband. I married the first time at twenty-one. In our somewhat brief marriage, we partied a lot, and we argued a lot. Then he got another woman pregnant, and that ended our seven-year marriage.

It wasn't long before I got into another relationship. That guy had a master's degree, and I thought that his education was the ticket to a better life. While I was never physically hit, he was controlling and emotionally abusive. He was great at isolating me from my friends and family, telling me how they were not good for me. He handled our social life in a manner that didn't include others. He had me sell my car so we only had one that he was in charge of. In time he controlled how I spent my time, even what I wore. He coerced me into engaging in sexual practices I didn't like or want. He often told me of women coming on to him at work, and that I was lucky to have him, since so many other women wanted him, too. He said that no one would love me like he did. Sad to say I believed him and accepted all of his reasons for everything he did. I didn't have any confidence in myself and thought I needed him or someone in order to be okay. He was masterful at manipulation. He was so good with words, so persuasive, that I never challenged him. I felt dumb in comparison. After eight years of berating me, when he left me for his cocaine and prostitutes, I was totally demoralized.

At the time of our divorce, I had two children under the age of four, no job, and lived across the country from family and friends. He was out of the house on cocaine and prostitute binges but still controlling me with threats of taking the kids away from me. I was immobilized. I didn't know how to take action on anything, and he left me with no money and no ongoing support. I had to work, but it was a struggle to keep up with the monthly bills on an office assistant's salary. I struggled with finding babysitters for my children. Fortunately, my sister showed up and took me to a doctor for antidepressants, enrolled me and paid for services at a counseling center, purchased household supplies, and paid for an attorney. With her help, I got mobilized. Within a year I was dating again.

Feeling better about myself, I decided I didn't need the antidepressants and stopped counseling. Then this guy came into my life and swept me off my feet. Like the last one, he was going to save me, and in this case also take care of me and my family.

Another Man to Fulfill Me

The first few years were good. We were both working, and my kids were being cared for. I had support with this husband in handling the threats that had continued by my ex-husband. But in time, there was too much partying. We had a lot of good times, and drinking was always center stage. This meant we were away from the kids more and more. We were married four years when I became aware he was having affairs. That's when my depression started to creep back in.

I started to gain weight. Not working, I would curl up on a couch for hours, not doing any housework, not volunteering, just spacing out on television and my phone. I got the kids to school, but once they were off, my day shut down. My husband was angry with my lack of initiative and how I looked. He was by now always critical of me. Finally, after nine years of marriage, he left to be with someone else. The kids were devastated, and I was numb.

I spaced out on life. The kids just sort of did what they wanted. In time, that meant drugs for my son, which he sold out of the house. I ignored it and pretended it wasn't going on. My daughter left to live with a girlfriend's family when she was seventeen.

One more time, my sister showed up and helped me get back on antidepressants and she put money into my household. While I had somehow managed to get a job, it was not enough to make ends meet, as there was no child support from the kids' father.

Needing to Be Rescued

While no longer that same attractive, vibrant woman, I started a phone and text relationship with a guy I had met much earlier in my life. He was a rescuer too, and I certainly was in need of being rescued, as I wasn't helping myself. After a year of long-distance dating, I moved from the Midwest to the East Coast to live with him. I blossomed. I found a new way of living. This was my first healthy relationship. He wasn't controlling or punitive when it came to my needs or wants. We enjoyed cooking together, sports, movies, and traveling. I also stayed on my antidepressants. I was happy.

Then he was killed in a car accident. It was horrific, the abruptness, the loss.

I tried to hang on to that happiness, but it wasn't long before the depression kicked in big time. While I got a part-time job, when not at work, I stayed in bed most of the day. I consumed movies. My screen time was at least eight hours a day. I didn't feel much of anything.

My sister, though I assume tired of coming to my aid again, one more time showed up. This time, she got me into treatment at The Meadows.

So Much to Learn

I was shocked to learn that I wasn't just depressed, I had love addiction and trauma. I learned how my early family life set me up for a desire to be taken care of by men, and that I had what they called "outer esteem": my ability to feel good about myself only existed in the context of being desired by another, specifically men.

I realized that I had a lot of negative self-talk and distorted thinking that created and fueled my depression. I told myself, "I need someone to take care of me," "I can't do life on my own, "I'm not smart," "I am not as good as others." I have learned to recognize that thinking and to stop it the minute I catch myself. I learned to replace it with affirmations—and this is something I continue today.

I also began to see the repetitive pattern of the men in my life having affairs, and that I might have a history of living with sexual addiction, beginning with my dad. I had not given much thought to my family life, but I began to realize that being emotionally abandoned by my father caused me to want men who I thought could fill up that hole.

I did a lot of work around my alcoholic dad not being there for me and scaring me so much. He did a lot of ranting and raving, called me names. He often drove while drunk with my me in the car and would deliberately swerve to scare me and then laugh like it was funny. He frequently accused me of being sexual with guys and made up these weird stories that he seemed to believe but were never true. He was wreaking terror in the family with his threats.

I certainly didn't get much direction when it came to life. I basically got up every day and tried to make the best of it. I stayed out of the house to avoid him as much as I could. My mom was a really nice person, but she was scared of my dad and she did what she had to appease him. Her way of parenting me was to let me do whatever I wanted to make up for what went on inside the house. I had a lot of freedom.

I have never thought about myself as having anger, but during Survivors Week, when we looked at childhood trauma, I was able to own and express being angry with my dad. I knew I was scared of him, but I thought my issues stemmed from my marriages. That week, I was able to recognize childhood and relational needs that were not met, safety being a big one. I learned that I had dissociated from a young age, and that I quickly go there when I feel vulnerable. Most important, I learned that I need to recognize inappropriate behavior and not excuse it, not tolerate it. That means having boundaries.

Family week was huge. Both of my kids came, and I was able to express my regrets about my lack of parenting. It was really painful; I have a lot of guilt. And while I can't go back, I can be there in healthy ways for them today. I hope they find some solace in my honesty. I was also able to tell my son the boundaries I was setting between us. My sister also came and we did this exercise where I released her from being my caretaker. Good for me, good for her.

A New Way of Looking at Life

Since my time in treatment, I have stayed on my antidepressants, which now include some antianxiety aspects. I attend a woman's support group, and I am currently seeing a therapist once a week. I have chosen not to drink. While I don't think I was addicted, there has been a theme of it setting me up to be in hurtful relationships and avoiding my pain and my responsibilities.

Today I have a sense of my own needs and realize I'm responsible for meeting them. It is not up to someone else to make me feel good about myself. I need and deserve respect, and that begins with me respecting myself. I need to recognize and honor my feelings because they often give me direction.

I also identified and follow through with boundaries I've set for myself and others. For example, I don't watch television or use any form of screens from 7:30 a.m. until at least 6:00 p.m. And I am off them by 10:00 p.m. I go to the gym and have a trainer. I am scheduled to do a grief workshop at Rio Retreat Center. I have a new way of looking at my life and what has happened now. And I don't beat myself up for the poor decisions I have made throughout my life.

I never realized how helpful therapy could be. I wish I had started it a long time ago and stuck with it. But that's okay. I'm here now.

♦ ♦ ♦

What Is Intimacy?
By Havi Kang, LPC (Willow House)

Intimacy can be defined as the level of safety, closeness, and trust two people can have between each other. It means being open and honest with who you are without the fear of rejection.

Intimacy exists on a spectrum, from little-to-no intimacy to high intimacy. Different levels of intimacy are required in different types of relationships, such as lover, parent, child, colleague, sponsor, therapist. For example, it is appropriate to have intimate sexual conversations with your lover, but not with your children. Here are some of the core ingredients that are important for relationships, especially intimate ones:

- Safety
- Honesty
- Love
- Emotional expression
- Intellectual closeness
- Religious closeness
- Trust
- Acceptance
- Emotional closeness
- Physical closeness
- Spiritual closeness
- Validation

- Sexuality
- Boundaries
- Nonjudgment
- Compassion
- Affection
- Communication
- Vulnerability
- Stability

Like the tangled roots of a tree, intimacy is complex, but it's the foundation of any relationship. Ultimately, intimacy is the willingness in which to be vulnerable, to share and to listen with respect for self and another.

COMMENTARY

From Stefanie Carnes, PhD, LMFT, Sr. Fellow
(Clinical Architect of Willow House, Clinical Sexologist)

For some individuals, the repetition of trauma can be a driving force in their life. This is not a conscious process, but by reliving aspects of our trauma, we understand it more, learn, and have a small measure of new understanding about it. The goal is to move beyond repeating the trauma story, which it sounds like Megan did.

One unacknowledged trauma for Megan was the ongoing episodes of *betrayal trauma* in her life. Betrayal trauma refers to the traumatic impact of being deceived, such as by gaslighting and other deceptive behaviors, by someone you loved, trusted, and relied upon. It is devastating and one of the most painful types of trauma, yet it often goes unrecognized because those who experience it feel so much shame that they feel as though they can't discuss their pain with anyone. It often leads to tremendous isolation. It also causes people to question their worth and value. They wonder if they are unlovable, not good enough, and not attractive enough. For Megan, these repeated instances of betrayal, starting with her father, her isolation, and her decreased self-esteem were likely the core features of her depression.

It is very common for women experiencing repeated episodes of betrayal to seek any method possible to escape the pain. For Megan, this was alcohol, food, and television. Unfortunately, self-medicating in these ways only leads to further isolation and depression. Megan's real healing began we she started rescuing herself, instead of waiting for others to do it for her. She went to treatment, stayed on her medication, and went to group. She started participating in passions that brought her joy. Doing the hard of work being there for herself and recognizing traumatic patterns in her life and having the courage to shift those patterns is true recovery.

From Tian Dayton, PhD, Sr. Fellow
(Developer of Relational Trauma Repair/Sociometrics)

Megan's hidden pain lay like a ticking time bomb inside of her. Growing up she appeared to function well by "looking good" and compartmentalizing pain. She found greater safety by staying out of the house as much as possible. She would also model her mother's tolerance for living with an acting-out, drinking man as well. Never having seen her mother openly deal with her father and not having done that herself, that horror of her father's behavior and her shut-down pain around it was relegated to a wordless world. It was never made conscious through feeling, naming, reflecting on, and talking about feelings of fear, pain, and anger. This unprocessed pain seems to have fueled her re-creation of one traumatic relationship after another. Wearing emotional blinders, Megan married not only without thought, but she also married without access to genuine feeling, which would have allowed her to know whether or not a man was right and good for her.

Therapy allowed Megan to directly experience the emotions that were at the core of her self-destructive choices and behaviors. It also gave her syndrome a name—love addiction and trauma—which appears to have helped her to distance from her shame and to feel able to access her righteous anger. Megan's unconsciousness around her father's hurtful behavior toward her, and her lack of a positive connection with him, interfered with her ability to make healthy relationship choices.

With the help of therapy, Megan was able to understand how she continually recreated past pain in current relationships and to see that she could choose to do things differently. She's taking responsibility for making the kinds of life changes that will allow her to consolidate her treatment gains, move in a positive direction, and create a support network so that when she feels herself sliding back into old patterns, she knows where to go for help.

From Jean Collins, LCSW

Having been covertly shamed as a child, causing her to not feel her worth, Megan grew up fearing she wouldn't get her needs met. She was naturally in a great deal of pain unless she was on a high with her love addiction. She was always looking to be rescued, and when the relationships ended, she became depressed. When she was engaged in her love addiction, she used sex and alcohol, and when she was in love addiction withdrawal, she used TV, food, sleep, and social media. While medication and her psychotherapy were critical in her healing, it wasn't until she did her underlying trauma work that she was able to sustain her recovery.

I Know Who I Am Now   BY AMBER

As a family, we were all struggling. But it was the 2011 crisis with my teenage daughter that was my first turning point. She was getting into trouble with boys, drugs, and staying out late at night. Then she ran away—and life blew up in my face.

What I wanted most in life was to be the mom I never had, but I had no idea how to be that. I loved my son and daughter fiercely, but not effectively. How was I supposed to handle their emotions—and support them in ways they deserved and needed—when I couldn't handle my own emotions?

When we found my daughter, we got her into treatment. There, a therapist suggested that I may need some help for myself; she suggested I was codependent. While I was a freaking mess, no way did I think I was codependent.

I had no idea how mentally, emotionally, spiritually, and physically sick I was. I had been living with undiagnosed PTSD, depression, and ADHD, and was drinking and abusing pain pills.

My daughter soon ended up in a second treatment program. Another counselor saw my severe codependency and recommended that I get help for myself. Over the next few weeks, I made that phone call many times and always hung up before anyone answered. Finally, one day, I allowed myself to talk to the intake staff and checked myself into a five-day workshop called Survivors.

Discovering My Value

I was forty years old with a mountain made up of layers upon layers of unresolved trauma and addiction. I was scared, so I vowed to myself that they didn't need to know all about me; I was going to keep my secrets.

When I got to the workshop, I was told I had value and that my needs were important—and they meant it, they believed it. In my childhood, there was such deprivation that I had not learned to value myself, let alone recognize my own needs. For example, at the time, I no longer had hunger or pain cues. Once, when I was a kid, I broke a bone in my foot and, because I was neglected by my parents, lived with it for years. I had learned to be needless, and as a consequence, my needs didn't get met.

During one exercise I was asked to place my hand on my heart and repeat after the therapist the words, "I have a right to be here. I have value and worth." I couldn't do it. I could only cry. On his hands and knees, the therapist looked up at my face with my head hanging down nearly to the floor and said, "Amber, your parents blew it. It's now your turn."

Those five incredible days of therapy led to a lot of good changes for me.

Getting Sober

One of the most significant changes was getting sober through Alcoholics Anonymous. I realized I had used alcohol as a medicator for my incredible pain, and in the process became addicted. The Twelve Steps are powerful, and applying those to my life gave me the basis to move forward. I did this with others who understood and accepted me without judgment. I found people I identified with. I began to let go of my shame.

Over the next few years, I attended AA on a regular basis and went to individual and couples' therapy. I was doing service work. I was putting my whole heart into AA. I even had three sponsees.

But while I was feeling some worth for the first time in my life, the impact of my childhood was beginning to resurface. I didn't know it at the time, but I was filled with existence shame. To cope, I lived in my head and continued to keep quiet about my secrets.

Owning My Reality

What I didn't dare tell anyone was that my dad had post-traumatic stress from Vietnam. He slept with a machete under his pillow. He was either full of rage—yelling, cussing, being physically abusive—or silent. On a daily basis he called my brother and I "shits." He drank all the time.

One night I was left home alone and got scared, so I went to the neighbor's house. When my dad got home, he grabbed his belt, held me upside down by my feet, and whipped me while I was naked. He often whipped me on my butt and legs. It was burned into my mind and bare skin: do not ever ask for help or tell the family secrets.

After the beatings, he would act so helpless, like a little kid. I would feel sorry for him. For years, I hung onto believing his moral compass was pointing to goodness and wanting to do the right thing in his heart. Yet his actions and lies were not congruent with that.

My mom had her own problems; she had tried to kill herself. She left when I was two years old, and my brother and I lived with my dad.

My mom's and dad's homes were both sexually charged. My mom walked around naked at her apartment and encouraged my brother and I to look at pornographic magazines when we visited her. As a little girl, she encouraged me to also go naked at home, even though her boyfriend was there. She took us to Bourbon Street, where we could see strippers through open doors.

There was a lot of pornography at my dad's house too. He drew pictures of nude women and hung them up in the house. All of this was normal to me.

I also had a stepmom who didn't want anything to do with me. She was emotionally cold and would lock me in my room for unending periods of time. This forced isolation was the most painful part.

I so wanted her to love me. I just wanted a mom and a dad who loved me. In my teen years, the way I got that love was through sex. By the time of my first marriage at twenty-one, I had been sexually abused by several people, including my dad, a female softball coach, and men at church.

I knew being taken advantage of sexually by my dad wasn't right; it hurt, and it was confusing because he was giving me some attention. When I was older, guys made me feel like I owed it to them. I didn't know how to say no—and I didn't know if I wanted to say no. I just wanted to be loved. Around this time, I crossed some line from being the victim to using sex to get my needs met, to soothe me, to feel a connection. I had developed a sex addiction.

I married an intern pastor who I thought had his act together and could save me. In reality, I would just be someone he thought he could control. The physical abuse began shortly after we were married, along with the emotional, mental, and spiritual abuse. I had been so used to other people, including myself, treating me as if I had less value than them that the abuse did not seem that unusual.

I had no boundaries and no idea how to take care of myself. My solution to this was an affair in my fifth year of marriage. When my husband found out, he said he wouldn't hit me anymore if I stayed. I didn't trust that at all, so I left with our two kids, one just a baby, and got remarried—to a man who was kind and respectful, who treated me like a valuable person where my voice, thoughts, and feelings mattered.

Another Turning Point

My grandson being born prematurely and my teenage son leaving home to live on the streets and use drugs in the same week was another turning point in my crisis. On top of feeling responsible for my daughter, now a mother, I felt hypervigilant about my grandson. I kept seeing this baby abandoned like I had been. My trauma from childhood was triggered. The pain and pressure of it all was getting heavier and heavier. I shoved it all down and went on autopilot.

I saw my son going down a hard path at a fast pace. In searching to find out about my son's behavior, I stumbled across pornography. My sex addiction was immediately reactivated. I began to compulsively masturbate while watching porn.

When the panic attacks started, I thought I was having heart attacks. I wasn't taking care of myself; I wasn't eating, wasn't changing my clothes. My depression was blatant. I lived in a state of dissociation. Finally, my daughter said my depression was so serious she couldn't leave my grandbaby with me.

So off I went to The Meadows, this time for a full treatment experience of forty-five days.

Willingness: The First Step

I arrived five years to the day I had attended Survivors. I was so ashamed. I felt like a failure. All I could do was cry.

I quickly realized that the first step was to be willing to ask for help. Asking for help meant trusting, and I trusted these people; I felt safe. I didn't have to worry that someone was going to harm me. I didn't have to think about anyone but me. And I was able to do that 100 percent without guilt. Within a couple days, I knocked on a therapist's door and asked for help. Through the tears, I told the therapist everything. My secret was finally out.

I showed up to groups. I participated in everything from trauma therapy to volleyball. The Meadows Developmental Model was validating to my recovery. I think of Pia Mellody, who developed it, as the grandmother to my inner child. I learned I could value my needs, that I had needs. I learned to distinguish when I was operating from my wounded, adapted, or functional adult. I discovered an inner child that I could nurture. I learned I had the right to my own body, that nobody else does. I learned that I had to have internal boundaries. This meant holding on to what I want and need and not allowing other people's thoughts and needs to override my own. This was crucial, and to this day I do visualizations to help keep boundaries intact.

The visualization I initially created was me in an ironwoman suit. There is a door over my heart and a handle on the inside, and I'm the only one who can open and close it. Now I use the Elastic Woman visualization. She is strong and brave and kind. She's not afraid to ask for help. She can honor herself and others in their diversity. She holds boundaries by being flexible, and when needed, she moves to wherever she feels safe. She knows who she is, along with her limitations.

During treatment, my husband of twenty years came out for a five-day family workshop. I was real scared. I thought if he saw me for who I was, he wouldn't want to be with me. I had convinced myself that he didn't really love me. These thoughts came from my childhood beliefs about my not being of value, not being lovable, of being damaged and rejected. I felt like a dirty, stained garment.

During one exercise, the outline of my body was traced onto a large piece of paper. On the outside of the outline, I had to write the derogatory messages I believed about myself. On the inside, I wrote affirmations or counter beliefs that contradicted the negative and shaming beliefs. Then I presented everything to the small group, of which my husband was a part. It was incredibly painful for me to share what I was fighting against every day. It was the first time my husband saw my pain. And although I felt very vulnerable, it was also an intimate and connective time.

In another exercise, we had to sit facing each other and share our concerns and feelings for each other and the relationship. I told my husband that I didn't think he loved me, that he was with me to validate himself. When I said that, I saw tears going down his face, the pain in his eyes. I finally knew that he really did love me. That moment of connection was very powerful for me.

The inner child work was also very helpful. I allowed myself to visualize going back and rescuing baby Amber. As I did this, I remembered what the Survivors therapist from five years ago had said: "Your parents blew it." I took advantage of this and imagined going into the delivery room and seeing me as a vulnerable, precious baby. I visualized telling my mom I was adopting this baby. I told her I was no longer dependent on her, and I was going to give this baby the love she deserved.

The Biggest Judge Was Me

Today I love this vulnerable part of me. I give her positive and empowering messages about herself. She is my wounded self. I take care of those parts of me with my newfound functional adult skills. Every day I do visualization exercises; if I don't, I feel off that day.

Since treatment, the entire foundation of my marriage has changed. It had to. Once a week we sit down and specifically talk about our feelings. We use the format they taught us for communication, for being able to speak and listen with respect. We talk on a heart level and hold space for each other. We listen to learn rather than listen to respond. It has saved our relationship.

I can take accountability for my mistakes, and I don't judge myself like before. I don't say self-deprecating or shaming statements. I don't degrade myself or make myself feel less than. A part of being in recovery is being with others who won't judge. But the biggest judge was me.

Before this treatment experience, I did not have a sense of self. The sexual abuse taught me that my body was not worth protecting and it was good only for sex, which was the only human contact I had growing up. Knowing I have a right to protect my body and my heart—what is on the inside—has changed my life. I know who I am today. I choose who I surround myself with and the behaviors I will allow. It has also taught me that I am equally responsible for the energy, words, and actions that I put out into the world.

While my adult kids don't live exactly how I want them to live, I am much better at recognizing what I can and cannot control, and I understand healthy boundaries. I don't lose myself in their problems.

Today I practice mindfulness. I take time to orient with my five senses, where I pause and I look, listen, feel, taste, and smell. This is helpful because the PTSD will never totally leave. The ability to be reactive, to be hypervigilant, to feel anxious, to see the dark side of things can come back if I don't practice the coping skills I have today. I also do a Seventh Step of the twelve-step related prayer, where I ask God to replace my denial, my tendency to minimize, with his truth and grace.

I want women, particularly women who have sexual shame, to know that they are worth getting help. No matter what was done to you, what you did, or who you came from, you are valuable and have worth. You always have and always will.

◆ ◆ ◆

From Stefanie Carnes, PhD, LMFT, Sr. Fellow

Growing up in a household where your parents were as likely to hit you as they were to hug you makes for a very insecure environment. The child, in these circumstances, has to develop attachments to caregivers who are not nurturing and are unsafe. For these children, as for young Amber, it leads to the confusion of pain and love. They desperately desire connection, and also deeply fear it. As is the case for most people with *complex trauma*, Amber's trauma continued into adulthood. Complex trauma victims will seek relationships with people who may further abuse them. And in Amber's case, it led her to project her *insecure attachment* onto her husband.

Amber has the further complication of the sexual trauma and incest by her father that fundamentally involves a deep betrayal. She learned at a very early age to use her sexuality to get her needs met for love, validation, and connection from men. Couple this with the shame and anguish of her complex trauma, and it is understandable why she developed addictions to sex, love, and alcohol.

Many trauma survivors have secrets that they feel they have to take to their grave. What they don't realize is that holding on to their secrets will surely take them to their grave. As in Amber's case, sharing her darkest secrets was a critical turning point in her healing journey.

Another critical point in her healing was finally being able to recognize love in her partner, likely because she had accepted her worth and value for herself. One of the incredible benefits of recovery is that we can learn intimacy skills and develop *secure attachments*. Amber and her husband were able to make a profound shift in deepening their attachment connection, providing Amber with the love she sought all of her life.

By the end of her story, Amber was not only showing up and being more emotionally available for her husband, she was also showing up for herself. Accepting her vulnerable, wounded "inner child" has allowed her to release the carried shame that was passed down by the intergenerational and complex trauma in her family. Reparenting her inner child will open up space for self-compassion and self-love. It serves as a solid foundation going forward to live in more vulnerable connection with her husband, be a more solid supportive mother, and be at peace within herself.

From Jean Collins, LCSW

Amber truly exemplifies the slogan "it works when you work it." She understood and implemented the Meadows Model, putting it into practice and integrating it into her life. In particular, Amber was able to identify the core issues of the model throughout her life:

- **Self-Esteem Issues:** Difficulty loving yourself
- **Boundary Issues:** Difficulty containing and protecting yourself
- **Reality Issues:** Difficulty being real or authentic
- **Dependency Issues:** Difficulty taking care of yourself
- **Moderation Issues:** Difficulty staying out of extremes

Desperate when she came to treatment, Amber hung on to the messages she began to hear about having been born precious and with value. She grew to understand that as a consequence of poor and abusive parenting, she was not able to integrate that sense of value. The "inner child" work was critical to her developing compassion for herself. Plus, a newfound understanding of boundaries led her to letting go of her secrets. The model gave her a framework for knowing herself better and a direction for what she needed to do in her recovery. Ultimately, it led to honesty with herself; when she shared her sexual abuse and subsequent sex addiction, her recovery really got traction.

Undaunted Hope

Intimacy begins with yourself. It starts with knowing your values and what is important to you, being able to identify your needs and wants and feelings, and putting that into words. You need to be able to trust your own perceptions and establish healthy boundaries. Attending to these issues is a radical act of self-care. By committing to yourself and your recovery first, you are primed for healthy intimacy.

CHAPTER SIX

Embracing All of Me
RECOVERY FROM
EATING DISORDERS

I hate the way I look.

I'm ashamed of how ugly I am.

I need to lose a few more pounds.

How often are you on a social media site and comparing your body to somebody else's? Do you like it when people tell you are skinny? Do you have a certain number in mind that you have to meet when you get on the scale in order to feel good about yourself? Do you talk to yourself frequently, telling yourself you are ugly, gross? Do you avoid eating when you are hungry or feel guilt when you eat? Do you feel a sense of power in exerting this control you have with food?

Just like with a substance addiction, our relationship with food can become all-consuming and take control of our life. And like other addictions, soon we are manipulating our schedule, being deceptive with others, rationalizing our behavior, and, irrespective of the consequences, do not want to give it up.

Sadly, society's ideal body weight and shape are more associated with fashion and sex appeal than with health. Magazines, television, and all forms of social media continue to impact people's perception of what makes them attractive and desirable to others. Being a compulsive eater has great stigma to it. Being restrictive or compulsive with exercise is culturally reinforced and even applauded.

We are much more apt to succumb to these outside cultural influences if there have been aspects to our lives that influenced the need to seek perfectionism, the need for outside approval, the need for control, or the sense of having no control. Having experienced various forms of abandonment often fuel a need to restrict, binge, purge, or compulsively eat. Our relationship with food may be the one thing we feel we can control, and may be the only thing we find that offers solace or relieves pain. The relationship we have with food is often related to an emotional hunger and it gets acted out with various forms and degrees of an eating disorder.

All eating disorders must be taken seriously. Anyone with any of these disorders is struggling with constant and progressive self- criticism, distorted thinking, the continual eroding of esteem and unrelenting perfectionism. This reinforces the belief that no matter what you do, it's not good enough, therefore you are not good enough, which only sets you up for self-defeating thoughts and behaviors. As with addictions or mental health issues, eating disorders are tragic problems, involving years of unhappiness. Obsessions with food and critical feelings about your body affect every aspect of your lives, from moods to work performance, physical health, to the ability to form and maintain personal relationships.

Irrespective of the degree to which an eating disorder interferes in your life, it deserves attention. The following narratives are reflective of female adults deeply embroiled in their eating disorder who sought treatment. As Sr. Fellow and author Jenni Schaeffer says in her book *Life Without Ed*: "Some people are deeply embroiled in their eating disorder, others are only casually dating." These stories reflect those who are deeply embroiled—and the possibility of a thriving, balanced life when in active recovery.

Skin and Bones BY KASEY

When I was in middle and high school, people labeled me anorexic because I was so tall and skinny. People would refer to me as "Skin and Bones." Yet, I was doing nothing to be skin and bones. I was just growing, and my weight couldn't keep up with my height.

But to me, this label wasn't a bad thing. I had gotten the idea in my head that being skinny was a good thing. It meant people liked me and wanted to be around me. So I was okay with my body being very thin, since I was likeable that way.

I wasn't outgoing, though. I was shy. I didn't have much exposure to other people, so I wasn't trusting of others. Being an only child, I was comfortable entertaining myself. While I had a small group of friends, I was okay being alone. I learned to not rely on other people. Of course, I relied on my parents, but I was very good at keeping myself occupied.

My parents were very loving, and my needs and wants were met. My dad worked and my mom was a stay-at-home mother. She did everything for me, so I was spoiled. I didn't learn how to be an adult until I went to college.

I took theatre arts in middle school and loved it. I did it every year. But in high school I kept being overlooked for the plays. I tried so hard, but I was never chosen. Every time the cast list came out, I wasn't on it. I really began to question myself. While I loved the theater, I didn't want to keep feeling the crushing rejection. By the time I was a senior in high school, I had no self-esteem, no self-confidence. I became so depressed and anxious that I was hospitalized for five days.

My parents came from a generation where mental health was not talked about, so they had no idea how to deal with what was going on.

The Hamster Wheel

At about age seventeen, I stopped growing and started to put on more weight. I was five feet eleven when I went off to college. I was still skinny, but since I wasn't as skinny as I used to be, and because I equated "skinny" with "good," I started to hate what I looked like. I saw myself three to four times bigger than what I actually was. I cried every time I looked in the mirror.

Social media had a big influence on me. I was so fallible to all the reflections of being skinny. I just wanted to be praised, and I knew skinny was good.

I stepped on the scale every day. I had a certain number in my head, and I told myself that if my weight ever went over this number then that would be it.

One day, the scale showed a number higher than the one I had set for myself. A switch flipped, and the hamster wheel of the insanity of the disease began.

In the span of only one year, I was restricting my food, starving myself into anorexia. I was overexercising, and it took a toll on my body. I was fatigued all of the time. I was also very depressed. I isolated myself and kept away from everybody. No one knew, I didn't tell anyone. I had no friends, so my eating disorder thrived in isolation.

My eating disorder had a lot to do with my need for control. I couldn't control what other people thought about me, or what they said. I couldn't control anything around me or my environment, but I could control my weight. I could control what I ate and what I didn't eat. I could control how much I exercised. The number on the scale meant more than what anybody else thought of me.

I was preoccupied with my body. Every time I tried to step off the hamster wheel, I would instantly get back on because the disorder was familiar, comfortable. I knew what I could expect.

Yet, I couldn't live like this. I knew that if I kept doing what I was doing, I probably wouldn't last much longer. There was an inkling of, There's got to be something better out there for me. I was desperate. So, on my own, at nineteen, I decided to enroll in treatment.

I was terrified because I didn't know what help would look like. The two biggest things for me were, How do I live my life without my eating disorder? and Who am I without it? Fear and anxiety defined me.

Yet, I had this deep feeling I was going to the right place, that I was going in the right direction. I had to try.

Stepping Outside the "Prison of Picky Eating"

When I started therapy, I thought my eating disorder and me were the same. But when I read *8 Keys to Recovery from an Eating Disorder* by Carolyn Costin and Gwen Schubert Grab, I realized that there was an eating disorder self and a healthy self—me. That was huge distinction for me.

Another defining moment was when I learned to detach from the scale. I learned that the scale does not define my worth. I am more than that.

I learned that there is no such thing as "good" or "bad" food. There's just food. In treatment, there were times when we would go to restaurants together, and a dietitian or staff would guide us through the meal. The structure was helpful. Now I just choose something I like and eat it.

I learned I would have to do things that made me uncomfortable, like eating a "full plate." At The Meadows Ranch (TMR), the full plate consisted of foods from all food groups. I had to learn to step outside of the prison of picky eating I had kept myself in to be able to move forward.

Learning to like things about myself that have nothing to do with my body was totally freeing. I found my creativity in the art room. In my art and other groups, I learned that I don't need to focus on what I look like, or what I thought I looked like, to be happy.

To finally be with people who could understand me and the insidiousness of restriction, my obsession with weight, and my distorted body image was critical for my self-acceptance. The women I spent hours talking with were empowering because we found similarities that had nothing to do with our eating disorders.

Living Life on Life's Terms

I was discharged from The Meadows Ranch on October 23, 2014. I'm very grateful to say that I've never had a relapse. I live my life one day at a time; if I get too far ahead or too far behind, then I am just not in the place I need to be.

Part of my recovery has been learning about hunger cues. The way I starved my body, it doesn't trust me anymore. It's like it says, "Oh, we're not going to tell her if she's hungry because she's not going to feed us anyway." So, it took me a while once I started to gain weight for me to register hunger. Now I eat when I'm hungry, and I stop when I'm full.

Today, I cope with my feelings by turning to other people: my therapist, my dietitian, my family, my friends. I learned to be very honest and say what I feel. If something comes up then I take care of it, and I talk about it. This is critical, because otherwise I might return to restriction or attach to another addiction.

Because my relationship with food was so much about control, today I practice the Serenity Prayer. It's a good tool for me. Sometimes it's a fine line between what I can and can't control and what I need to hand over and let go of. Trying to control just doesn't turn out good for me. I will dip back into my old behaviors if I start to hold on to things. I've learned to live life on life's terms.

But recovery is not linear, it's a lot of ups and downs. It's not butterflies and rainbows all the time. It's trial and error for me.

When I began to gain weight, learning how to live with a new body and accept it was difficult. But today when I try on clothes, I don't think about whether I'm pretty or cute or attractive. I think about how I feel. How do I feel in this dress? Is it a little tight? If so, I take it off and go up a size.

I also tend to not use the word "healthy" in my recovery. I think that word is too closely linked to toxic fitness culture. For instance, society tends to label you "not healthy" if you are in a bigger body. I think of "healthy" physically in terms of things like my blood work or whether I have a headache. Instead of "healthy" eating I think of intuitive eating or mindful eating.

Now I work at a wellness center, and recently I decided to try a new fitness class. The trainer was shouting at the class and pushing us. *Do more! Feel the sweat! Not enough yet!* My body was crying out, Please stop! I'm not comfortable! I know my limits, and that was pushing past it.

I do not need a group fitness class. But I wouldn't have known that if I hadn't tried. So, lesson learned.

I don't need negative messages from trainers or anyone else. While I can't escape the internet, when it comes to social media, I have learned to scroll past content that doesn't support me in recovery.

You Can Change Your Way of Thinking

It's okay to not know what your future will be. What you really need to know is that it can be different from what it is today. You don't have to stay where you are; you have a way out. You do not have to live in pain, in delusion. You don't have to live your despair.

Anybody of any shape or size can have an eating disorder. Even though you aren't thin, you still can have an eating disorder. It's not about the size—it's about what's going on inside in your body.

So remember this: What the disease tells you is not true. You have to build new neural pathways by practicing new behaviors over and over. You can change your way of thinking. I did.

Carolyn Costin and Gwen Schubert Grab wrote in *8 Keys to Recovery from an Eating Disorder*, "Being recovered is when a person can accept his or her natural body size and shape and no longer has a self-destructive relationship with food or exercise. When you are recovered, food and weight take a proper perspective in your life and what you weigh is not more important than who you are, and in fact, actual numbers are of little or no importance at all. When recovered, you will not compromise your health, or your soul to look a certain way or reach a certain number on the scale."

Yeah, that's my life today.

♦ ♦ ♦

Society Has an Eating Disorder
By Jenni Schaefer, Sr. Fellow (Author, Recovery Advocate)

Hangovers don't get complimented. Neither do overdoses. But society applauds rigid diets, compulsive exercise, and, of course, thinness. This can make it difficult for someone with an eating disorder to know that their relationship with food and their body is a problem. Someone with anorexia might receive continual compliments for having a serious, life-threatening illness: "I wish I could eat like you! You look great!"

Society has an eating disorder. And people, like the three women in this chapter, who go through the grueling work of recovery gain what many people *without* eating disorders never do: true peace with food and their bodies. So, ironically, those with eating disorders can become better than most at coping—and thriving—in an eating-disordered society.

$$\boxed{\text{COMMENTARY}}$$

From Jenni Schaefer, Sr. Fellow
(Author, Recovery Advocate)

A lot of people weigh themselves, but obsessively checking the number on the scale is a form of *body checking*: anything you do that "checks" your body. Think trying on those "skinny clothes" in the closet just to see if they fit. Or using a tape measure to gauge the size of your arms. Or pinching fat or staring into the mirror at perceived flaws.

Body checking fuels bad body image. When we narrow our self-image to these types of measurements, reinforcing their importance each time, the view of ourselves can become very narrow. It is easy to miss what we aren't looking for: the glow in our skin, the sparkle in our eyes, the energy and light that others might see when they look at us.

It is easy to be completely off about how you look when *body image dysmorphia* takes over, as happened for Kasey. This is a very real experience of having a distorted self-image. Imagine looking into the mirror at a fun house and seeing yourself as taller and thinner or shorter and larger.

Mirror exposure work with a therapist is one way people can begin to see themselves more clearly. This includes someone with an eating disorder looking into the mirror and describing their appearance in neutral objective terms: "My eyes are brown. My hair is short." By dropping eating disorder language like "My thighs are too big," and using neutral terms, space can open up for noticing positive features. "My thighs are strong." To heal from body image dysmorphia, you can't just avoid mirrors. For one, avoidance only fuels anxiety. Plus, mirrors can be useful when it comes to getting dressed in the morning.

As the brain slowly rewires, which can be aided with the help of neurofeedback, an individual's view of themselves normalizes. They also begin to see that appearance doesn't define someone's worth. As Kasey described about shopping and trying on clothes, she doesn't think about whether or not she's pretty or cute, but she focuses on how she feels.

Kasey didn't choose to have an eating disorder, but she chose to heal. Specifically, she chose to be "recovered," as she shared in the quote at the end of her story. This is a common term used among the eating-disorder community. Kasey isn't "in recovery" maintaining abstinence, as many describe recovery from substance use. But she is "recovered," maintaining a relationship with eating and exercise that no longer allows these things to control her.

From Kara Fowler, LPC-S, RD
(Executive Director of The Meadows Ranch)

Kasey's story reflects some of the struggles common to many young people in today's world. For instance, our mobile devices—unthinkable for most of us to be without these days—supply a constant barrage of images depicting thinness and other stilted perspectives of what makes one desirable or acceptable. While social media is not solely responsible for the development of an eating disorder, it certainly can add fuel to the fire in a person with other risk factors and predisposing traits.

Kasey refers to herself as being shy, a common trait in those who have anorexia nervosa, along with worrying and perfectionism. Another common trait is difficulty trusting and relying on others, which Kasey learned growing up. But the fact is, we are all wired for connection. We are designed on a nervous system level to be our best when we can *co-regulate*, which means to reach a calm or soothed state with the help of another. This inherent need for connection can get easily minimized, or dismissed altogether, in our overachieving, individualistic, and "just do it" Western culture.

As an only child with a shy temperament, Kasey may have engaged in fewer opportunities to learn co-regulation, even though her parents were clearly positive and available resources, and even though she had plenty of opportunities for peer interaction. Her temperament also may have made it more difficult to communicate her emotions and needs to others. In perhaps not feeling known to others beyond what was "seen"—the thinness that she experienced growing up—she may have struggled more than some teens in developing an identity beyond her appearance and eating disorder.

In treatment, skills related to self-regulation as well as co-regulation, can lead to profound shifts, especially for people like Kasey. Peter

Levine's Somatic Experiencing therapy (see sidebar "What Is Somatic Experiencing?") emphasizes the importance of developing *interoception*, which is our ability to sense our own bodily experience. The transformation is palpable as Kasey learned to connect with herself and her body in a new way. Most people in the process of recovering from an eating disorder find learning to sense and respond to natural physical signals of hunger and fullness scary at first. That's why, as Kasey recalled, it's often helpful to have the support of peers and members of a treatment team at meals. This process also leads to real empowerment. Being able to know what we need and respond to it helps us maintain equilibrium and can replace the false experience of "control" that the eating disorder often seems to provide.

Developing interoception, as well as gaining confidence in trusting herself through interactions with supportive others, appears to have been essential in Kasey ultimately having the discernment and empowerment to reject an exercise class that didn't work for her. Kasey's story shows how building these tools in her day-to-day life can allow for true change and growth beyond her eating disorder. Instead of relying on external cues to tell us who we are or who we should be—whether it be social media, other people's comments, a diet, or a number on the scale—we can know our own reality and define ourselves more authentically and fully.

Desperate to Fill the Hole   BY DANIELLE

I began drinking when I was fifteen. When I drank, I drank to get loaded, and over the years I mixed drugs with my drinking. My mom was an alcoholic, so it was probably in my genes. In my twenties, my blackouts became more frequent and longer. It didn't matter if I drank two drinks or twenty-five. It didn't matter if I flipped my car in an accident and cut my head open, or passed out for minutes at a time. But for all the years of drinking and using, it was the eating disorder that took over all aspects of my life.

More Interested in Exercising than Furniture

I grew up in the '90s, so the Atkins diet was perfect—a certain number of calories and no carbs. I had even more food rules: no carbs, no sweets, minimal oils and fats, no sauces, nothing fried, no sandwiches, no drinks with calories outside of alcohol. This led to anorexia, the restrictive type. Plus, in high school, my mom got me a trainer who I saw five times a week. It must have been important to her that I be fit. That was the beginning of my compulsive exercising, which was a part of my eating disorder.

Years ago, I purchased my own elliptical, before the days of Peloton. I had a tiny apartment, so the elliptical was the center of the living room. I was more interested in exercising than any furniture. I would work out early in the morning, go to the gym later in the morning, and, if I had any food guilt—thinking I had eaten too much that day—I'd work out some more. I always made a point to have a gym membership that gave me access twenty-four hours, and I was frequently at the gym at 3:00 in the morning. I also used a trainer in between all of these activities.

In many ways, living in a city the size of Chicago strongly supported my eating disorder. I got a membership to a group cycling/spinning gym, and the friends I made also went there and worked out the same way I did: obsessively. This is literally where I lived and breathed. I was in an environment where my excessive workouts were easily accessible—and applauded.

I bought an Apple watch and became obsessed with tracking my steps and calories. The rule I set for myself was to eat fewer calories than I burned in a day. Over the years, this ranged from 500 to 1,000 calories. It got to the point where, if I took a spin class and didn't burn off the calories I had eaten earlier, I would go to the gym and make up the remaining calories. Then I'd drink the rest of the day, and then start all over. I knew that what I was engaged in wasn't okay, but I couldn't stop. At one point I did a three-meal-a-day delivery service to monitor my calories, which cost me about $3,500 a month. And there were times when my drinking was so out of control, I tied the fridge handles together with rope.

I was very successful in my career in the fashion industry. I was able to keep things in order because, like many addicts, I was great at manipulating my schedule. That knack started in college and continued throughout my adult life. In college, I'd configure my classes around my training and gym time. It wasn't much different at work. I would put fake meetings on the calendar—and those meetings were the gym. I had negotiated working at home so that I could have more control over my schedule.

True Desperation

There were people who definitely questioned my exercising. When I was in my mid-twenties, my mom brought up that she was worried about me and my weight. I had friends who periodically would say, "You're not eating" or "You're working out too much." I had boyfriends who called my parents concerned. I once went to an outpatient clinic but controlled who I worked with, what I would work on, and what I shared. So, I had some sense that I was in trouble, but I was never willing to wave a white flag and surrender.

But then in early 2018 I went on a work trip and woke up in a hotel room surrounded by the trappings of extensive room service. I didn't remember anything. I sat there looking at the leftover pizza, the pancakes, the syrup, the green tea, the empty alcohol bottles. I walked to the mirror and looked into it and said, "You can't do this anymore." That's when I hit bottom with my drinking. My mom was ten years sober by then, so I and decided to give Alcoholics Anonymous a try.

Without the alcohol, I spent more time working out and focusing on food. I went from doing two cycling classes a day, followed by boot camp, to spending four or five hours a day on the elliptical—plus more classes and boot camp. That's when the eating disorder *really* kicked in. The twenty-four/seven eating disorder voice was so pervasive and so strong, yet I couldn't shut it up because I didn't have the alcohol anymore to numb it.

On paper I would say my fear of stopping these behaviors—giving up restrictive eating and exercising—was that I would gain weight. But the real fear was that I'd lose control of my whole life. My compulsive working out, my counting steps and calories and carbs, kept my life in order. I was afraid that if I gave up control, there would be this downward spiral into I didn't know what, and I couldn't go there. My perfectionism had ramped up as much as the eating disorder.

It was apparent to me that I wasn't going to kick my eating disorder on my own. So three months into my sobriety I made my own referral to the eating disorder program The Meadows Ranch.

I Found What I Was Looking For

When I got to the Ranch, seeing women on feeding tubes in treatment was a wakeup call. Any resistance I had left me because I realized this was life or death. That said, I also remember crying over having to eat a sandwich.

I had the most wonderful therapist; she was a complete game changer for me. She shared a little bit of personal disclosure, and knowing she was in eating disorder recovery made it easier to trust her. She made it safe for me to not just be honest about my eating disorder but look at what it was I was trying so hard to control.

I didn't know what I was looking for when I went into treatment, but when I found it, I understood I was looking for people who genuinely cared about me. I was looking to feel respected, and I got that vibe literally beginning with the intake calls. I finally felt seen and heard— and in my family, I had never felt seen and heard.

A Chaotic Upbringing

I was raised with affluence. On paper, again, I had everything I wanted and needed. My parents and I looked very good on the outside, very buttoned up, with nice things. So in my mind I convinced myself that everything was fine. But it wasn't fine, and my drinking and eating disorder reflected that.

From an attachment standpoint—from a place of feeling valued, feeling connected, and having a sense of safety and security—I didn't get what I needed from my parents. I had an alcoholic mother and a father who was compulsively working. With my dad not around so much, and me being an only child, I was the one dealing with my mom passed out on the couch or passing out at the dinner table or vacillating between crying and yelling. I never knew what I was coming home to when I entered the house. I also had to do chores that should have been hers, like running to the store or the dry cleaners, going shopping.

Periodically I tried to bring attention to some of what was going on, but I was quickly shut down. We lived by the Don't Talk Rule: You don't talk about anything that is hurtful or confusing; you pretend everything is okay even when it isn't. My dad ignored my mom's problems, and my mom would deflect and say, "At least I'm not as bad as so and so." Because neither seemed interested in handling problems or concerns, I certainly didn't feel like I could go to them with my own. All of the chaos made me feel out of control.

Whole-Person Treatment

What was so significant about the Ranch is that they really treat the whole person. I had acute things that needed to be taken care of: my obsessive thinking, my rituals, my rationalizations, my use of exercise to feel in control. For example, I wasn't allowed to exercise, which I found a lot harder to accept than getting sober from alcohol and drugs. And they certainly helped me take a look at underlying family trauma.

Another really important piece of work I did had to do with recognizing my values and whether or not they aligned with how I was living my life. I became aware that my true values didn't align with the men that I was allowing to be in my life. I had dated a string of terrible men before I went to treatment—and a couple afterward—because my self-worth was so low. But the work I did helped me get out of those poor relationships.

Sr. Fellow Jenni Schaefer's book *Life Without Ed* was a game-changer for me. It was another moment where my experience was seen and heard. Also, the book *8 Keys to Recovery from an Eating Disorder* was eye opening because I was able to see that it was time to make a commitment to change.

In treatment I connected with the Adult Children of Alcoholics (ACA) material, as I see myself as a double winner: an ACA and an alcoholic. Reading books about codependency was very helpful, as was anything that tapped into perfectionism.

I was serious about my work when I was in treatment. I did not want to go back; I didn't want to be a repeat offender. I wanted this to be my one shot, so I was willing to do everything I could to move forward in my life.

I spent a full year focused on my recovery. I was at the Ranch sixty-two days, and then did aftercare in a PHP and then IOP program for seven months. For the remainder of that year, I saw a therapist twice a week and a dietitian weekly.

Healthy Boundaries

Recovery isn't just about how much food I put on a plate; it's equally about exploring and identifying what is important to me, what I want to attach value to. It's also about emotional connection: knowing my feelings, having self-esteem and self-confidence. It's about addressing the little "t" traumas. I was able to grieve the mom that I never had; I was allowed to be angry with how my mom and dad hadn't shown up for me. I've come to peace with that and I am fortunate that my mom has gotten sober, which has led to healing.

I no longer weigh myself. I also have boundaries around movement. I use the word "movement" not "workout." I do not go to gyms or have gym equipment in my house. I hike and walk, but never longer than forty-five minutes. This is to protect myself.

Yes, the eating disorder voice is still in my head. But 97 percent of the time the voice is a recovery voice, and the other 3 percent of the time it's the addict voice. The key is to know my intentions. When I eat a treat I ask, Am I compensating for something or simply enjoying it? If I choose not to have a dessert, is my intent to lose weight or am I not hungry for it? If I see a red flag, I talk to my therapist.

I live with the model that all foods are equal and no foods are off limits. I can eat processed foods, unprocessed foods, whole grains, fruits, vegetables, tortilla chips, cupcakes, whatever. I now eat three meals a day and two snacks. It may sound regimented, but these are healthy boundaries.

Following my true values also meant making a career change. I have left the fashion industry and am now a licensed therapist.

Beauty on the Other Side

I think it makes a real difference where you get help and what therapist you choose. People with eating disorders don't want to give up behaviors that work because they provide comfort and that feeling of safety. A good therapist understands this and helps you find healthy ways to self-soothe and feel safe.

Walking through the healing process is a tough journey, but there is so much beauty on the other side. Beauty you don't even know about. You just have to give it a chance.

◆ ◆ ◆

COMMENTARY

From Kara Fowler, LPC-S, RD

Danielle's story underscores how powerful it is when an eating disorder fills the need for consistency, predictability, and reliability. As children, we need our caregivers to be attentive and helpful a majority of the time to allow us to develop a feeling of safety, the embodied experience that we are protected and seen, and the sense that we can count on our needs being tended to effectively. These overall experiences contribute to the development of what is called *secure attachment* and teach us how to be in healthy relationships with others. Danielle didn't have enough of these experiences due to her mother's addiction and her father's travel. In fact, she often experienced interactions with her parents as frightening and confusing.

This causes our nervous system to stay in survival mode, either ramped up in fight or flight, or shut down in freeze or collapse. The implicit rules in Danielle's family to not talk about problems or address her own needs further locked in trauma responses in her nervous system. People with these experiences often find themselves acting impulsively and unable to delay gratification. No wonder—they are holding energy related to long unmet needs and a sense of danger. In many ways, it makes sense that Danielle's eating disorder served some of the same functions that a secure attachment could have. Her eating and exercise rituals provided an illusion of structure, reliability, and predictability.

Danielle admits to feeling that her eating disorder helped her feel in control of her life. The problem is that eating disorder rituals aren't stable and are often progressive. Her focus on numbers—on the scale, calories consumed, calories burned—became a never-satisfied obsession, clouding all judgment. It seems as though Danielle's relationship with food allowed her to stay removed from much of the awareness of the impact of her chaotic childhood until she reached treatment, where she wasn't able to mask her distress or trauma-related symptoms. In treatment, she was able to have the support that she needed to begin to learn to own and regulate her emotions, sort through her experiences, and identify her actual vision for her life.

It's also significant that Danielle realized that the eating disorder voice is still with her, but that she can be recovery-focused the vast majority of the time. Her story reflects being able to heal that part of the self that was in survival mode for so long, and being able to learn that there can be security in developing healthy boundaries and connections with safe people.

From Jenni Schaefer, Sr. Fellow

According to the National Center on Addiction and Substance Abuse, an estimated 50 percent of women with eating disorders abuse substances. For Danielle, alcohol meant chaos. Counting calories was the antidote: control. But Danielle was never in control, the eating disorder was.

Maintaining abstinence in substance use recovery is often compared to "leaving the tiger in its cage." Danielle's "tiger" of drinking could no longer be a part of her life. Period. But recovery from an eating disorder means taking the tiger out of its cage—several times a day, every single day: eating is required for survival. Moving is necessary, too, yet, as with Danielle exercise is a dangerous compulsion.

Eating disorder recovery means "petting the tiger." An excellent example is when Danielle chooses not to have a dessert and asks herself, "Is my intent to lose weight or am I not hungry for it?" In terms of exercise, she hikes and walks, but she no longer goes to the gym.

Danielle has befriended the tiger.

As a therapist, Danielle now helps others to do the same. She has taken her power back from the eating disorder and the addiction and has transformed her pain into passion and purpose.

Finding Wholeness   BY VICTORIA

When I arrived at The Meadows Ranch nine months ago I was desperate. My PTSD was active with flashbacks related to sexual abuse when I was a child. My cutting and thoughts of suicide had returned. And my lifelong struggle with eating disorders was fully activated.

Trauma Begins Early in Life

I am the youngest of three children. My sister is five years older, and my brother was seven years older. It was he and his friends who sexually abused me for three or four years starting when I was about six. Their abuse and torture as a group was extreme. They did things like cover my head with a plastic sack to cut off my ability to breathe; they used electric cattle prods on me until I threw up from the pain. I was thirty-two years old before the memories returned and I told anyone. My brother had told me he would kill me if I told, and I believed him. I was also sexually abused when I was slightly older by a seventeen-year-old who worked on my parents' property. It would take me several years before I told anyone, and that was mostly because I blamed myself. I already thought I was bad and this reinforced it. In my recovery, it's best for me not to go into more detail.

My self-harm, which began when I was seven, was directly related to trying to detach from the emotional pain. I would do things such as burning myself. My unhealthy relationship with food was also connected to the abuse. At age seven, I believed that if I could reach 100 pounds I would be strong enough to stop the bad stuff from happening to me.

So while I wanted to be big, my sister, who has a different body build and was always very thin, relayed the message that I was fat and lazy because I was not as thin as her. She was the one to first teach me about restricting my food intake. She would tell me how many calories everything had and how much I had to exercise to get rid of the weight I was gaining.

I grew up in what they call the Bible Belt, and that meant churches that were fire and brimstone. The ones I attended as a child were terrifying, and I was sure I was going to hell since I was seven or eight. I saw God as just waiting to hit me with a lightning bolt.

By my teenage years I was restricting and binge eating, doing more cutting, and becoming suicidal. My self-loathing was huge. I just didn't want to be here, yet at the same time I did. I trusted the staff at our small school and let a teacher and counselor know about my depression and suicidal thoughts. The staff called my parents and told them they needed to get me help or the school would call children's protective services and report me as a danger to myself. My dad responded with rage screaming I was being dramatic and nothing was wrong with me, but my parents made an appointment for me to see a psychiatrist. He prescribed my first medication, an SSRI. After I was given the meds, I was never taken back for a medication check, and my parents never asked me about taking the medications or about me.

Shortly after, my counselor and I decided that a change in my living situation would be helpful. So I graduated early by taking correspondent courses so I could get to college more quickly. But that plan backfired because I was not officially a senior when I applied, and I ended up taking classes at a community college and living at home. My depression and suicidality escalated. I wanted to die, and I kept telling myself I was depressed because I wasn't trying hard enough to get out of the sadness. I told myself I wasn't praying hard enough. After seeing another psychiatrist, Paxil was added to the mix and I had an adverse reaction, and it escalated the suicidal thoughts.

In time, I moved to another community where I attended a state university to give me some breathing room from my parents. In spite of the fact that I was depressed, active in restricting and bingeing on food, and binge drinking, my grades were okay. But I had become a professional in self-loathing. I continued to see a counselor and psychiatrist throughout this time and began to talk about the sexual abuse with the older teenager. I still had no memories of the abuse with my brother and his friends. Suicidality was a way of life. I spent most of my teen and young adult years trying *not* to kill myself from week to week. My self-talk, now what I call my inner critic, was in a continual state of blasting me.

Then, in the middle of making plans with a friend to move out of state after college, my friend was killed in a car accident. With no obvious other recourse, I moved back home and worked in my family's business while pursuing my master's in business administration.

By now, in my early twenties, I was gaining more weight. At one point my parents offered me money for every pound I could lose. I didn't take them up on their offer, but I entered serious restriction mode and lost the weight they were going to pay me for. I was also doing triathlons while restricting my food.

Oscillating Between Living Life and Wanting to Die

At twenty-six I married. I still never felt good enough, but I was trying to fix myself by being in a relationship. But over the next few years, family tragedy occurred. Several elderly citizens in our community were being terrorized, and my father-in-law was murdered and my mother-in-law kidnapped by a meth addict. All of this triggered serious PTSD for me.

When I was ready to have my first child, I needed an emergency C-section. I was immobilized and didn't leave my house for six months after he was born. By the time I was thirty, my brother's meth addiction was full blown, with paranoia and violence. It was after the family did an intervention that I learned my sister had also been abused by our brother. When she told me that, my memories started coming back—and with it my weight. I finally told my parents about my brother's abuse. He denied it, and they believed him. Then I began to get threats from my brother unless I retracted my statement. This pushed me back to significant bingeing, regaining all of the previous weight, and then ultimately back to the triathlons.

By the time I had given birth to my second child, I was oscillating between living life and wanting to die. I was severely plagued by the memories of my childhood sexual abuse. I sought out a Christian counselor and was led to believe that if I prayed hard enough, I would be fixed. Prayer was good, but it didn't relieve me of my PTSD. I started to go to a prayer-led yoga class, and the female pastor inspired me to go to seminary. This female pastor was the first person to introduce me to a loving God. It was through conversation with her I realized I read the Bible with God and Jesus screaming at me instead of speaking in loving and tender voices. I would go on to obtain a masters from a Methodist seminary while obtaining a masters in counseling from a state school. I was trying to fix myself through the acquisition of knowledge. I wanted this loving God to be my magic fix.

My research focused on the efficacy of treatment protocols while mitigating factors of shame and the image of God. Recognizing the impact of shame and the image of God was important to me. My image of God was developed from an early age and looked and sounded a lot like my raging father or teenage abusers. The research also guided me to contemplative prayer, guided meditation, and yoga as new ways to experience the love of God instead of the older ways of trying to be perfect. Diving further into the research as it related to childhood sexual abuse survivors showed me that I wasn't alone, I wasn't the only one. And it planted a seed of gratefulness for that part in me that worked so hard to protect me and help me to survive.

It was after my brother's overdose in 2018 that I then began to see a therapist who did trauma work. As a result of Bessel van der Kolk's book *The Body Keeps the Score*, I did my first round of EMDR therapy. I became familiar with a lot of different modalities, but by going through cognitive processing therapy (CPT) and starting to use acceptance and commitment therapy (ACT), I was able to hold my eating disorder in check.

Then Covid-19 hit. I was struggling at home with kids and two jobs when my husband began to have serious health issues. Due to my parents' business expanding and health issues, I was taxed with longer work hours.

My self-loathing started to escalate, and I slipped into self-harming and passive thoughts about suicidal ideation. And the binge/restrict cycle began to take over. In time, I was bingeing and drinking nightly. The last straw was when one of my childhood abusers moved down the road from us. I had made up in my head he was dead, but there he was, a half mile from us. The PTSD storm hit. I was having flashbacks; I couldn't concentrate. Then more self-loathing and restricting and bingeing and drinking. My therapist intervened and said I needed to think about treatment. Since I had been impressed by the work of the Sr. Fellows Peter Levine and Dick Schwartz and Bessel van der Kolk, I decided to go to treatment that they influence.

A Leg Up to a New Life

At first, I wasn't comfortable there. I didn't understand or like all of the treatment. But I rode it all out. I realized I was in treatment and it wasn't like home, where I could do what I wanted when I wanted. I was also horrified when they said I had to eat everything on my plate at meals. I didn't understand why, but I came to understand that I needed to eat on schedule and in moderate amounts. I wouldn't be allowed to deny myself food. My time there was clearly a springboard into wholeness. While not a fix or cure-all, it was my leg up to a new life.

Doing Somatic Experiencing (SE) was the turning point for me. I had done somatic processing but not SE. In one pivotal session, my legs were wanting to run, and I realized I was running from my life, running from the trauma. Allowing my legs to move translated into an ability to care for myself. Before that experience I would be frozen and dissociate when asked to care for myself. After that exercise I felt empowered, capable. Trust in myself was restored. That combined with finding my safe place, this cocoon inside my mind and body where all of the parts of me were protected. I learned to be still with my pain and to offer comfort to it. That combined with self-compassion work and parts work brought me to a place of acceptance I hadn't known.

Also, one day I was engaged in a mindful exercise that invited us to make scribbles on paper. Suddenly I drew scribbles with such depth— landscapes and people. It was an artistic awakening. Now I draw twice a week as a recovery practice. It allows my brain to go to a certain spot where it can process my thoughts and feelings.

There was another exercise where I had to carry a clear bag full of food that I would typically binge on before coming to treatment. Mine was so heavy with salsa, chips, fruity pebbles, candy, etc. I had to carry it everywhere for a whole weekend. It was like carrying my dirty underwear for all to see. I felt compassion for others when they had this exercise, so that is what I did for myself. What I got out of the exercise is the realization that I have a disorder and will live my life with this tendency of disordered eating. So hiding this part of me doesn't help, it only makes it harder. I could move into integration. I was no longer telling myself I was bad because it was there. It just was.

I had a wonderful experience with equine therapy too. In one self-exploration exercise, the horse and I had to walk to each of four quadrants that represented myself: The first was what I know about myself, second what I don't see, third what others see, and the last what no one is able to see. I was scared to do this, but being dutiful, the horse and I stepped to each quadrant. We were fine until we got to the quadrant that represented what no one sees, including myself. My depth of self-hatred I had carried for so long was in that quadrant. The horse would not move. I cried and cried. So the horse and I had a conversation and said we are letting that go. It was with relief and gratitude in that moment I allowed myself to see how strong, capable, and beautiful I really am.

Combine those experiences with being in a setting with so many women of different shapes, sizes, and backgrounds. They were all struggling with eating disorders and various trauma, and I heard my words coming out of their mouths. The thoughts they had about food and body were not unique but were ways we were all trying to cope and make sense of the world. That too was important in my finding gratitude for that part that was trying to protect me no matter how maladaptively. It allowed me to accept and offer kindness to that self-loathing part instead of trying to exile it.

The Gift of Self-Respect

My greatest gift in recovery is respecting myself. Today I can acknowledge frustration and anger, and I don't go into self-defeating thinking, which was my old way.

I do really well with the concept that all foods are okay. I don't skip meals, and I eat snacks. I eat out in restaurants, and I don't overthink it; it's more about enjoying the company. My inner running commentary about food is a lot quieter these days. If I start to notice restriction urges, I email my therapist and dietitian.

I agreed to not drink alcohol the first ninety days after treatment. While in treatment, we explored whether or not this was an addiction. At this time, I don't think so. Now I might have a drink only if social, maybe once a week. I struggle some with body image. Some days I am more okay than others. I need to have grace and patience with that.

Today my exercise is thirty to forty minutes of walking each morning. There is no speed, no distance goal. I do some yoga and stretching.

I've looked at my work as an addiction. I work on it a lot in therapy right now. There will always be work to do, but now I know I don't have to do it all. It's not tied to myself worth. My internal boundaries allow me to set external boundaries. For example, continuing to work in my family's business, I work eight hours a day with a lunch break. I step away from my workstation to eat. My husband and I don't talk work after work. In our board meetings, if my dad starts to go into a rage, I simply say, "We aren't going down that path; in this meeting we don't talk like this. We can calm down and find a solution or can stop and take a break." I am not going to be the punching bag, and if he doesn't stop the meeting ends.

The presence of the past abuser doesn't bother me anymore. If anything, I see him as kind of pathetic. He is not the monster that he was.

Being at The Meadows Ranch gave me time to learn about myself, to be me with me. It allowed me to explode old thought schemas and to let go of them or reframe them. I came away from the Ranch with a knowing of wholeness and belief in me. With the PTSD managed—and with healthy eating, rest, and letting go of my perfectionism—I didn't realize life could be so freeing.

• • •

What Is Somatic Experiencing?

By Peter Levine, PhD, Sr. Fellow (Developer of Somatic Experiencing)

Somatic Experiencing is a body-oriented approach to healing trauma. It releases traumatic shock from the body and restores connection, which is key to transforming PTSD and the wounds of emotional and early developmental attachment trauma. It helps individuals create new experiences in their bodies—ones that contradict those of tension and overwhelming helplessness.

Somatic Experiencing is an alternative to dredging up the details of your trauma history. In fact, that can be retraumatizing. I believe that what causes long-lasting trauma and an imbalanced nervous system isn't the traumatic event but the overwhelming trapped response to the perceived life-threat that is causing an imbalanced nervous system. This means that healing isn't about reclaiming memories or changing our thoughts and beliefs about how we feel, it's about exploring the sensations that lie underneath our feelings and beliefs, as well as our habitual behavior patterns.

Somatic Experiencing's aim is to help one access the body memory of the event, not the story. The objective is to diffuse the power of the narrative and remap the body memory to regain aliveness and flow. It is my conviction that Somatic Experiencing helps practitioners to do more effectively what they do. I think that this synergy is one of the strengths of the many Meadows'programs.

COMMENTARY

From Kevin Berkes, MA
(Director of Spiritual Services)

Victoria's story beautifully demonstrates several key elements of the spiritual aspect of the recovery journey: growth, transformation, purpose, and peace.

The significant trauma that she experienced at such a young age and the resulting "coping behaviors" of cutting, self-loathing, deprivations, and suicidal thoughts could be seen in some way as attempts to remove herself from existence—while her religious upbringing led her to the belief that she would go to hell. Spiritual distortions often result from abuse and can sound like, I'm no good, I don't belong, or I shouldn't be here. These strike to the core or the essence of one's being, creating quite a spiritual bind.

Unfortunately, for someone with her trauma history, the messages from her early religious upbringing and the way they were delivered reinforced the negative messages that enveloped her rather than served as a source of strength and encouragement.

The remarkable testament to her growth is that when Victoria was powerless to get out of her situation on her own, yet nevertheless driven by the desire to feel better, she made small decisions with extraordinary courage to say yes loving herself. This led to a trusting relationship with a female pastor that led to an awareness of a loving God, which led to acceptance of the possibility that she is lovable and worthy of being.

As she transformed from "self-loathing" to "respecting myself," her image of God transformed—and as her image of God transformed, she transformed. Her prayer transformed from a dutiful, shame-ridden chore to a comforting, safe activity of being still. She found a loving connection with self, a loving connection with God, and spiritual freedom and peace.

From Dick Schwartz, PhD, Sr. Fellow
(Developer of Internal Family Systems)

No matter how severe and pervasive the abuse we may have experienced, we *can* access a state I call the *Self*. That is because the Self can't be damaged, no matter the trauma we suffer. The Self is our core essence, our true identity. It lies just beneath the surface and manifests in qualities like calm, courage, curiosity, and compassion, especially toward the parts of ourselves that have been plaguing our lives. Victoria was able to access her Self when she allowed a part of her that was frozen in an abuse scene to run out of that scene. Afterward, she described feeling relieved, empowered, and capable—and able to comfort herself rather than run from the vulnerability, thanks to channeling her Self.

Victoria describes other activities she participated in at the Ranch that allowed her to access her Self. The scribble exercise, for example, allowed her to express through her hands thoughts and feelings that she had suppressed. She was able to extend compassion to herself from her Self as she drew. Similarly, the bag exercise helped her feel less ashamed and more empathic toward others doing the exercise and also toward her own bingeing behaviors. Her experience with the horse further cemented her shift in identity; as soon as she was able to let go of her self-hatred, her true Self emerged spontaneously.

From Peter Levine, PhD, Sr. Fellow

I was naturally touched when Victoria reported that doing Somatic Experiencing (see sidebar "What Is Somatic Experiencing?") was a turning point for her. Victoria had become stuck in an immobility response; in other words, her body had literally resigned itself to a frozen state from which she could not escape. What she needed to do and what occurred was to be freed from her symptoms and fears by arousing her deep physiological resources and consciously utilizing them. This experience assisted in helping her tap into her power to change the course of her instinctual responses in a proactive rather than reactive way. After Somatic Experiencing, her trembling legs were the discharge of energy she experienced when she flowed out of her passive, frozen immobility response into an active, successful escape.

From Kara Fowler, LPC-S, RD

Victoria relays how her eating disorder served as a hope of protection, of making her "strong enough" to be able to stop the abuse she went through at the hands of her brother and his friends. She likely used food and bingeing as a way to stuff her voice down, having been conditioned by the invalidation at home and in church to believe that she was the problem, and that she was bad and unworthy. In addition, disordered eating may have been a familiar way to attempt to manage the intensity of her flashbacks and activation. In contrast, learning to count calories and restrict was a way to connect with her sister who valued dieting and rigid food rules.

Part of what was most crucial to Victoria's recovery process was learning to allow all parts of herself, and all of her emotions and needs, to be seen, heard, and responded to, day to day, in the present. Victoria's story promotes hope in that during treatment she finally had the space to safely make room for herself, to separate from her abuse and the false messages she had received growing up. This was foundational for allowing her to learn how to start living from her own values and needs.

Residential treatment can sometimes be the first place that someone experiences that safety is possible. Once the possibility of safety exists, connection with the Self, the resources of the body, and a healing relationship with a higher power, become more accessible.

Undaunted Hope

It takes courage to address the impact of any eating disorder. Along with that bravery, it takes honesty and a belief in your worthiness to let go of self-defeating thinking and behaviors and embrace a new way of living. In recovery, the hunger that you have been experiencing— the hunger for connection, to be understood, to feel your own empowerment, and for safety—can be satisfied with a commitment to recovery practices. And when you are willing to allow others to walk with you and guide you in the recovery process, your eating disorder will no longer be a driving force. You deserve this.

CHAPTER SEVEN

Coming Out of the Shadows
RECOVERY FROM SEX ADDICTION

Well, I am certainly not going to give up sex!

What my wife doesn't know can't hurt her.

What do you mean sex addict? Nobody can be addicted to sex.

We are all sexual beings, and our sexual interests, desires, and behaviors can exist on a broad spectrum. Some of us believe that sex is only to be expressed with a romantic interest or in a committed relationship, while others are comfortable being sexual with someone without a commitment. Many people enjoy self-stimulation, others don't engage. And we certainly vary as to what we find enjoyable. Sex is a form of not just physical intimacy, but for many emotional and spiritual intimacy as well.

While sexual mores have changed over the generations, advances in technology have greatly influenced and created another sexual landscape. Today on the web and on social media sites there is greater exposure to visual stimulation. You can also meet someone anywhere in the world at any time with the tips of your fingers on a screen. Coupled with the ability to stay anonymous, the web has tempted people in ways not previously available. There's now greater ability to hook up with more people for casual sex. It has also meant sex exposure to a population younger than ever before, strongly influencing desires and impacting sexual interests and behavior.

In a society where people are increasingly looking for quick fixes, sex is easy to come by. Unfortunately, this greater access to sexual stimulation comes with an increasing number of risky behaviors, resulting in severe negative consequences. While initially exciting and pleasurable, compulsive sex and compulsive engagement in pornography becomes a major problem. When sexual behaviors become hard to control, it sabotages our relational and emotional connection in sexual intimacy with another. We find ourselves lying, manipulating, losing sight of our values, and betraying our loved ones. We may be putting ourselves at financial, legal, and health risks.

Sex addiction, also referred to as *sexual dependency* or *sexual compulsivity,* can be defined as a pathological relationship with a mood-altering experience. Sex becomes the organizing principle in the life of the addict, who prioritizes temporary pleasures and unhealthy relationships over healthy intimate ones. Sex becomes more important than family, friends, and work.

Sex addiction is a very personal struggle that can manifest in a number of ways. Some people experience compulsions ranging from pornography and internet sex to masturbation. It frequently involves turning to online interactions, pursuing multiple relationships, engaging in anonymous encounters, and soliciting prostitutes and escorts. In time, sex addiction turns sex into something that is empty, demoralizing, and robs the person of the ability to experience real intimacy.

Sex becomes a way to anesthetize fears, loneliness, shame, helplessness, and other intense pain. Sex can give us a false sense of power when we feel we have none, or a sense of confidence when it is lacking. It may enable us to feel greater worth, at least in the moment. It can allow us escape from daily life stressors. Those are frequently the initial payoffs, but when we continue to act out, we lose ourselves and so much that is important to us in the process.

The sex addict doesn't engage in risky behaviors intending to risk what they value or get to the point of self-loathing. They don't think to themselves, I want to lose control over my behavior or I want to engage in sex and have sexual secrets to the point I lose my family, my health, my job, and my finances. As with substance addictions, sex addiction involves the same brain neurochemical process. As far as the brain is concerned, a reward is a reward, regardless of whether it comes from a substance, behavior, or experience. In the brain of someone who is repeating behaviors over and over, the reward system overrides one's ability to make rational decisions. This leads to more impulsiveness.

The good news is the brain has *plasticity*. With a combination of different therapeutic modalities, new skills can be learned to deactivate what is triggered in the reward center of the brain. The rational thinking part can come back online and become increasingly stronger. You can learn ways to have healthy intimacy.

There are many scenarios for what sex addiction looks like, as varied as our own desires and sexual identities. No matter your situation, you can find hope and experience the promise of a way out of living a life of deception—just like the men in the stories you'll read.

A Lifetime of Punishing Myself   BY SCOTT

There were many times in the fifteen years I had been married to my third wife when she would corner me with her suspicions about my activities. But this time I was caught.

My wife and I had just returned home to Switzerland after spending the Christmas holidays in the United States. She had left her iPad on the airplane, so the next day, as I was heading out the door for a three-week work trip, I offered her mine. I was only minutes down the road when I wondered if I had deleted my search history.

I waited, anxiously expecting to hear from her. One week went by, then two weeks, and by the third week with no questions, I figured she wasn't looking. So, I started to troll websites for prostitutes and text them about arrangements. It was then that I got a FaceTime call. My wife asked, "What the F are you doing? What are you involved in? I can see everything that you have been doing over the past week on your iPad."

She asked me if I knew what sex addiction was, and I said no. She told me to look it up. My head was spinning. I was caught and there was no way out.

Building a Facade

My first—and nearly all—childhood memories are of my parents fighting. They would drink, fight, scream, slam doors, leave the house for long periods of time. They said horrible things to each other. I learned that conflict meant "fatality"—there was always a win/lose ending, never any compromise or healthy negotiation. Their actions left me with an overwhelming fear of being left alone, of not ever being loved, and certainly of conflict.

I truly thought I was the reason they drank. I tried to stop the fighting, tried to reason with them, tried to distract them. I tried being a clown and bringing humor into all of the chaos. Then I tried being perfect, because if I were good enough, they would not drink, they would quit fighting, and focus on giving me the love I needed. As a young boy, I cried so much they told me repeatedly I was overly sensitive and that I needed to grow up. By the time I was a teenager, I had become a hypervigilant rule follower who had shut off all of my feelings. I didn't want them to see me vulnerable, thinking something even worse would happen. Suppressing my emotions was a part of my building a façade to help forge peace in the family.

Although I didn't want to be a problem child, I still wanted their attention. Maybe unconsciously, I thought hanging myself was a way to change a neglectful parental pattern or maybe it was just my last effort to flee a life I couldn't bear to live. I was old enough to know I wasn't supposed to climb the fence along the highway because it was dangerous. I knew that if I slipped—which I did—the Y prong would hang me—which it did. It narrowly missed my jugular vein. A man driving on the freeway stopped, ran across the field and pulled me off, and yelled for my mom. If he had not seen me, I would have died. To this day we have no idea who that person was.

Seeing what alcohol did to my parents and their friends, I decided I was not going to drink—and I did not—until I went to college. There, I went from zero drinking to blackout drinking in a month. I didn't know what normal drinking was. I had turned into my dad lock, stock, and barrel. It was a complete and quick collapse into drinking, sex, and drugs.

Master of the Universe

My career was in global sales of private jets to companies, wealthy individuals, and various governments. For years my office was either a hotel room or on an airplane. I would make it home every couple of weeks for a few days. Then I would change bags and hit the road again, going to amazing places that most people don't get to visit, like Pakistan, Dubai, Nigeria, just to name a few. I was good at my work, and I loved it, but I would wake up every morning on my knees in despair because of my behaviors the night before.

After having dinner with coworkers, and after everybody went off to their respective rooms, I would head down to the bar and connect with sex workers. The next morning, I would bargain with my higher power saying, I'm not going do this again if you will make sure no one finds out. All through the day, I'd wait for a phone call informing me that I'd been found out. But it never happened. I would return to work, take calls, attend meetings, thinking I had control. By late afternoon, I would take out what money I could from my ATM and blow it on dinners, drinking, and prostitutes. I felt I was the master of the universe.

I figured all of the shenanigans of my addictions would come to a stop when I retired, whenever that would be. I felt entitled to do anything I wanted. *It's my money, I make it. And I'm choosing to do this. I see other people do it, so why not me?* I thought I could live this dual life of drinking and acting out. And I did for decades, through three marriages, three divorces, affair partners, and countless one-night stands.

A Dual Life

I stopped drinking three years into my third marriage after my then-wife caught me in an affair. Well, she only suspected an affair because she couldn't reach me by phone. I had been drinking all through the night with an affair partner, so when I called her drunken there was no denying my return to drinking, but I held onto my lie of who I had been drinking with. I told her I got to drinking with a bunch of people and left the phone in the car. But I felt I had come too close to her really knowing, and in an attempt to appease her, I told her I would quit drinking. I thought taking this action would distract her from the affair and let up on the pressure I was feeling with her suspicions. So I stopped drinking.

But I didn't stop any of my affairs; in fact, they intensified. Now I added one-night affairs to my list of infidelities. I was out of control, building a fragile house of cards.

In place of my drinking, I got into compulsive exercising. I began competing in triathlons. I lost weight and was looking good. Then I began to spend money compulsively. All of it was about trying to feel better about myself and to get approval from others. I couldn't feel joy, so I manufactured what I thought would bring joy. But it never came.

I compulsively moved from one addiction to another trying to find the pleasure or the dissociation or the escape. I just wanted to numb out, and I did that with alcohol, drugs, sex, and spending. I could walk through any airport and act all of that out. Like trauma specialist Gabor Maté, MD said, "I put all of my addictions in a bucket and then I would pull out whatever was at the top to relieve me of pain and put me into pleasure."

After seven years of sobriety, (never connecting the dots between my own drinking and sexual acting out or to my parents drinking) I started to drink again. Thinking I had it in control, I felt it was my right. Before I initially quit drinking, I typically drank to get drunk. This time the drinking was more about disinhibiting my decision-making ability to be able to do the things that I knew were wrong. I would drink just enough to get buzzed and then go out and hire somebody for sex.

I began extending work trips into the weekend. After a while, my wife was getting upset and wondering why I was prioritizing my weekends with business as opposed to spending time with her. Then the day of reckoning occurred, when she discovered me trolling for sex on my iPad. She wanted details, and this time all of the details of my secret life. I was caught, and I knew it.

To help us manage our conversation, she and I asked my brother, who was in recovery from alcohol addiction, to help us handle this. Little by little, my honesty came to the surface. It was the beginning of giving up my secret life of addictions. I was about 75 percent honest with my answers to their questions. I owned up to the affairs and the prostitutes, but I didn't give the full story.

My wife and I then set up a meeting to talk to a therapist. He was not a specialist in sex addiction, but he knew enough to get us to open up. It was like we were on the operating table with our hearts splayed wide open. We were bleeding out. When we left that meeting, we both knew we would not make it through the weekend; I knew that I would get back into my habits that very weekend. I also knew I would not find recovery one session at a time week after week. I thought maybe I would make it an hour, but the moment I left therapy, I knew my mind would shift back to work, and that I would be seeking this momentary pleasure. We decided that I needed time away, right away. I got on the internet, typed in "sex addiction," and Gentle Path (GP) at The Meadows showed up.

I contacted my fellow coworkers and told them that I was going to treatment. Not one of them asked why. Every one of them was supportive.

One Big Class

I didn't know what to expect. Maybe a bunch of guys in trench coats and boots? But that's not what I saw. I saw men who were physically fit, well-spoken, and nicely dressed. They ran the gamut of every possible career. There was no socio-economic class system; every color, every faith was represented; there was just one big class.

In the early part of my stay there were a lot of tears. I was wondering, "Where is my life going to end up?" "Where was my relationship going to go?" "How could I do my job?" "What in the F was I doing all of those years?"

Those first several days were a blur, but the morning meditation that was a part of the schedule helped me to get focused. I realized that I usually think with my head, so I reasoned that I needed to think more with my heart. So while meditating, I would also ask myself, Where is my heart? As well, I would take a run early in the morning when it was still dark. Under the desert sky with the moon out and falling stars, I felt a connection with a higher power, which had a grounding effect on me. I also read a variety of meditation books. They helped me with clarity and to be centered. If I didn't start every day with a meditation and reading, I felt like I was behind the power curve.

When I first shared with the therapy team and my peers about the constant fear I had as a child, hanging myself on the highway fence, my sense of emptiness, the many marriages and divorces, my complete collapse into my addictions, I gave the presentation as if I was telling someone else's story.

"You just shared the most traumatic events of your life that landed you here and did it as though you were selling an airplane to the CEO of a major company," my therapist said. "It must be exhausting to maintain such a facade."

That's when I broke down, the breakthrough started.

I learned to look at myself through an analogy—if I aimed a firehose at the flames of addiction, I would run out of water before the fire was extinguished. I needed to aim the water at the coals, at the base of the flames. I needed to face my feelings, fears, my truth. I realized that I had significant issues around the fear of abandonment and trust, that the people who were supposed to be there for me were not going to be there for me. That, plus the fear of conflict, led me to be a people pleaser and constant affirmation seeker. I became a compromiser, never sticking up for myself, never believing that maybe I was right and someone else could be wrong, or that I could even have a distinct opinion from someone else's on the same topic. Being so disconnected from myself, having completely covered my true self up, I didn't know who I was or what mattered to me. I was just running. I have come to realize that a lot of my acting out was really about my own self-harm, about punishing myself.

I also learned how much self-loathing and anger I had. I so wanted to be seen, to feel valued, to not be alone. For instance, I would say I love you to my wife even if she was just going down the street. It wasn't intended to show my affection; it was to hear her throwback "I love you." I was seeking reassurance and hope that she was my forever with her comment, yet it only gave me confidence for five seconds. Even though we shared I love yous, they were hollow expressions, and like my addictions, could never fill the hole inside.

I wanted and expected treatment to cure me in forty-five days and simply go home and believe that all of life would be wonderful. But there was no way my wife was going to have me at home, and at the end of forty-five days. I also had to consider everything in my life.

Patrick Carnes, the founder of Gentle Path, asked me, "How are you going to stay sober traveling the world and not being able to drink? Who will you be accountable to while you're traveling? Are you going to spend X amount of money on sober escorts to make sure you stay in recovery? Or can you retire?"

I didn't have answers, but I knew retiring was my best chance of living a life of fulfillment. So, I retired.

In doing so, I made a commitment to myself. I went on to an extensive aftercare program for forty-five days. I was able to live in a sober living house and attend groups for several hours a day, where I explored more deeply the many feelings that I was running from and how to let go of entitlement. And still, this was only the beginning, and I knew I had a lot to address yet.

I Am Worthy

When I returned home, even with the next few years of individual and couples therapy my wife still didn't want to have sex with me. I believe it was so hard for her because I'd had sex with so many other people, and maybe she could only see me in my past. We never became sexually intimate, and I accepted that. Then in the fifth year of my recovery, after twenty years of marriage, as we were holding hands and had just awakened, she said, "I'm out."

I am grateful that she tried to stay in the marriage. Her leaving certainly created a lot of vulnerability for me. I don't know how I would have coped had she left early on in my recovery, but today I have the tools to cope with the sense of loss and grief. I have never relapsed.

Today, I work with a sponsor; I have my own recovery coach; I have support from the peers I met in treatment and from others whom I've met in twelve-step meetings since that time.

I am now a recovery coach and I have a purpose, intent, and a vision. Today my recovery and my life are the same. I live in the moment, and I have to forgive myself. I remind myself that I am worthy, that I have value as a human being, and I do matter. The things I did are part of my past, they're not my present.

I work on being a better person every day, staying in the uncomfortable moments in life. My flight response, my wanting to flee from myself, is so intense and so pervasive that it will take me time to heal.

Today nothing good can happen for me late at night, so I am in bed early. I start my day early, in peace and solitude, with reading recovery books, journaling, and exercising with my dog. I know then that I have started my day right, grounded, balanced, centered, and focused. It is harder for me to be bumped off balance—or caught up in the speed, intensity, and chaos ramping up during the day if I start this way.

In hindsight, I wish I had not waited so long to get help. But I was so blind about my addictions. I didn't know I was deep in them. This attitude of entitlement and believing that what others don't know doesn't hurt them led me to think that somehow my actions were acceptable.

No Half-Assing It

Once I made the choice to live a healthy life, to make decisions to live a life with purpose, integrity, and intention, there could be no half-assing it. The first three years had to be 150 percent all in, meetings, reading, and understanding addiction and recovery, talking about it with other addicts, seeking therapy, using every possible tool available to me to turn the corner. Relying on willpower alone got me into addictions. I cannot let myself believe only in the power of my will. I need a power greater than me as my guide.

It's scary to walk into the shadow side of self, the side that contains all those negative and traumatic life experiences. No amount of medicine can relieve the pain; there is no quick fix; we must I must do the work. Avoiding the work is like walking on a slack line: tense, stressful, close to the edge of falling back into my addictions. My choice today is to do the work and live in recovery, allowing my core qualities to shine bright in my life.

• • •

What Defines a Sex Addict?
By Patrick Carnes, PhD, Sr. Fellow (Pioneer in Sex Addiction, Founder of Gentle Path)

Even the healthiest forms of human sexual expression can turn into self-defeating behaviors. If a behavior has become unmanageable to the point that it's taken over a person's life, it's likely a sign of addiction. Here are behavior patterns that can indicate the presence of sexual addiction:

- **Acting out.** This is a pattern of out-of-control sexual behaviors that is hurtful to self or others, and great effort is made to keep the acts hidden.

- **Experiencing severe consequences.** Due to sexual behavior, repercussions can be severe, such as marital or relationship problems; health problems, such as increased risk for sexually transmitted diseases, genital injury, unwanted pregnancies, depression, suicide obsession; legal risks, such as from sexual harassment in the work place, to illegal behaviors such as voyeurism or exhibitionism; and financial consequences, such as travel for the purpose of sexual contacts, purchase of pornographic materials, or hiring of prostitutes.

- **Persistent pursuit of self-destructive behavior.** Even understanding that the consequences of their actions will have dire consequences does not stop addicts from acting out.

- **Ongoing desire or effort to limit sexual behavior.** Addicts often try to control their behavior by creating external barriers to it, such as moving to a new neighborhood or city, getting married, or immersing themselves in religion. Although they have a desire to stop, without inner change, in time they resume their behaviors.

- **Spending inordinate amounts of time in obsession and fantasy.** By fantasizing, the addict can maintain an almost constant level of arousal. Together with obsessing, the two behaviors can create a kind of analgesic "fix."

- **Regularly increasing the amount of sexual experience.** The brain gets saturated so it needs more than it needed before. That is why there is "never enough." This escalation is a sign of the reward system of the brain continuing to grow in its influence. The brain actually is transformed and cannibalized to feed the growth of the reward system. What used to be thrilling now becomes blunted. The dopamine transfer genes become more and more powerful.

- **Having severe mood changes.** The intense mood shifts are driven by the binge purge cycles of a shame-driven and shame-creating behavior. Also common is depression most often in the form of hopelessness.

- **Spending inordinate amounts of time obtaining sex, being sexual, and recovering from sexual experiences.** In addition to time spent initiating sex and actually being sexual, addicts also spend time lying, covering up, and dealing with shortages of money, problems with their spouse, and trouble at work.

- **Neglecting important responsibilities.** As more and more of addicts' energy becomes focused on relationships that have sexual potential, other relationships and activities—family, friends, work, talents, and values—suffer and atrophy from neglect.

The good news is that there are interventions proven to heal pain and past hurts, and to train the brain to have a healthy coping response.

COMMENTARY

From Patrick Carnes, PhD, Sr. Fellow
(Pioneer in Sex Addiction, Founder of Gentle Path)

Scott participated in a culture that purported to be "masters of the universe." Those who travel by private plane (CEOs, the privileged, and the extremely wealthy) and pilots in general (both military and civilian) all talk about that feeling of being above the rules of what most people must observe. This view is not just about skipping the TSA line. This is about extended travel, little accountability, and abundant opportunity. And great talent. Which can add up to entitlement and problems with addiction.

Business, excitement of the big sale, and constant exposure to rich and famous customers increased Scott's endorphins to a level of stimulation that made him vulnerable to addiction—that is, the more excitement he had, the more he craved it.

In this fast life, Scott was going to great lengths to dodge his emotional pain. He went from his first drinks to blackouts in a month's time. This is a sure indicator that alcohol was filling an empty and hurting spot inside himself. Over time, with continued use, the prefrontal cortex—the part of the brain that assesses decisions before they get made—becomes harmed. Addicts basically lose the ability to make the next right decision. And choice making continues to decline. Scott's persistent engagement with some form of addiction—drinking, sex, compulsive exercise, drugs, or spending—despite risks to career or marriage, is a further sign of addiction brain damage.

Addiction and trauma specialist Gabor Maté, MD, who Scott mentions in his story, observed that no addict sets out to be so destructive to themselves and others. Rather, they are seeking to solve a problem. They are not bad people. Rather, they are wounded. They are people who have brain dysfunction, which is a medical condition. (See the sidebar in Chapter Four, "Addiction Is a Learning and Memory Disorder.")

Fortunately, the brain can repair itself. Discovering ways to self-regulate is a foundational step to healing the brain and stopping addictive behaviors. Scott referred to meditation as the first helpful strategy he encountered. The Meadows' programs teach tools in how to set aside your overstimulated self and be still—sometimes euphemistically called the "here and now." Through new tools, he learned the beginnings of how to be his true self and not an image he projected to others. Acquiring tools are the first steps to self-regulation and honesty. Scott is a valuable human being who how has the ability to make the next right decision.

By Claudia Black, PhD, Sr. Fellow

*(Pioneer in Addictive Family Systems, Clinical Architect
of Claudia Black Young Adult Center)*

At the core of addiction, we often find abandonment. While Scott did not experience physical abandonment, he clearly suffered from emotional abandonment. The consequence is the shame belief, I am not loved. Through his jet setting career and the materialism that was the byproduct, he set about to prove to himself and everyone else his worth.

Scott is like so many people who grow up with active substance addiction who live a life of unspoken fear, then become disconnected from themselves and engage in self destructive behaviors. Scott was running as fast as he could from himself.

To experience recovery, it was critical that Scott explore his trauma and challenge his distorted, shame-based thinking. In this process, he would be able to develop skills that allow him genuine connection with self and others. It allows him to be seen and heard, and to be there to see and hear others. These skills of emotional intimacy are also the foundation for healthy physical intimacy when that time comes in his recovery.

For someone who felt such rejection as a child, his rigid self-reliance was about survival. A powerful gift of recovery is letting go of self-will, and as Scott did, finding a power greater than himself to be his guide.

Scott is a changed man today. While his marriage did not survive in this transition, he is still able to embrace his life. To sustain that though he must be vigilant to his recovery practices. They will always need to be his first priority. While that may sound overwhelming to those contemplating or in early recovery, those very practices lead to finding your worth, liking this Self you have found. Scott like others, has been humbled in the recovery process, but humility is a virtue that will help to sustain his recovery.

Finding Emotional Intimacy   BY KEITH

I don't ever remember feeling good about myself. Growing up I never seemed to fit into my family. I had two younger brothers, and I was supposed to be the little adult, helping my mother, fathering my brothers, and doing whatever my father dictated in the moment—and doing it right. But nothing I ever did was good enough for my dad.

Our family was Christian, which meant church on weekends, prayers at meals, and a lot of do and don'ts. Mostly don't touch: don't touch the girls, and don't touch myself sexually. Masturbation was a clear sin.

I often heard that I was good looking, but I found no confidence in that. I was a really good athlete, mostly basketball and baseball, so I was popular. But I was also really shy when it came to girls.

My dad was a successful businessman; he owned an electrical firm with about twenty employees. As a teenager, I had afterschool and weekend jobs that taught me his trade. But I didn't want to work. I wanted to play ball, I wanted to have friends, so I juggled pleasing him and trying to please myself. Going on to college or getting a scholarship for sports was not in my dad's vision, so after high school I went to work for him.

Hiding Behind the Portrait of the Perfect Marriage

At twenty, I married a girl from church; we were both virgins. Looking good was a part of my family portrait, and my wife and I repeated that. We are both physically good looking, and we and our two kids dressed well. Every Sunday we showed up at church, the perfect family, and sat in the same aisle. We participated in church and other community activities that allowed us to look good. At home we were polite and caring toward each other. But between our children, my wife's had two miscarriages. She struggled with a fear of not being able to have more children, so our sex life was often about procreation. I was insecure in the sex department, so sex wasn't really fun or special or, what I learned in recovery, intimate.

I worked long days, I provided well for the family, and I loved my wife and my children. But when she and the kids went to bed and I was alone, the internet became a part of my private routine. Within five years of being married, I was using the internet for relaxation, mostly gaming. But then without a lot of thought, I found myself on porn sites. In the beginning I learned a lot about being sexual. When my wife and I were sexual, I had to be careful not to move too quickly with my new moves or desires. But our sex life wasn't nearly as frequent as I wanted, and so porn became a nightly way of relaxing.

In the beginning I watched porn only late at night from home. I was careful to make sure that I hid the sites and files I watched; I used my work laptop, and it was always with me. I kept up this pretense for years. In my heart I knew it was wrong, but as long as my wife was not complaining about our sex life or lack of it, as long as I continued to take care of her, and as long as I enjoyed being a dad and participated actively in their lives, I could rationalize it. I always told myself it wasn't hurting anybody.

Escalation

As addictions do, mine escalated. Within a few years, I was on porn sites in my work truck during the day. I found myself hating going to church. I was getting angry with my wife but couldn't tell her why. There are professionals who say that the use of porn in a marriage can have some benefits. I don't know anything about that. I do know it didn't help mine, and it didn't help me. It ultimately drove my wife and I apart and only fueled my self-hatred. The porn was just one more reason I was inadequate and not good enough.

So at age thirty-eight, I decided to go to therapy. Of course, I didn't tell the therapist about the porn. Instead, I talked about the pressure at work, never feeling good enough for my dad, the stress of my wife's illnesses. In my mind I was in therapy for porn addiction, but just didn't mention it. I thought that by talking about these other issues and making an effort to not get on the computer at night I could handle it.

I liked having someone to talk to about my stressors. One of them was being in constant struggle with my dad. He had been making some upper management decisions that were very invalidating to me. He was disrespectful to me in front of employees I supervised. He didn't want to spend any time with me or any of the family outside of work; he had his own work addiction. I stayed in therapy about eight months and felt a bit better about myself.

While I felt better talking about my stress, being in therapy and lying didn't help it all. The porn was getting more out of control. As I got bored with certain types of porn, I found myself searching sites for something more enticing. There are sites for finding sexual hookups with just about any desire you have. My addiction escalated to visiting massage parlors. Eventually it led to hookups with guys. Initially I was really scared, but after talking to a couple of guys on the phone, I was convinced that they seemed like regular guys, like me—guys who were heterosexual and just did this sometimes without their wives knowing.

I got good at living in two different worlds: my secret life and the family man. But after a couple of years of that, I got scared my wife would find out. At that point, I was no longer responding to her sexually at all. I was feeling more and more disconnected from her and chronically lying to her. I knew my wife would divorce me if she discovered what I was doing. So, I decided I needed more than a therapist: I needed treatment. It didn't take a lot to convince my wife I wanted treatment to address the lifelong issues of not feeling like a success, struggling with dad issues. She readily accepted I was depressed.

Honesty Among Men

The first thing I realized when I got to treatment was that the guys looked normal, so that helped me to not feel like I was some freak. I can honestly say I never felt judged by another person there, staff or clients. I was the one judging me. I was taken back by the honesty of the men in my all-male group. I had a lot of secrets, but most of them had secrets too. And they were talking about them. And they talked about feelings. I had never seen or heard that among men.

While some had been and still were successful professionally, they didn't necessarily feel strong on the inside. They doubted themselves, maybe didn't even like themselves. And all of that was true for me too. I didn't know how to talk about a feeling and certainly had a lot of secrets. But in time, my secrets came out, my fears came out. And the things I was going to need to do to have recovery—like be honest with my wife, learn to like myself, develop self-confidence, set healthy boundaries with my dad—I felt I could do, even though they seemed scary.

The hardest part of treatment was telling my wife about my porn addiction. Family week was critical, and for those of us with sex addiction, only the partner comes. Gentle Path gave us formats for healthy communication and for being able to recognize when you are getting into distorted thinking or misperceptions, and how to get out of them. This helped my wife recognize that she was not responsible for my behavior. The dynamics of her many surgeries and recoveries put up a barrier in the bedroom that could easily be blamed, but my addiction was not her fault.

The childhood trauma workshop helped me to let go of a lot of negative messages I had internalized from my dad: I am not good enough. I need to be someone other than who I am. I'll never be successful.

In a small group we had the opportunity to do an empty chair experiential where you get to talk to someone significant to you, and it can even be yourself. You get to say things that are important to own for your recovery. I imagined my father in the chair. I told him I was angry that he did not support me in going to college. I told him I needed more personal attention when I was a kid; his ignoring my accomplishments made me feel I wasn't of value to him. These comments and others I shared that day in group would be feelings and thoughts I had never felt safe to share before and allowed me to own and give voice to them. Whether or not I would share them in real life with my father would ultimately be my choice, but they immediately gave me the courage to set some needed boundaries to not internalize disparaging comments from him and external boundaries about what I would do should he disparage me again.

Staying in the Green Area

I never could have imagined recovery giving me so much of what I never had before: self-respect, healthy communication, boundaries, and intimacy skills.

Today I am three years into recovery, and I have not had a relapse. My wife and I are still married—twenty-five years. But it wasn't easy. It took several months post-treatment before I became fully honest with her about acting out with other people. She was outraged and confused, so we took a six-week break from living together. We needed a lot of help to navigate that. Fortunately, she was very willing to go to couples counseling with me, and we did it with specialists trained in work with sex addiction and partner betrayal.

We also did individual therapy. All of that helped my wife feel supported. But we had a lot of basics to learn. We had to learn how to listen with respect, how to talk honestly about our feelings. We didn't know much about healthy sexuality, so in time we focused on that. But we needed emotional intimacy first. When I left treatment, I had a plan for how to stay in recovery. We had done a relapse/recovery circle with a plan for what supports recovery, what are absolute non-negotiable behaviors, and how to know when I am in "yellow territory," that slippery slope where I can quickly relapse if I don't immediately move into the green area, active recovery behavior.

My non-negotiables are: no getting on a computer at home other than to shop on Amazon or help the kids with homework. No gaming. No masturbation. No new, inventive access to porn. No outside relationships. Work with a sex addiction trained therapist weekly for at least the first two years of recovery.

My yellows—those behaviors or feelings or thoughts that could trigger a relapse for me—are looking for excuses to not go to therapy, avoiding potential conflict with wife rather than telling her when I was upset or frustrated about things, and backing down from boundaries I had set in regard to working with my dad. The yellows tell me I have to move into green areas and address the issues immediately.

My green is doing a daily meditation reading, attending aftercare activities with other guys in treatment, attending therapy for self and with my wife. Honoring the non-negotiables.

Today I actively listen to my own voice, not my father's. I have separated my part of the business from my dad's. The church has stayed important for both my wife and me, but we changed churches. We found a church that for us is more real, where they understand addictions. They even have twelve-step groups on campus. I found Sex and Love Addicts Anonymous helpful for me. I don't see myself as a love addict, but nonetheless, I like the groups and the program.

But the most wonderful gift of my recovery is that I am a different kind of father. I had always participated in the kids' activities; I was proving I wasn't like my father, who never made time. But I couldn't really show up emotionally for them when I was so out of touch with my own feelings. I don't want them to feel alone like I did. I don't want them to feel they can't come to me with concerns or fears or having made mistakes.

With my wife's agreement and full support, I shared with my kids who by then were in their late teens my struggles with porn. I didn't fully disclose; I just told them it became a problem and that I got help. We talked about healthy intimacy and how porn got in the way of a good relationship.

My wife and I still have healing to do, but our relationship is so much healthier today. When we look at each other, we really see each other. I am so grateful my behavior did not destroy our love. And so grateful that recovery is giving us this path forward.

♦ ♦ ♦

From Stefanie Carnes, PhD, Sr. Fellow
(Clinical Architect of Willow House, Clinical Sexologist)

While many recovery stories such as Keith's are kept secret, they are not uncommon. As a matter of fact, sex, pornography, and love addiction (see Chapter Five, Intimacy) occur in approximately 10 percent of men and 7 percent of women but are often underrecognized and overlooked.

Many clients like Keith will enter treatment believing they have no trauma history. But Keith's history is rife with "little t" traumas of invalidation, emotional abuse, parentification, never being able to meet expectations, and feeling worthless. These little t traumas accumulated, leading Keith to internalize messages of shame and feelings of being unlovable. This toxic shame is common for those with compulsive and addictive sexual behavior.

What began as escapism or stress-relief escalated in frequency, intensity, and risk, eventually leading to experiences offline and in person. One unique aspect of Keith's story is that his offline behavior escalated to sex with men. While for some client's this behavior may involve some questioning of orientation and a supportive and affirming exploration of bisexuality or homosexuality, it appears in Keith's story that he identifies as straight. There can be many reasons that straight men have sex with men, including things such as males being more available for anonymous sexual encounters, traumatic repetition of a past event, and looking for male nurturance that was lacking in a father figure. Any of these reasons could have been a possibility for Keith given his history.

It is imperative that clients in recovery from sex addiction get honest with their partners and do the hard work necessary to heal the wounds of betrayal. Disclosing information about the sexual acting out, while difficult, is a necessary part of healing. Understandably, Keith's wife was devastated by the news of Keith's infidelity. Many partners of sex addicts experience betrayal trauma when they learn of their loved ones acting out behaviors. Intensive couples therapy to heal the wounds of betrayal is often required.

Keith also took the additional step of sharing his recovery with his children. Older teens and adult children can often benefit from appropriate sharing about the addiction. When considering whether to disclose to children, it's important to consider the child's maturity level and stability, and whether sharing is in the child's best interest. In this case, Keith shared with his children about his recovery without sharing details about his sexual behavior, which was appropriate. This sharing gives them important information about addiction in their family and their father's recovery, and likely deepened their relationship with their father. It can be very important for older children to recognize that family history so that they can recognize that they may too, have a vulnerability to addiction. Involving the family in the healing process, when appropriate, can allow for growth throughout the family system.

From Patrick Carnes, PhD, Sr. Fellow

Growing up was an emotionally abusive and intensely critical period for almost all sex addicts. As Keith did, most come from rigid and extremely controlling families. Oftentimes these families were excessively religious and at times even cult-like. They were also typically sex negative, meaning that sex was a taboo subject and activity. No intimacy or vulnerability was tolerated. It's no wonder that hidden sexual behavior, then, escalates into loss of control under clouds of shame.

Another path to addiction starts with gaming. Gaming teaches a set of rules around conquest, novelty, and distancing from others. When applied to sexuality, these rules fit the world of porn. Nowadays the abundance and easy access to porn and sex is more than humans have experienced historically. Porn, like crystal meth, is considered a super stimulus and can quickly overwhelm and start changing the brain.

Keith started down the gaming and porn path because it gave him immediate but temporary relief from emotional pain and stress. Like many, he found himself experimenting in ways he never dreamed possible. Although not true for Keith, it's important to note that if someone has a dopamine deficiency in their brain they are very likely to be diagnosed with attention deficit disorder. Consequently, Adderall is prescribed with the intent of improving their focus. However, porn on a stimulant accelerates the addiction process. Quickly people seek out more powerful stimulants to watch porn, all of which maximizes the power of the reward system.

Keith finally got honest in therapy. Now, he and his wife are part of a church community that is affirming. He now owns his own business, gaining significant distance from his father. He and his wife are practicing skills they were never given when growing up. Today they've taken what they've learned about emotional intimacy and have incorporated it into their sexual intimacy.

Simply Not Enough

BY KIRK

I was seventy-one years old when I walked into treatment four years ago. I had two fears: My first was that I couldn't stop my drinking and sexually acting out, and second, I would be the oldest guy there and I wouldn't fit in because of it. Fitting in had been what I had been trying to do my whole life.

Needing to Fit In

As a child, I desperately wanted approval from my father. He was born in the era when men did not hug, kiss, or show any affection. In addition, he was an engineer, so he was very pragmatic, logical, disciplined. Everything had to have a purpose.

When my uncle would come to visit, he would get down on the floor with me and play. Or we would bat balls or play football. I loved it; I couldn't get enough of that attention. To my dad, playing for fun wasn't purposeful. I started to feel like I would never be enough in my dad's eyes.

When I was twelve, I became friendly with this boy who was very popular, two years older, and quite a bit bigger than me. He was a lineman on the football team. He was cool and had a cool scooter. I really looked up to him, so when he made sexual advances toward me, I was afraid I would lose him as my friend if I didn't do what he wanted, so I participated in oral sex. I hated the act and felt a lot of shame about it, but the thought that he liked me overrode everything else.

Because I didn't stand up for myself and stop him, or tell anyone, this just reinforced the belief I already had about myself: that I was weak and unworthy. By the time I graduated from high school, I believed I wasn't smart enough, wasn't manly enough, wasn't strong enough.

I entered into marriage at twenty-one, secure in my inadequacies. I chose a woman I felt inferior to. She was accomplished, she had gotten accepted into a major college with honors. She had awards for her high intelligence.

I also chose to befriend guys who had positions or degrees that were immediately associated with smartness. I constantly compared myself to them, and of course I could never measure up. It didn't help me believe that I was smart, but it was an outward symbol that other people thought I was.

Therefore, I fit in. I just needed to fit in.

The Stabilizer

Within a year of marrying, I was having affairs. Sex was the tonic I thought I needed. If I was fearful, my sexual behavior would temporarily take my fear away. If I was angry, it would soothe my anger. If I was awarded a big project at work, I celebrated using it as a reward. If I lost a big project, I drowned my anger and despair with an affair. I was hard working, and my sex addiction would level me out; it was a stabilizer.

I did get caught, and on more than one occasion. The many affairs hurt a lot of people.

My feelings were strong and quite varied. Shame was the dominant feeling. It was a tough time, and my drinking accelerated. But as an addict you are pretty selfish, and in time, affairs took too much effort. I started going to massage parlors, hiring escorts, and engaging with people I didn't have to think about or act like I cared about. I was forever searching for the sense of intimacy I never had as a kid from not being touched, hugged, or kissed. That was a huge driver for me. I felt like I needed it, and I justified it. I thought I couldn't be a successful businessman without it.

So when my now-second wife caught me going to a massage parlor, and threatened divorce, I struggled to explain this to her, as we had been married all of a year. So, I threw myself on the gauntlet, saying it was my drinking. That was my entry into Alcoholics Anonymous.

I had a lot of good growth in AA, but I carried my sex addiction in my back pocket the entire time. My acting out continued all of the next twenty-four years. I was in denial and full of entitlement. I thought, I deserve this. This is what men do. I was afraid to think of it as wrong.

Acceleration

After seventeen years of sobriety, I resumed drinking. It had seemed so natural—my wife and I were on a vacation. Just this one night, I told myself.

Over the next few years, I convinced myself I was controlling the drinking, but I wasn't. It got to the point that when I wasn't drinking, I was preoccupied with the anticipation of the next drink and was lying to keep the secret. My drinking accelerated, and my sex addiction along with it.

My wife attempted to make our marriage last, but she was pulling away from me and building a shell around herself. My behavior was beating her down. As a result of my addiction, I was dealing with two totally separate blackmail attempts. She discovered that I had taken more than a hundred thousand dollars out of our retirement. But that wasn't even the tipping point for her. That came after she caught me looking at pictures of a former acting-out partner. So, either I went to treatment for sex addiction or I was headed for another divorce.

The thought of living without her was unfathomable. She is smart, strong, and attractive, just like my first wife. I truly believed that I could not carry on alone.

So I drove eighteen hours to the Gentle Path, and I drank the whole way there. I had never felt that down in my life.

Leaning into the Therapy

For me being in treatment, meant I would have to wage a battle with myself about who I was. I wasn't very excited about having to do that.

What shocked me the most about being at GP was that I felt no judgment. I wasn't seen as a bad guy. The other men in treatment seemed so normal, and the therapists treated me kindly.

The therapists worked with us around our core beliefs. My main belief, I realized, was that I was not good enough, smart enough, athletic enough. I was simply not enough, period. When they asked me what I liked about myself, I had to think about it for a bit. But then I identified one thing, and then another and then another. I had this sudden realization that I am not evil or simply a piece of shit. I do have some worth.

They gave us a lot of homework. Initially, I had a mental block. But then I took on this attitude: I am just going to jump in. I don't know what will happen, but I am ready. That approach carried me throughout the rest of my time there. And I carried that into my work after GP too.

I was introduced to twelve-step sex addiction programs. I had already been in AA, but these groups, following the same steps, were focused on the behavior of compulsive sexual behavior. Today I have a sponsor, and I sponsor others.

I discovered that nearly every man in these groups was dually addicted, so we discussed it a lot. We worked with Dr. Carnes's book, *Facing the Shadow*, and addressed how our addictions interacted. I saw how anger and fear were a part of my addictions, and if I didn't address the underlying issues, those feelings would pop up in other self-destructive ways.

At some point during my stay, it was suggested to me that I needed to extend my treatment, that I wasn't quite ready to be on my own without the strong support and structure. My reaction was, Oh no, I am going home! Choosing though to go directly home, I stopped for dinner on the eighteen-hour drive. Feeling tired, I ordered a glass of bourbon. Yep, after all that treatment, that was a sign to me and everyone else— including my wife—that I wasn't ready to be home.

The next day I checked into a sober living house and entered an intensive outpatient program. For three more months, I was afforded the ability to really get my sobriety and recovery off the ground. Then one weekend, when visiting my wife at our home, I poured myself a drink, just a little bit of bourbon. I wasn't a quick learner. She saw it and asked me to leave. I went back to the sober living house and told the men in the home and of course my therapist. By the time I completed that program and my stay in sober living, I knew I had been blessed and grateful for the staff and the program for giving me my life back.

A New Beginning

Recovery for me is more than stopping my drinking and acting out sexually; it has to do with addressing anger and fear, being willing to be vulnerable and honest, and addressing my codependency—how I was looking to others to bolster me up, make me feel better about myself.

Getting out of the toxic shame cycle was a huge battle for me. The more I worked and the deeper I went with my therapist, I realized how poorly I thought of myself. I have come a long way to let go of that thinking. It took a lot of work, and many people held my hand through this.

Recently, I attended a retreat where a man talked about emotional sobriety, knowing your fears and angers and learning how to deal with them. For me, that means putting stress or problems in perspective— that these too will pass. I tell myself, I will figure it out. It may not be what I want, but it is not the be-all to my life. I can handle this. I am not alone in this. My life isn't going to stop.

Every day I have something I could be fearful of. Instead of reaching for alcohol or sex, today I work with my fear predominantly through prayer. Every morning I have a conversation with God. I pray for strength to handle the situations and be accepting of the outcome. I pray to be my authentic self. I don't need to be a low handicap golfer or an engineer, just me. My conversations with God are often of gratitude, and I need all of the gratitude I can get. I ask God to allow me to be me, today, in the present—and that is good enough.

I stick to my recovery practices religiously: morning prayer, meditation, and several readings. I have two sponsees and facilitate a phone call for Gentle Path alumni weekly. I also keep in touch with my peers during my treatment. This brotherhood is uplifting and amazing.

Today my relationship with my wife is based on no secrets and a lot of communication. She too is active in her recovery process. For a long time, we held our own meetings once a week to make sure we shared our feelings about each other and about life in general. Now it's just an organic part of our relationship. I don't hide my fears, my vulnerability, from her. Nor do I let them keep me up at night. There is a lot of freedom in sharing yourself. These are the blessings of recovery.

That said, life still happens. My wife has had serious health issues, and I've had two major surgeries. We moved out of state; our dog died. I get stressed out. But when I begin to slip back into feelings of being unworthy, when self-pity appears, I have to become more specific and more frequent with my prayers. I practice radical acceptance. I inundate myself with positive affirmations. I focus on staying in the moment. I let go of what is required. All of this allows me to pull myself out of a lengthy funk.

There Is Light

I am a sex addict, alcoholic, codependent, and internet addict. I wasn't born an addict. I didn't choose to be an addict. In my addiction, I made very bad decisions. There has been a lot of damage. But it is a battle I survived. Not all do; but I did and am stronger for it.

I have gone through my life not believing in my worth, and today I think I am a good person, and I am doing good things. And I am lucky. Going to treatment for forty-five days is not enough; it is just a beginning. But it's a beginning to what can be a good life.

I want other addicts to know there is hope, and that they are not bad people. When you are ready, you can do this with the help of others. And for those in recovery, when things get tough, just keep at it, keep working what you have learned. You will see progress.

Whether you are nudged like me or arrive at the point of wanting your life to be different, you need to make change. With those changes can come a lot of wonderful things. There is a lot of work along the way, but there is light and we can do it.

I have gone from not believing I could recover to being in recovery.

◆ ◆ ◆

Being in the Recovery Zone
By Patrick Carnes, PhD, Sr. Fellow (Pioneer in Sex Addiction, Founder of Gentle Path)

The objective of any good treatment plan is to teach individuals the skills that allow them accountability for their behavior and to supply them with tools that help them to be more emotionally honest with themselves and others. Here is a sampling of practices identified as Resilience Master Skills that move people from the chaos and challenge of initial recovery to a firm, grounded platform on which recovery can be sustained for the long term.

- **Vision.** The capacity to picture your intentions and future can make a big difference in attaining them.

- **Persistence.** The pure tenacity of picking yourself up eight times after seven falls builds resilience over time.

- **Acceptance.** It's important to have the capacity to cope with the realities in front of you.

- **Knowledge.** Feeding your brain is a nourishing practice.

- **Emotion Regulation.** Keeping yourself in a state of calm and maintaining the capacity to restore calm is critical in everyday life.

- **Boundaries.** One of the most important self-care skills is establishing clear definitions of what works and what does not— and maintaining your boundaries consistently.

- **Listening to Fear.** One of the hardest but most valuable practices is the ability to pay attention to things that bother you, assess true levels of danger, and then use your best intuitions to react wisely.

- **Inner Observer.** We all have a "wise mind" that can rise above the turmoil of the brain, filtering out extraneous thoughts so you can focus on what really matters; you just have to tap into it.

- **Flexibility.** The ability to explore and expand options, and adapt to surprises, is another hallmark of resilience.

- **Inner Coherence.** Achieving an inner stillness is possible when you integrate your body rhythms with what matters most.

- **Empathy.** The ability to look at a problem from another person's perspective and experience appropriate feelings is a resource you can strengthen, like a muscle.

- **Flow.** The capacity to stay in a range of behaviors that challenge you, matter to you and generate happiness.

From Jerry Law, D. Ministry

(Executive Director of The Meadows)

Kirk, at age seventy-one, was still active in his sex addiction. Many erroneously believe that this disease is only active in younger men and women. Addiction is no respecter of persons, be it age, gender, ethnicity, faith, or any similar factor. The goal of addiction is to inform its victim that they do not have the disorder and then to kill them.

Struggling with self-worth, Kirk was desperate to fit in. This desperation led him, at a young age, into acts he did not want to participate in, and furthered his shame and lack of self-worth. He therefore sought validation in relationships unhealthy as they may be.

Kirk mentions the rapid acceleration of his addictions, fueled by anticipation. The power and influence of anticipation cannot be understated. fMRI studies demonstrate that the *limbic system*, or pleasure center of the brain, lights up when merely thinking about or seeing photos of "the next." This anticipation can take the prefrontal cortex, the judgment seat of the brain, offline while the desire for the next high takes over. This may help explain how Kirk had spent in excess of one hundred thousand dollars from his retirement account chasing the high.

Many people use addictive substances or behaviors to numb their emotions and avoid the pain that life often involves. In his recovery journey, Kirk learned the power and value of allowing himself to "feel the feels" and not turn to self-destructive behaviors, such as excessive drinking and sexual acting out, to numb those emotions. The only way out of "The Valley of the Shadow of Death" is through it.

The hallmark symptom of all addictions is denial. Kirk's denial both to himself and his wife were indicative of impaired thinking. His brain had been hijacked. He honestly believed he could manage the addiction and keep the secret from all others. Inevitably, the house of cards collapsed, as we saw when Kirk's wife drew a line in the sand.

A critical part of Kirk's story is that he has learned that those in recovery don't shoot the wounded. His time at Gentle Path taught him many things, including the fact that a slip does not mean he is never accountable for his actions, he is. But the recovery community can be a place of hope and healing rather than retribution and failure.

From Patrick Carnes, PhD, Sr. Fellow

As people graduate from treatment, one of the most common sentiments we hear is "I wish I had started earlier." They realize that every day has great value. It also becomes clear that treatment is the platform for beginning the work. Kirk is a good example. The key issue for Kirk was never feeling enough. He jumped into his treatment and made real progress. He faced difficult truths about himself and did the work asked of him. He saw a lifetime of sexual acting out and secrets. He realized that he never really had a successful long-term relationship. At seventy-one that is difficult to admit to oneself. Further, he realized that alcoholism was a core factor in his sexual addiction. Both were used to "even things out" emotionally. Not many people grasp that so quickly.

Treatment can go very well for many but can be sabotaged by not having a plan that staff, families, referents, and patients can all follow. Leaving a structured, warm, caring, and resource-filled environment to being totally on your own can be precipitous and abrupt. Translated it means that being in recovery is living in consultation with your caregivers.

That Kirk cared enough for himself to find support after leaving treatment is testimony to the sense of self-value he retained from his work. Now he has a different life, and his wife has joined him in sharing the abundant consciousness of recovery.

Kirk learned that he was worth finishing his work. It starts with that first leap of faith, and then other leaps follow. When you face the difficult truths about yourself and you do the work asked of you, people say that you earned a chair within the circle. Kirk earned his chair, even with some bumps on the way. He was more than enough.

Undaunted Hope

Recovery from sex addiction can seem unfathomable. Yet as these stories reflect, you can transform your behaviors. And as discussed in the commentaries, there are reasons your behavior has taken over your life, and it is not because there is something wrong with you. In recovery you get the opportunity to make behavioral amends to those you have hurt, plus the opportunity to let go of your fears and shame. You will discover your inherent worth and value. And you don't have to do this alone. Recovery offers you a genuine connection to yourself and also a brotherhood of support.

CHAPTER EIGHT

Finding the Courage
RECOVERY AS A FAMILY MEMBER

I thought treatment was only for my son.
I really didn't expect I would personally benefit too.

By the time my wife went to treatment, I was so conflicted I didn't
know what I wanted from our marriage anymore.

I was afraid to leave my husband at the treatment facility,
I thought he would probably leave, or be so angry he would
just try to punish me and the kids for intervening.

We all have our own family story. Whatever is happening, the bottom line is we love our family member and want them to get better. Some of us have been trying to make a difference or change our loved one's behavior for years. It's also possible we didn't know what was even occurring until recently. Perhaps you have spent years confused or frustrated by their thinking or behavior. Or you may have lived with a lot of fear—of losing your relationship or of their dying due to their behaviors or illness. You've endured embarrassment, anger, disappointment, or sadness because of their actions. And often that is topped by feelings of guilt for something you did or didn't do, or for even having these feelings in the first place. Right now, you may be in shock, outraged, or numb and tired.

While your loved one is responsible for their recovery, as a family member, it is likely you can use some support and an opportunity to address dynamics of your own that will lead to more serenity for yourself. Engaging in family work when a loved one is in treatment is not about blame but about creating a healthier family system.

Being focused on your struggling loved one can often lead to letting your own self-care go to the wayside. You may have lost sight of what you want or need for yourself. If you have reacted to your loved one's behavior, you may have inadvertently caused more disruption or disconnection among family members. Your communication style may be ineffective or expectations unrealistic. Healthy boundaries may have flown out the window. You could be caught up in the drama and don't know how to get out.

Whether it's a mental health, trauma or addiction issue that a family member is struggling with it is usually a family member who is the impetus for getting professional help. It's also important to know that those who have the support of family members have an increased chance at long-term recovery.

The following narratives are by family members of individuals who caused varying degrees of hurt, but who ultimately committed to healing and recovery. The stories reflect the openness and growth that can happen for a family when we embrace treatment for struggling loved ones that also includes therapeutic support for ourselves.

Kidnapped by Addiction
BY MARK

Kelly and I met at a bar when we were in our mid-twenties. It was love at first sight for both of us. We spent a lot of the next two years having a good time, partying with friends, with my wife being the center of the party.

We lived in the Pacific Northwest, where I had grown up. Kelly had moved there from Austin, where she had grown up, and told me it was best she didn't live near her family. While we were dating, we visited her family a couple of times, and they weren't good visits. There was a lot of arguing, and her brothers and father smoked weed and drank heavily. All of them—her mom, dad, stepdad, brother—seemed really negative. I saw why Kelly was content to live apart from them. Happily, my family embraced Kelly.

Kelly and I had good jobs. She was working in graphics for small start-up companies. I was working in tech for Amazon. As we watched our friends getting married, and as they started to have kids, we decided that's what we wanted too. However, Kelly didn't want to get pregnant as early as I did. She said she wasn't ready to give up her independence yet. But she got pregnant in the second year of our marriage, so we had our daughter sooner than she wanted.

Head in the Sand

I figured Kelly had settled into her role as a mom by the time we had our son, two years later. But I had my head in the sand. Over the next few years Kelly complained about being cooped up and wanting to go out more. I felt her unhappiness at home. Her nights out with girlfriends were important. She was often critical of me and saying I wasn't as much fun as I used to be. I was really into being a dad and content to be home with the kids, which made it easier for her to keep her independence. I began to feel her distance, her evasiveness. But I figured that this was the kind of stuff that changes in a relationship when you start having kids and developing a profession. I didn't see it as a red flag.

At times, when I told Kelly that I thought she needed to pay more attention to the kids, she would get defensive and tell me I should give up some of my work time and do more with them. I tried to manipulate her subtly into getting involved in kid events. I'd buy tickets for her and the kids to do something, or for the four of us to go out, but she always figured out a way to get around the manipulations. For example, she'd give the tickets to my mom to take the kids or come up with last-minute excuse as to why she couldn't go. I wanted to take family trips, but Kelly always managed to talk me into trips with just the two of us, saying we could have more fun, like in the old days.

The Signs Were There All Along

By the time the kids were in junior high school, the signs of a problem became more blatant. It started one day when I came home from work and found her high. Then I noticed how often she would come home drunk after a girls' night out. She started being short with the kids, and she wouldn't join us at the dinner table. Instead, she would stand back in the kitchen drinking.

"I'm unhappy," she would say.

"Why?" I'd ask.

"I don't know why! I just am," She'd answer.

I was happy, and I just wanted her to be happy too. So, I started to send the kids more often to their grandparents' house on the weekends. I tried to make her happy by going out with her at night, but she would get so smashed that I wound up having to take care of her by the end of the evening. I would see her flirting with other guys, and I began to wonder whether what she was doing now with me was also what she was doing when out with her girlfriends.

During all of this time, Kelly was still working. But she had changed jobs three times in five years. It was another sign I missed, because it was easy to rationalize it when I saw other friends switching jobs too.

Then one day when she was in the bathroom, a text came through on her phone, and I don't know why but I picked up her phone. It was a sext from a guy. When I confronted her, she tried to laugh it off, making an excuse that she didn't really know him. I wondered, did this have anything to do with her evasiveness, distancing, and critical nature?

Of course, I didn't say anything to anyone because I was embarrassed. What was wrong with me that I couldn't keep my wife happy?

Nobody's Happy at Home

The next couple of years, everything escalated. She began to drink more at home, not just when she went out. When she did go out, she would drink at home beforehand. When she didn't go out, she openly drank before dinner and kept it up all night.

Then I noticed that things in the family checking account weren't adding up. In addition, I noticed that our kids weren't happy. Our son was isolating in his room, and our daughter—who had begun arguing with and being disrespectful to her mom —was staying out of the house whenever she could.

Yet surprisingly it wasn't Kelly's behavior that got my full attention. It wasn't until her brother died of an overdose and her father died from liver cancer due to his drinking, within a six-month period, that the light bulb in my head turned on. *Oh my god she has a drinking problem,* I realized. *Why didn't I see this before?* If I had to put it all on paper, I'd have seen that the signs were there all along, since we first met.

I felt so stupid, so ashamed.

I knew I had to get my wife help. If not for her sake, definitely for the kids. I didn't think Kelly would listen to me, since she was always so defensive when I tried to talk to her about even little things. So, I called my mom, and her social worker friend agreed to do an intervention under the guise of concerns about our daughter. When we gathered, and the focus went to Kelly and her drinking, I was surprised to see that she appeared to be listening. We each shared our concern and our love for her and then ultimately, I requested she go to treatment. She cried, she was quiet, she looked away a lot, and a couple of times she tried to make excuses, blaming things on her brother and dad dying. But the truth was this was years of her manipulating, lying, and using. To be honest, I was shocked that it worked but it did. She went to treatment that evening.

I felt immediate relief. I was happy to come home to my kids and not have this dark cloud over the house. My kids said they knew she drank too much; both said they knew for a long time. I wasn't sure how things would go, but at least now I had a name for what was happening in our family: addiction.

Moving into Family Recovery

Family week was important to me on a lot of levels. Kelly wanted my mom to come because she wanted a "mom" presence. She said she didn't feel that my mom judged her, and she wanted that kind of support. So, my mom attended along with our kids—a junior and senior in high school. I felt the kids had been impacted enough that they should be a part of the family program. Kelly was hesitant, but agreed to their participating.

Before Kelly's going to The Meadows, I had already made a connection between my wife's family and her drinking problem. But the staff there had a name for it: *generational repetition*. I understood then that she was going to die from her addiction just like her family members if she didn't quit.

On my second day, during one of the exercises, Kelly had to show us her timeline regarding drinking, and sure enough she was also using pills and had at times used cocaine. Kelly described for me what The Meadows calls the *symptoms of addiction*: her preoccupation, her denial, and what she had come to recognize as loss of control. She realized that she had a history of being out of control going back to before we met. But, she said, having me—someone she trusted and loved—in her life, along with her work, gave her some stability that helped her manage for quite a while, in spite of the fact that the addiction was still there.

Kelly described how she was consumed with planning how she would get out of the house, hiding her behavior, and manipulating me, the kids, and my family to make it easier for her to use. I was dumbfounded that the addiction had taken total control of her everyday life. For the first time I got angry. I didn't want to be angry because she was finally telling me the truth, but I was.

After that session I wasn't sure if I would return to group the next day. I was like a kid not wanting to go to school. I wasn't thrilled to know that the family work was mostly done with other families, either. I didn't want to share our secrets with anyone. But my mom made me go back. And by the end of five days, I could not have been more grateful for the other families. I really got that I was not alone and that Kelly's addiction was not about me. I got that I wasn't a bad husband. And I really only understood that as I put myself in the shoes of the other participants.

The kids were pretty quiet the first couple of days and just listened. I was too focused on myself, so I was really glad my mother was there for the kids as well as Kelly. But on the third day, when the counselors asked that we all write a letter to the addiction, everyone opened up. Both kids laid out all of their feelings—the anger, the fears, their guilt, even though they had nothing to feel guilty for. They talked about their feelings of betrayal as the addiction grew. Their pain, their vulnerability was so raw. There wasn't a dry eye in the group. That day I realized that I had gotten so caught up in my own confusion and pain that, in many ways, I had ignored their pain too.

The letter-writing exercise helped me separate Kelly's behavior from Kelly as a person as well. She is my beautiful wife with this horrible addiction that had kidnapped her. And I wanted her back. But she had to be willing to walk away from the kidnapper. Did she have Stockholm syndrome, meaning would she stay attached to the addiction? Time would tell.

I also learned that a lot of my enabling was by what I didn't do rather than what I did. I enabled her addiction by making excuses for her to my kids, friends, and family. I enabled her by not forcing the issue and backing down when she got defensive. I enabled her by not asking enough questions when she changed jobs at work. I enabled by being so silent.

What My Family Needed

There isn't a lot of time in a five-day workshop to do and say all the things I wanted, but family staff gave us a format for weekly family meetings. The kids really liked that, as it allowed them to see we were taking recovery seriously and that they were important to us. We wanted them to continue to have a voice and the skills for talking about what was important to them in a manner in which they could be heard.

It has been five years now, and recovery is a natural part of our lives. Today Kelly thrives in her work and attends a lot of twelve-step meetings. Sometimes I go with her, but I also decided I needed a lot of support to get out of my shell, to learn some skills I didn't have. So, I ended up seeing a therapist myself and going to Codependency Anonymous and Al-Anon meetings. I like them both, and they meet different needs. In Codependency Anonymous I address my "niceness," which for me is about not wanting to talk about my feelings, and not recognizing my own needs and losing myself in my wife's needs. In Al-Anon I address my need of "staying on my side of the sidewalk," meaning not trying to subtly manipulate my wife to do her recovery the way I think she should. Or trying to manipulate how she relates to our kids. Al-Anon helps to keep me honest with myself about the seriousness of this disease. Both programs support me speaking up.

Our ability to communicate, which we learned through healthy communication exercises, has made all the difference in the world. For instance, our son got heavily into gaming and got in trouble over it while at college; but we recognized something was seriously wrong and intervened. This time we did not wait years to get help. Our daughter's life has been challenging as she navigates relationships and choices about work and school, but it's amazing how mature she can be due to her recovery skills. She talks about boundaries; she communicates well.

In spite of coming from a relatively healthy family system, I still had a lot to learn about being in relationship with another, be it as a partner or a parent. My life had a lot of superficial qualities to it, including wanting to ignore the problems. Today a problem doesn't scare me so much. I take an attitude of, *we will figure this out.* I know that I may not have all the answers, but there are also people who will help.

◆ ◆ ◆

What Does a Dysfunctional Family System Look Like?

Thinking of a family as a system, here is what a functional vs. dysfunctional family system can look like:

Functional	Dysfunctional
The family system is open, expanding and changing	The system is rigid, closed and secretive
All emotions are allowed and shared	The system controls which emotions are allowed
Mistakes are forgiven and disciplined when appropriate	Mistakes are punished, judged and shamed
Individual awareness is based on an expanded reality	Individual awareness is based on denial, delusion and shame
The system serves and exists for the individual	The individual serves and exists for the system
Boundaries are heard and supported	Boundaries are distorted or rigid or lacking
Each generation redefines the family dynamics	Intergeneration dynamics repeat
Family Roles are flexible	Family Roles are rigid and ascribed to support the dysfunction in the system

COMMENTARY

From Jerry Law, D. Ministry
(Executive Director of The Meadows)

Mark, like many family members, was oblivious to the signs of his wife's addiction. Because Kelly was capable of holding a good job, wanted a family, and was fun to be with, he had no reason to question her fun-loving nature (which he would later come to recognize was always centered around her drinking). Their lives were busy, he was developing a career, they were raising children—there were many distractions that kept Mark from noticing what was occurring, trusting his intuition, or questioning his wife.

Remember, addicts are usually masters at deception. And substance use disorder, particularly alcoholism, is often a slow, insidious process.

Wanting those we love to be happy and wanting to please another are admirable qualities. But needing to please our partner, putting their happiness in the forefront, actively avoiding conflict, and desiring their approval—as Mark did—are codependent traits. Crossing the fine line from stand-up traits into self-defeating behaviors is as insidious as moving into addiction. Denying one's own needs and feelings in the process is what makes these actions self-defeating.

It is important that family members not judge themselves for how they react to what is happening. Recovery is not about blame. It is about being accountable to yourself. As his wife's addiction escalated, Mark started to blatantly accommodate her, thinking that would make her happy. Accommodating, using the silent treatment, never asking questions, manipulating, and lecturing are all common enabling behaviors for a family member, often done in attempt to help or to make sense of a confusing situation. Enabling assists the person with addiction to not feel or take responsibility for their behavior, often delaying the crisis needed for them to be willing to reach out for help. Kelly's primary enabler was Mark, and while the story does not reflect others, most people who are addicted have more than one enabler.

Men are more apt to leave a woman with a drinking problem than vice versa. This has a lot to do with men not being as dependent financially on their female partners. and their esteem is more often related to their work than a relationship. But as seen in this case, Mark did not consider leaving. In fact, he supported and was a part of initiating Kelly getting help.

One of the values of multifamily group as Mark experienced it is that it can be a quick shame reducer. Mark had the ability to put himself in the shoes of other participants, other family members. He saw that he wasn't alone, and if he could see they were not at fault, they were not bad, then neither was he. He also no longer felt alone in handling the crisis.

From Claudia Black, PhD, Sr. Fellow
*(Pioneer in Addictive Family Systems, Clinical Architect
of the Claudia Black Young Adult Center)*

While it is common for parents to believe that their kids aren't affected by the addiction and that they don't notice how it is impacting family dynamics, Mark had less denial about that. He wanted his kids to get help too. Children may not know what is causing the problems at home or why, but they experience the impact. And given permission and safety, they will talk.

When asked to talk about what they are experiencing, family members often struggle with the issue of loyalty, thinking they are betraying their loved one, even if they have been hurt by that person. Kids think that by expressing their feelings and sharing their experiences, they are implying their loved one is a bad person or that they don't love that person. To create safety, treatment professionals talk about separating the disease from the person, which makes it easier for families to speak their truth. We also address the issue of loyalty and betrayal by explaining when expressing your feelings, you aren't betraying your loved one, you are betraying the addiction—and by not speaking your truth, you will betray yourself.

Mark learned an important part of his recovery is taking the focus off of his wife, being accountable for his own behavior, and being willing to speak his reality. This was strongly reinforced in Al-Anon. Even with recovery, life continues, kids have struggles, and Kelly and Mark are finding their way, and have a path that gives them the tools to be able to look forward to handling whatever comes their way.

We Just Thought He Was Lost

BY DIANA

My son Will rarely drew attention to himself. He never appeared to have any problems. But when he was nineteen years old, he nearly died after cutting his wrist. He ended up in a hospital for nine days. But I'm not sure if it was really treatment. Mostly they kept him safe until they assured us that he was no longer suicidal.

I'd like to say that that was enough for us to get more help, but he was pretty convincing that he was okay and had learned his lesson. He told us that he had been feeling lost about his future and wasn't sure what there was to look forward to; because of being isolated during the pandemic, he hadn't felt a part of anything important—but he really didn't want to die. My husband and I accepted that a lot of young people are lost at this stage, and that Will had just had a moment of being overwhelmed.

As horrible as this sounds, we had so much going on in our lives and, in retrospect, had come to rely on Will to always be okay, that we simply *needed* to believe things would get better. At the time, Will's stepfather of ten years was recuperating from a bad car accident. My elderly mom had Alzheimer's, and my dad couldn't take care of her; since I was an only child, I was having to make decisions about their care. Plus, I was looking after Max, four years younger than Will, who had Down's Syndrome. I needed to help him with activities that relied on his motor skills, such as basic grooming and dressing. Max also had health problems that were related to his GI system, so we had a lot of doctor visits.

So, it was easier for me to hope that, with some counseling through college student services, Will would be okay and that the suicide attempt was just a blip. I checked in on Will every day by text, and he sounded okay; he actually sounded pretty good for a long time.

Then one day we got a call from the campus police. Will had been rushed to the hospital after an apparent suicide attempt by cutting his wrist again. When we visited him in the psychiatric department, he was noticeably depressed. He was a lot thinner. He didn't want to look at his stepdad or me. When we started to bring in his brother, Will got really agitated and started crying and screaming at us. We learned that he wasn't polite to the doctors or staff, that he just wanted to be left alone.

This time we were told that he needed more than outpatient counseling. So, we chose the young adult program at The Meadows. Will had just turned twenty-one three weeks earlier.

Growing Up

Will had always been a pretty quiet kid. He was a sweet boy yet reticent around peers at school. His father and I separated when he was seven. I was remarried two years after my divorce, and so I was busy in this new relationship. I was also busy with Max, but Will was always really helpful in attending to his younger brother.

My new husband was good with the kids, and he engaged with Will a lot in the beginning. Together they went on errands, spent time in the outdoors, fixed things around the house. But around the time Will was in fourth grade, his biological dad insisted on seeing Will on weekends. I wasn't happy about these visitations because his biological father drank a lot, was drunk a lot, and I suspected was using some kind of drug too. But I had no legal recourse. Will was always despondent when he returned from weekends with his dad. I suspected his dad didn't pay him much attention on those visits.

Over the years, we saw a shift in Will; while he continued to be loving and paid attention to Max, he was emotionally isolated. Socially, Will was more on the outside looking in. When he would be invited by kids in school to some type of party, he would go and always said he had a good time but also seemed relieved to come home. He seemed to be content at home with his brother and his pets.

Will made a few friends in chess club and at his part time job at the recreational center. He became very close to one friend in particular. But then, in Will's senior year, the boy moved out of the country. In retrospect, he seemed moody and he didn't want to talk to us about his friend and got short with us if we asked. He didn't ask much of his stepfather or myself, and time just passed. We expected and he always planned to go to college, saying he wanted to be a veterinarian. This seemed so natural, as we always had pets. He grew up with one dog in particular, and they were inseparable.

Eye-Opening Week

At CBC, I went into our family workshop really confused as to what would make Will's life so horrible he wanted to die. We were not a family who talked about problems; we just handled them. We didn't talk about feelings much either. Certainly, we were sad about things, and there were things that were scary or frustrating. But we didn't overtly express our feelings, which is why family week was so eye-opening for us.

During one exercise, Will and other patients role-played aspects of his depression until, ultimately, they painted a visual portrait of his depression. I was shocked at how verbal he was and also horrified to see how terrible he felt about himself, and just as bad, where that thinking came from. I wasn't totally surprised that he felt upset about his biological father's relationship, or rather lack thereof. But Will got the message he was not important to his dad and had developed the belief that he was not important in general. Self-loathing was a big part of his depression.

Another role-play exercise, called *Family Sculpt*, showed us the way the family works as a system. While ours was not portrayed in the group activity, we all were asked to reflect and share how we saw ourselves within our family system. Clearly Will was the Lost Child, the invisible child. I saw him as a content, easy going kid. But in his quietness, in his never asking or requiring much attention, his needs didn't get met. He didn't feel noticed either. So, his belief that he didn't have value just grew and grew.

The therapist and Will showed us a timeline of what they considered little t traumas, aspects of Will's life that were traumatic to him in his development. It began with a subtle form of neglect by me not being available to him as much as he needed, plus his father's hurtful behavior, then the loss of his good friend due to the move, then the death of his dog. The next year, Will moved 225 miles away to college, holding in his feelings, not feeling good about himself, not easily being able to connect with others. It was obvious then how lonely and miserable he was when he attempted suicide at nineteen.

Then came the communication exercise. He had something to tell us that was obviously hard for him to say. He was very afraid of us rejecting him, but he told us anyway: he was questioning his sexual orientation.

The family team had taught us how to listen before we speak, and they taught us how to speak without discounting the other person's words. Individually and spontaneously, both my husband and I looked at Will, listened, and simply said, "Will, I love you." His stepdad stood up and put his arms out and asked Will if he could hug him and simply said, "I am here for you, Will."

All of Us Changed after CBC

After treatment, Will attended an outpatient therapy program for six months. It's been two years since then, and Will has found himself in so many good ways. He switched to a smaller school that's closer to home. He comes home on a regular basis, and we go to the school regularly to visit. This was part of our agreement for what we would change as a family. He sees a therapist and gets a lot of support from the local LGBTQIA+ community. He will never be an extrovert, but he has friends. He no longer questions his worth, his value, or his sexual orientation.

I can't do much about Will's lack of relationship with his biological dad, but he worked on that when in treatment and since he has been involved with the twelve-step program ACA. His stepdad and I have shifted the focus and energy in the family so Will has equal space. Having our own time with him, we have come to learn how interesting he is, how well-read he is.

As a mom, I must say I have felt a lot of guilt. I was trying to be everything to everyone and I allowed this one child to not get his needs met. But the family team was quick to point out that while I may feel guilty, I cannot sit in it. They reminded me of my humanness and they also let me know I had to create space for my own self-care. What a concept!

My husband and I attend meetings of PFLAG, a support, education, and advocacy group for friends, families, and allies of those in the LGBTQIA+ community. We also attend a Couples Recovery group. We are now a couple who talks about challenges, about our feelings, about what we are individually needing. The communication exercise we did offered us a format that we still use in our conversations. Who would have ever thought treatment for my son would lead to couples' therapy? Only one of my elderly parents is alive now; my youngest son will always require our added attention, but we have redistributed our attention to ourselves as a couple, ourselves individually, and made sure that Will gets attention too.

We also have an agreement with Will that his stepdad, myself, and he will have a check in monthly to talk specifically about any feelings or signs of depression. We have shared how devastating our lives would be without him, how much we love him and are there for him. Will agreed to be honest with us about his life. The frequency of this specific check in will lessen in time.

I have a lot of compassion for other parents in similar situations. My husband and I didn't see Will's pain; we were distracted. The thought that Will could have died while we were oblivious still pains me. But I don't go there too often in my thoughts. I tell other parents, don't wallow in your guilt, be there for your child. Be open to clinical staff saying they don't blame you, they are there to help you figure out what will help you be a better functioning family.

• • •

COMMENTARY

From Claudia Black, PhD, Sr. Fellow

As with substance use disorders, depression doesn't just show up overnight. It was easy for Will's parents to view his quietness as just part of his temperament.

Will's mother and stepfather knew it hurt Will that his biological father wasn't making himself available, yet it was only normal they didn't see the full impact. Will was not only experiencing abandonment on the part of his biological father, but he was also increasingly lost in the family system due to his brother's needs being so great and his mom and stepdad being in a new relationship. In becoming the "Lost Child," Will would come to believe his needs and wants were not important, and that would translate into his believing he wasn't important and didn't have value.

The Family Sculpt exercise helps family members understand the various roles they adopt for themselves. In Will's family, his brother played a central role in which the mom's behavior culminated in her being the family Hero, his stepdad the Placater, his biological father the Acting Out Person, and Will the Lost Child. When these identities are role-played, it is a powerful experience to witness the various distorted beliefs and thoughts that go along with them. While it is common for family members to adopt roles, in a healthier functioning family they are not so rigid and severe. In unhealthy functioning families, the role ascription is based in fear and often shame. The roles typically bring greater stability in the moment and provide a sense of psychological safety. While it is critical to see the impact of rigid roles, a part of the goal of the exercise is learning what one can do to get out of the role completely, or out of the rigid aspect of the role.

The bulk of family work done in treatment is closer to the close of someone's stay in inpatient. Will likely would not have felt secure enough to disclose to his parents about his questioning his sexual orientation any earlier in his treatment process. As well, being in a safe space where he felt seen and heard, he also felt more confident about his questioning. While many parents and helping professionals would like to think our families and community have become more inclusive of gender and sexual orientation differences, a lot of young adults don't feel it. Suicidal ideation and attempts are more common among those questioning, such as Will and those who are a part of the LGBTQIA + community. Not wanting to be alive is not only fueled by the systemic homophobia, but additional traumas, such as the many small t traumas that Will had. There was enough of a foundation of strength and love in this family; Will's mom and stepdad are going to love him irrespective of his sexual orientation.

While Diana and Will's stepdad regularly engage with Will with their newfound awareness, Diana and her husband are also using their new skills within the family unit as a whole. Diana is engaging in more self-care rather than trying to meet the needs of everyone else above her own. Continuing to use the communication skills that had been totally foreign to her and her husband has allowed them an intimacy with all members of the family.

From Jack Register, MSW
(Claudia Black Young Adult Center)

In Diana's family there was a lot happening all at once. Between the concerns with Will's brother and his medical needs, her new relationship, and her children's biological dad's addiction, she turned a blind eye to Will. As a Lost Child, Will struggled to see and understand himself in relationship to others. When Lost children are also LGBTQIA+, there is an added layer of silencing. Diana's distractions created another layer of silence that fueled Will's inner conflicts.

The literature on LGBTQIA+ development tells us that often there is no external source of validation of identity for this child during their developmental years. The lack of validation is sometimes subtle other times blatant from media and in the community. As a consequence, for Will this caused painful issues to seem "sharper" or harder to process. As important as it is for Will to find support within the LGBTQIA+ community, it is equally as helpful for Diana and her husband. While they were readily accepting of Will's sexual orientation, they nonetheless felt isolated; joining PFLAG offered them the opportunity to meet other parents, which reinforced the pride they already had in their son.

I'm very hopeful for Diana and her family. She took the treatment experience very seriously and was willing to make changes for herself. Her recovery will not only be of great support to Will but impacts all of her relationship in a healthy way.

From Trusting Blindly to Trusting My Gut   BY CANDACE

One day, I found a note in my mailbox and opened it up as I was heading into the house. It read, "Your husband is a scumbag, and you don't even know it. He tells me he loves me. He buys me lovely things. We have even taken a few trips. But after three years of telling me he is leaving you, I am no longer waiting."

I dropped to the ground and just sat, numb, frozen. How could he? My head was spinning. I felt sick to my stomach. Who was this woman? How had I not known for three years? From shock I moved into rage. I didn't know what I was going to do, but this had to stop and he had to leave. But what about the kids? In the moment, I hated Brian—this really nice guy, so well liked by everyone, and my closest friend. But he was betraying me, lying to me, and manipulating me. What was wrong with me? How could I be so stupid to not know?

We had gone through this sixteen years ago—and back then I trusted he wasn't going to do it again. That time, Brian's coworker's husband showed up at our doorstep with the evidence of their affair on a road trip together. I was devastated, confused, and six months pregnant with our first child. Once confronted with the evidence, Brian told me it was a mistake, it meant nothing. He reasoned that he was just stupid and young and just let things get out of control.

Then all I could do was cry. I didn't want out of the marriage—I loved him. But how could he do this? I just wanted to understand *why*. And to know he would *stop*.

That first time, he did all he could to appease me: calmed me down, said over and over that it meant nothing, begged for my forgiveness, talked about our baby that was coming. He cried too, fearing I would leave him. He said he really loved me. I thought he was sincere. It was easier to accept his excuses and apologies.

There Were Times I Wondered . . .

For the next several years, I thought things were going well. He was a good provider and supported me in my professional work as a headhunter. He coached various sports for all three kids, and we attended every school play. We enjoyed being parents and were on the same page about parenting.

But there were times I wondered. He periodically traveled in his work, which would sometimes trigger my feelings of insecurity, and which made me question whether he was really being honest with me. At times, he seemed distant from me. Sometimes he was agitated when it didn't make sense. We would be somewhere as a family, and I had the sense that he wanted to be elsewhere. I would point out that he seemed distant or agitated, and he always apologized and simply said work had him stressed. I found myself looking for reassurance that he loved me.

Everyone once in a while he wanted to try different things sexually, and while I know you need to spice up your bedtime behavior to keep the romance, it felt off to me—as if he wanted me to be someone different, someone else. Through all of this, I never allowed myself to fully question his behavior.

Standing My Ground

Now, sixteen years later, I was devastated again. But I still didn't want to leave the marriage. I simply wanted to be able to trust him again. So I said we had to go to marital counseling. He didn't want to go to therapy, and suggested church. I backed down, happy he was willing to do *something*. In the meantime, he was doing what he did the first time he was caught, being the ever so dutiful husband, catering to everything he thought I wanted or needed.

One day at church, I saw a flyer about a support group for partners of sex addicts. I really didn't think Brian was a sex addict, but I was intrigued. The flyer spoke about the trauma of betrayal. It spoke to me. I began to attend, without telling Brian.

I didn't say much during the first few meetings, I just listened, but I so identified with the women and their feeling overwhelmed, confused, humiliated. Some were blatantly angry, others were more like me, immobilized. But a few of them talked about finding themselves in this process. I wasn't sure what that meant, but they seemed to be happy.

What I heard that was important to me was that I wasn't trusting myself. I wasn't paying attention to those passing moments of wondering. They talked about living in a fantasy, and I began to wonder how much of my marriage was a fantasy.

Within a couple of months, this all led me to approaching my husband with questions. I wanted to know more about this woman who wrote the note. Brian didn't want to talk about it, saying it was behind us, reminding me of how good things were between us now. He said he was making it up to me, that guys just did this, and maybe it was a midlife thing for him. He assured me it was over.

I let another month pass and continued to attend group in secret. To his surprise, I finally told him he needed to see a therapist who specializes in sex addiction. He was enraged and told me I was ungrateful, that he was a good husband and he loved the kids and me. He challenged me, asking me what was wrong with me that I couldn't trust him, after all he was really trying. I realized I had never ever really challenged him, and I had this newfound confidence in myself and I stood my ground.

After he yelled at me, which he had never done, he left the house for a few hours. When he came back, he wanted to know if I had come to my senses, and again told me I was making something out of nothing. I think he expected my old behavior, for me to acquiesce and shut up. Instead, I handed him a flyer with the names of people who specialize in treating sexual addiction. I told him I didn't have the answers, but I no longer trusted him and wasn't going to stay to have another woman write me a note or another husband show up on my doorstep.

Some Time Apart

After Brian had been seeing a trained counselor for four weeks, he came home and told me he wanted to go to treatment for sex addiction. Suddenly, I panicked. What did this mean? Was there more acting out that I didn't know about? How serious was this? As much as I wanted the truth, I wasn't sure I was ready for it.

He told me part of the treatment would include family programming, and there would be people there to support me. *What?* What did *I* need support with? I was terrified. I didn't know where this was leading us. I wanted to keep my marriage, but I needed to know who I was married to, and we needed help, so I agreed to go too. But I also agreed knowing that maybe it would be best for me to not be married.

Our kids—ages twelve, fourteen, and sixteen—had their own questions, too, like were we getting a divorce? We told them that we were not planning to get a divorce (because we weren't, not that that couldn't change, but at the moment no) and that it was best for their dad and I to have some time apart and get some help on being better at being honest with each other. Brian assured them they would talk on the phone after he was there a week.

I Too Have Choices

During the fourth week of his stay, I arrived for five days of family programming. I was frightened of what would happen to us. I was also afraid of being judged. I didn't want to hear them tell me to leave my husband, nor did I want them to tell me that men do this, and that now he has been caught twice he will just stop. I wondered if the staff would blame me for not being attentive enough to Brian. I was afraid they expected me to forgive him without being able to trust him.

But I quickly bonded with the other family members around our emotional pain. Outside of my group at church, I had not told a soul about my husband's infidelities, not even my sister who I was close to. She knew I was struggling but thought it was with depression and anxiety. I had depression and anxiety, but they were just the symptoms of the trauma.

Nor having seen Brian for several weeks, I immediately sensed he was different. He seemed happy to see me, but he wasn't trying to appease me or act like everything was okay. I saw him be vulnerable in a way I had never seen without begging for forgiveness, without trying to please me. I felt a hesitancy on his part, as if he wanted to listen to me, not talk over me.

Brian talked about his feelings of inadequacy, things that led him to seeking out other women—he had been having one-night affairs with women he met while traveling and multiple longer affairs with various coworkers over the years. Then he shared how he rationalized his lies and deception. These were not excuses but a part of his being accountable to me. He described how he gaslighted me, how he made me question myself versus him, which helped him to be able to be so deceptive.

By the end of the family week, he shared with me his plans for recovery and talked about accountability to self and to others, his support team, and accountability to me. He let me know he also knew I had choices in what happened to us as a couple.

I was still in a state of shock when I left. I didn't know how I was going to make sense of all of this. I even wondered if I had been better off not knowing so much. But we did have an initial plan.

The Plan

This plan included what I needed to do for me. I had learned about boundaries during family week, and Brian and I established some initial boundaries that would allow me to feel more emotionally safe in our marriage. I needed to know his daily recovery practices, and to know he was engaged in them. At first, I preferred we not be sexual. I was willing to sleep in the same room if he would give me that space until I felt I wanted to be more intimate. This was not meant to punish him, but sex implied trust and I didn't have it yet.

We agreed to have daily check ins with each other. They were very structured; we had them each evening after dinner. What feelings did we have that day? This was new, as we had never talked about feelings in this manner before. In the check in we could talk about feelings about anything: the kids, work, each other, ourselves. The goal was just to be honest, to listen with respect. It was a practice in being emotionally intimate. Then we were to talk about what we were grateful for that day. Once a week we had a longer check in. We shared with each other what our recovery practices had been for the week, and then our intentions of recovery practice for the upcoming week.

I also asked for transparency regarding the credit cards, and that blocks be put on his cell phone. I asked that he speak to his boss about not traveling for work for at least the next six months. Having boundaries was what I needed to go forward, and I did this by speaking up for myself.

In the meantime, Brian was in a virtual alumni group (due to the pandemic) with several of the men he was in treatment with. He saw a sex addiction therapist weekly. He attended Codependency Anonymous groups once a week in addition to his sex addiction related twelve-step groups. Now, two years later, he is still going to some men's only groups. That was another a boundary of mine. And he accommodated.

In time, I accepted Brian's behavior was not about me. It was about his inability to be honest with himself, his genuine fear of rejection, his insatiable need for validation and approval. And he had a lot of distorted beliefs about what intimacy was. He grew up in a family where people didn't openly talk about problems. I thought his family was nice, but underneath that niceness they had a lot of their own secrets.

A Focus on Me

About eight weeks after he came home, I enrolled at the Meadows' Rio Retreat Center and spent five days with other partners in a workshop called Intimate Treason. I was still feeling very shaken and confused about where my life was going, so I was happy to have my own time to focus on me.

This workshop took me to the depths of exploring my attachment to the perfect family fantasy, my fear of questioning, and how I diminished my own needs and wants. It helped me to be more honest about my anger, and it reinforced the need for boundaries. Boundaries were still new to me, so it was helpful to see how some boundaries remain, others flex, and others are let go of. I realized I had a lot of codependency and began to attend Codependency Anonymous regularly. I also attend ACA meetings and see a counselor on a regular basis individually with Brian and I seeing one together monthly.

Today

It's been two years since Brian was in treatment. Brian and I have stayed together. We continue to see a couples therapist who specializes in betrayal trauma and sex addiction. The relationship is different; we are both different. We are more real with each other. We both like our recovery and our support.

I feel strong in a way I never did. A lot of that came from honoring myself with boundaries, knowing and valuing my needs, not being afraid of feelings, and trusting my gut. I had to get to a place where I felt a choice and the confidence that if needed, I would leave the marriage.

What Brian did was not okay. It was so hurtful, and I hated him for it. I so needed him to be my knight in shining armor. I blindly trusted. Hard to explain but there is a depth of love we have never had before. It comes from knowing each other more intimately, respecting each other. Will I trust ever him fully? I don't know. But right now, I can live with trusting life a day at a time.

◆ ◆ ◆

COMMENTARY

From Christine Herrera, MA
(Clinician, Rio Retreat Center)

It's common for the betrayed partner to hesitate accepting the truth about the betrayal, as they tend to give their partner the benefit of the doubt. Plus, the truth can be too painful to accept. In addition, most partners tend to blame themselves or feel some toxic responsibility for their loved one's hurtful behavior. Also common is feeling stupid and shameful, as if it was their responsibility to recognize the problem and have a solution.

By attending family week, Candace was able to be in a safe, guided setting, where she and her husband could talk and listen to each other respectfully. She came to understand the nature of sexual compulsivity and intimacy avoidance. And while she was given a framework for understanding what fueled Brian's deception, it did not discount the impact of betrayal she was experiencing. It reinforced that his behavior was not a statement about her; Candace was not at fault or to be blamed.

This, of course, takes time. As family members are typically still in shock, as Candace was, during family week, her seeking out her own intensive treatment eight weeks after family programming was extremely important in her recovery.

Candace learned how to establish boundaries and to hold Brian accountable for his actions. She left treatment with more tools to help her not spiral into depression and anxiety.

Having their own aftercare support, independent of each other, was another best practice. They each needed their own recovery plan, and in doing so, could ultimately come together in a much healthier and stronger relationship. When both partners courageously move into their healing journey, the possibility of experiencing healthy, authentic intimate relationships is greatly enhanced.

Setting Family Boundaries

By Claudia Black, PhD, Sr. Fellow (Pioneer in Addictive Family Systems, Clinical Architect of Claudia Black Young Adult Center)

A lack of boundaries is one of the most prevalent contributors to dysfunctional family systems. Boundaries provide structure and a safety container that helps you to not stay in a constant state of traumatic stress. Without them, family members struggle to get their needs met, to feel seen, and to be authentic. A lack of healthy boundaries is a set up for victimization and offending behaviors, and chaos and drama are the natural consequences.

Fortunately, with commitment to change and taking responsibility for one's own actions, setting boundaries can stabilize a family.

From Claudia Black, PhD, Sr. Fellow

However a family member becomes aware of a partner's behavior, it is traumatic. When Candace first became aware of her husband's infidelity early in their marriage, her response was a common one. She was overwhelmed, went into a freeze state, and believed that if her husband felt guilty enough—and sounded convincing—he would immediately stop and not do it again.

As painful as it is, in the short run it is so much easier to accept apologies, particularly when a partner is begging for forgiveness. After all, we want to be able to trust those we love. And sometimes, in the moment, the apology is sincere. They may mean what they say, but their addictive behavior eventually overrides intent. Over time, Candace noticed subtle signs of sexual acting out, but as she wrote, "I never allowed myself to fully question his behavior." It is very important for family members to not berate themselves for wanting it "just not to be true."

In addition, the person acting out is a master at manipulation, at *gaslighting*, at being deceptive. They have a skill set that they have been using for most of their life that makes it possible to stay in the addiction with little exposure and few consequences.

It takes courage to no longer discount your own perceptions and to trust yourself. Courage often comes when there is hope, and for Candace that hope came when she allowed herself to attend her first group with other women who had similar stories. That act alone does much to help lessen the depression that partners often find themselves experiencing. Desperate for answers, Candace listened with a willingness to hear. Coming to realize she was very possibly living in a fantasy, and had not been trusting herself, she found the courage to set limits with her husband, insisting he see a qualified therapist who dealt with chronic sexual infidelity.

When Candace arrived at family week, like many partners, she wondered did she really want to know the full extent of her husband's betrayal? In the long run, it benefits the partner more from knowing than not. This honesty is a vital aspect of the recovery process for both members of the couple ship and for the relationship. There is a therapeutic tenet that secrets not only interfere with recovery, but they also preclude the possibility of recovery. Knowing the truth gives the relationship the potential for an honest foundation. The partner deserves to have the information to make objective choices about the future.

While Candace didn't want to divorce her husband, it would become critical in her healing that she allowed herself that choice. In the long run, the decision to stay or leave often involves incremental steps to garner a stronger foundation to make that decision. While love is unconditional, relationships are not. Candace came to realize that.

Allowing herself to be witnessed, validated, and led by others who have been on a similar journey and found a path out of their dark time, she found the strength to take the self-care actions that were necessary for her healing. She availed herself of help and found tools to practice on a daily basis that have made a difference in every aspect of her life. She also discovered what most people must: she needs to heal with community. With the support of others, she will continue to grow.

Undaunted Hope

There is so much potential for individual and familial health when everyone takes responsibility for their part in what they can do to make the family dynamics healthier. Obviously as a family member you have no control over partners or other adult family members, but you do have a choice about what you do.

The impact of a structured intensive family workshop is invaluable for families in crisis. Therapeutic support acknowledges and repairs the disconnect you may feel with your loved one and yourself; it also brings awareness to the need for greater self-care practices. You can develop many of the same skills your loved one may be learning, such as healthy communication, the identification and healthy expression of feelings, and boundary setting. You can leave this experience with your own map and tool chest of vital coping mechanisms and skills.

CHAPTER NINE

Gifts of Recovery

What happened to me? This is the question to ask yourself, not, What's wrong with me? There is nothing wrong with you. You aren't having these struggles because you are willful, stupid, or whatever demeaning adjective you want to use. Something has occurred in your life that set you up for self-defeating behavior.

As we enter this world, we come into it with an innate sense of wholeness. We don't begin our lives questioning our worth and value. But for so many, the questioning begins at a young age, when our identity is developing. In the stories shared, you read about how early life experiences shaped the storytellers' lives. You read about how they felt an emotional hunger, often sought outside validation, and engaged in unhealthy coping mechanisms that would either plummet them into depression or set them up for various ways to numb their pain. You also discovered that no matter how deep or painful the impact of trauma, healing is possible.

For the storytellers, finding their path to recovery meant it would take great despair to ultimately reach out for help, and in their cases, it warranted an inpatient treatment experience. To create boundaries for safety and stop their acting out behaviors, they needed the structure an inpatient setting provides. This level of care allows for a more thorough assessment in a shorter period of time, as it involves working with a team of clinicians and a variety of clinical modalities. It also involves peer support, which, for the storytellers, was usually not something they initially wanted but ultimately became one of the greatest gifts of their treatment experience.

Finding and being in recovery is not a clear-cut, preprogrammed, one-size-fits-all path. For most individuals, opportunities for help are readily available before the problems become as severe as those reflected in *Undaunted Hope*. You may find your answers in self-help groups, individual or group work with a therapist, intensive workshops, or intensive outpatient programs.

If you would like to get better, feel the fear and ask for help anyway. You do not have to continue to live with secrecy, shame, and judgment.

Finding Connection

Healing and recovery are about connections with yourself and with others. In order to walk back through the pain—be it of trauma, addiction, depression, or relationship struggles—you must be able to trust at least one person with your healing process. No one heals in isolation. Every time I sit in graduation groups at various Meadows programs, I am reminded of this truth; without fail, individuals tell me that the number one factor to turning their life around was the support of people they met while in treatment. Why? Because for these graduates, who were once consumed with self-loathing and fear, what they feared most was being seen. Seeking the support of others is a sign of strength, not weakness. With the right allies in your corner, you can be heard and hear; you can be seen and see. If you are willing to share your story, there will be people willing to listen. Whatever your healing journey, there will be people ready to walk beside you. They can shine the light and provide the hope when it is difficult to garner for yourself.

Gifts of Recovery

If you or someone you care about is struggling, it can be nearly impossible to envision a better life. But it is possible. Here are some of the gifts recovery can offer if you are willing to accept help:

- You will come to understand what has happened to you, and why you think, feel, and act the way you do.
- Aspects of your life that used to confuse or elude you will suddenly make sense.
- You will no longer seek perfection or hide behind a façade in fear of being judged as inadequate.

- You will no longer need to hide from or fear your feelings. You will be able to express feelings in a healthy manner.
- You will learn to recognize and avoid (or end) toxic relationships.
- You will no longer see yourself as a victim.
- You will no longer need to remain constantly vigilant and closely defended.
- You will let go of your painful past.
- You will know when to say yes, and when to say no, and when to say, "Let me think about it."
- You will set healthy boundaries.
- You will make wise choices about whom you allow in and whom you keep at a distance.
- You will learn to accept and forgive yourself. You will accept and learn from your mistakes and failures.
- You will have compassion for yourself and others.
- Your life will have direction. You won't feel out of control or frozen in place or like you are spinning helplessly.
- You will approach each day with greater ease.
- You will become a healthier, stronger partner, parent, sibling, grandparent, or friend.
- You will live your life from a position of strength, confidence, and clarity.
- You will learn to meet life head on without succumbing to despair or crushing fear.
- You will discover the help you need is close at hand, and you will learn to ask for it, accept it, and make the most of it.
- You will live life from a position of strength, confidence, and clarity.

These are the gifts of recovery, and I invite you to join the millions of others who have walked this path.

Healing is possible, one moment, one step at a time.

GLOSSARY

Acute Trauma. Trauma that has occurred due to a single event.

Adverse Childhood Experiences Study (ACEs). A groundbreaking study that emanated from Kaiser Permanente health care system in 1995 that continues to be expanded today through the Center for Disease Control. It has demonstrated the relationship of adverse childhood experiences to mental and physical health problems. See ACES.org for more detail.

Anhedonia. The inability to experience pleasure from activities usually found enjoyable.

Arrested Psychological Development. Term that describes when a person is stuck at an early phase of emotional development. It often results from trauma, neglect, or grief.

Autonomous Nervous System. Component of the peripheral nervous system that regulates involuntary physiologic processes including heart rate, blood pressure, respiration, and digestion.

Betrayal Trauma. Refers to the emotional distress that occurs when a loved one, an intimate partner violates another's trust.

Bipolar Disorder. Formerly called manic depression, it is a mental health condition that causes extreme mood swings that includes emotional highs and lows. These mood swings can affect sleep, energy, activity, judgment, behavior, and the ability to think clearly.

Bodies of Culture. Refers to all human bodies not considered white, a term coined by Resmaa Menakem.

Body Checking. The habit of seeking information about one's body, shape, weight, or size.

Body Image Dysmorphia. Also called Body Dysmorphia Disorder (BDD). Mental health condition characterized by persistent and intrusive preoccupation with an imagined or perceived imperfection in one's appearance. In reality, a perceived imperfection may only be slight difference or nonexistent.

Body Memory. Sensory recollection of trauma in the form of arousal, tension, pain, or discomfort held in the body; refers to memories held in bodies on a cellular level; the body itself is capable of storing memories, as opposed to only the brain.

CES (Cranial Electrical Stimulation) Machine. Apparatus that recalibrates the nervous system so that someone becomes unstuck from hypervigilance and the flight-or-fight response to be able to experience a state of relaxation and inner calm.

Cognitive Behavioral Therapy (CBT). Widely used form of talk therapy that assists clients in becoming aware of negative thinking to be able to view challenging situations more clearly and to respond in more effective way.

Collective Trauma. The psychological distress that a group, usually an entire culture, community, or another large group of people, experience in response to a shared trauma.

Compartmentalizing. Defense mechanism in which people mentally separate conflicting thoughts and emotions to avoid discomfort or be able to focus on other experiences.

Complex Trauma. Describes both a person's childhood exposure to traumatic events and the wide-ranging, long-term effects of this exposure.

Co-Occurring Diagnosis. Having two or more mental health and or addictive disorders at the same time.

Developmental Trauma. Ongoing relational trauma that occurs in one's growing up years, interchangeable with the words complex trauma.

Dissociation. Mental process where a person disconnects from their thoughts, feelings, memories or sense of identity. It ranges from a mild emotional detachment from the immediate surroundings to a more severe disconnection from physical and emotional experiences.

Dopamine. Known as the "feel good" neurotransmitter, playing a strong role in experiencing pleasure. It also contributes to motor function, mood, and decision making.

Dysthymia. A persistent and mild form of depression; low mood occurring for at least two years, along with at least two other symptoms of depression.

EMDR. Eye Movement Desensitization Reprocessing is a form of trauma therapy; it focuses on a thread of subconscious thought and reprocessing the traumatic memory so it can be stored in a more organized and coherent way.

Emotional Abandonment. When one is not valued for who they are and learns to hide parts of themself in order to protect themselves or to garner acceptance.

Emotional Immaturity. A term describing how childhood trauma causes immaturity, then drives unmanageability, creating problems with being relational; comes from the Developmental Model of Immaturity developed by Pia Mellody.

Epigenetics. The study of how behaviors and environment can cause changes that affect the ways genes express themselves; also the study of how cells control gene activity without changing DNA sequence.

Family Sculpt. A role play exercise where the roles that family members ascribe to are demonstrated by participants; this exercise allows participants and viewers to see the purpose of certain roles, their vulnerabilities, and what is needed for a healthy shift within the family unit.

Family System. A term used when recognizing that individuals within a family operate as a unit. What one member does or doesn't do affects not only that person but everyone else in the family.

Faulty Neuroception. Limited or missing capacity to evaluate relative safety or danger in one's environment.

Fight or Flight Strategies. Universal and primitive survival strategies in response to trauma.

Freezing. A frozen or numb state of the mind or body that occurs when neither the survival strategies fight or flight ensures safety; it's a universal and viable response to threatening situations.

Gestalt. Form of therapy that focuses on the present moment rather than past experiences. Instead of talking, clients are encouraged to engage in intellectual and physical experiences that include role playing, reenactment, or artistic exercises.

Glutamate. Most abundant excitatory neurotransmitter in your brain and central nervous system. It is needed to keep your brain functioning properly and plays a major role in shaping learning and memory.

Historical Trauma. Intergenerational trauma experienced by a group of people because of their race, creed, or other identifying features due to systematic oppression. It is cumulative and collective.

Hypervigilance. Elevated state of constantly assessing potential threats around you.

Inner Child. Spirit within you that reflects connection you have within yourself to your child self and your childhood memories.

Inner Child Work. Form of therapy that addresses needs not met in childhood and heals attachment wounds; involves exploring your true feelings and parts of yourself that may have been rejected or abused in an effort to develop healthier coping mechanisms.

Inner Critic. An inner voice that judges, criticizes, or demeans a person whether the self-criticism is objectively justified.

Insecure Attachment. A type of bond that develops in childhood if a child feels that their needs are not being met by caregivers, causing them difficulty in all relationships; styles of insecure attachment include avoidant, ambivalent, and disorganized.

Intergenerational Trauma. The specific experience of trauma across familial generations.

Internal Family Systems (IFS). Therapy modality developed by Richard Schwartz. It combines systems thinking with the view that the mind is made up of relatively discrete subpersonalities, each with its own viewpoint and qualities. It employs strategies to effectively address issues within a person's internal community of family.

Interoception. The ability to sense internal signals from your body, such as when your heart is beating fast or when you are hungry; it's the sense that allows us to answer, How do I feel? in any given moment.

Intimacy. A level of trust, safety, and closeness two people can have between each other.

IOP. Acronym for Intensive Outpatient Program. It is a level of mental health and addiction treatment that allows someone to live outside of the treatment setting but participate in three-to-four-hour of therapy experiences for up to five days a week for several weeks, usually ranging from six to twelve weeks.

Limbic System. Part of the brain that is largely responsible for regulating emotions. Its components support a variety of functions, including emotional, behavior, long-term memory, and olfaction.

Listening Boundary. A communication guardrail that allows one to listen to another with curiosity and take in what is real and true for them and discard what is not.

Love Addiction. A process addiction whereby a person feels excessively dependent on their romantic relationships, interfering in significant other areas of their life.

Love Avoidance. A state of emotional distancing from or emotional unavailability toward others, typically because the thought of relying on another creates anxiety, distress, and discomfort; a love-avoidant person often wants to be in a relationship but fears becoming lost or overwhelmed.

Major Depressive Disorder. Mental health disorder characterized by persistently depressed mood or loss of interest in activities causing significant impairment in life.

Moral Injury. The damage done to one's conscience or moral compass when that person perpetrates, witnesses, or fails to prevent acts that transgress their own moral beliefs, values, or ethical codes of conduct.

Neuroception. The process by which neural circuits distinguish whether situations or people are safe, dangerous, or life threatening.

Neurofeedback. A therapeutic intervention that provides immediate feedback from a computer-based program that asses a client's brainwave activity and presents it visually or audibly in order to consciously alter such activity.

Outer Esteem. A temporary sense of esteem garnered by validation from others or achievements that provides a moment of self-worth.

Perinatal Depression. Depression that occurs during pregnancy or up to a year after childbirth.

PHP. Acronym for partial hospitalization program, a level of mental health and addiction treatment with more hours per day and more days of week than an intensive outpatient program (IOP). It commonly offers or requires a secure living environment, such as a sober living house.

Physical Boundary. A relational guardrail that delineates closeness and touch, and respect for the physical boundaries of another.

Plasticity. Refers to the brain's malleability or ability to change.

Post-Traumatic Stress Disorder (PTSD). Mental health disorder that may occur in people who have experienced or witnessed a traumatic event, series of events or set of circumstances; symptoms include flashbacks, nightmares, disturbing thoughts and feelings, intense feelings of sadness, fear or anger, detachment from others, depression, and substance use disorder.

Process Addiction. A compulsive, chronic, physiological, or psychological need for habit-forming behaviors such as gambling, gaming, and sexual activity; the neurochemistry of a process addiction is similar to that of using alcohol and or other drugs.

Progression. A state reflecting a predictable pattern of escalation due to the mental, emotional, and physical aspects of being addicted to a process or behavior.

Psychodrama. Type of experiential, action-based therapy in which clients use props, role-playing, and other elements of theater to help people gain greater perspective on emotional concerns, conflicts, or other areas of difficulty.

Psychostimulant Psychosis. Mental disorder characterized by psychotic symptoms such as hallucinations, paranoid ideation, delusions, disorganized thinking, and behavior typically caused by the ingestion of stimulant drugs.

Relapse. A recurrence of self-defeating behaviors after a period of improvement and work toward recovery.

Secure Attachment. A type of bond that develops in childhood if a child's needs are met by caregivers; securely attached children grow up with consistency, reliability, and safety.

Serenity Prayer. Prayer attributed to American theologian Reinhold Niebuhr and popularized by Alcoholics Anonymous and other twelve-step programs, commonly quoted as "God, grant me the serenity to accept the things I cannot change, the courage to change the things I can, and the wisdom to know the difference."

Sex Addiction/Sexual Compulsivity/Sexual Dependency. Interchangeable terms that describe a state whereby sex becomes the organizing principle in one's life and priority is given to temporary pleasures over healthy intimate relationships, despite ongoing negative consequences.

Sexual Boundary. A relational guardrail that delineates one's right to determine with whom, when, and where they are willing to be sexual and to respect the sexual boundaries of another.

Sociometrics. A quantitative method of measuring social relationships that explore and reveal the hidden structures that give a group alliances, subgroups, relational preferences; developed by the founder of psychodrama, J.L. Moreno.

Somatic Experiencing. A body oriented approach to healing trauma that releases traumatic shock and restores connection; developed by Peter Levine.

Sponsee. A person in a twelve-step program who has agreed to be mentored by someone who can offer wisdom and direction.

Sponsor. A person in a twelve-step program that agrees to mentor another person who most typically has less time in the program.

Talking Boundary. A relational guardrail that delineates a framework for sharing one's reality with another while not controlling or manipulating.

Toxic Shame. The painful feelings associated with the belief that one lacks value.

Trauma. A disordered mental or behavioral state resulting from a grave mental or emotional stress or physical injury that exceeded the body and brain's ability to cope.

Trauma Repetition. Repeating physically or emotionally painful situations that have happened in the past.

Traumatic Energetic Loads. Energy one carries related to unresolved trauma.

Twelve Steps. Set of guidelines designed as steps toward recovery utilized in self-help groups. Most commonly focused on those struggling with and impacted by substance and behavioral addictions.

White-Body Supremacy. Falsehood that the white body is the supreme standard against which all other human bodies are measured and judged structurally and philosophically.

ACKNOWLEDGMENTS

I cannot thank enough the incredibly courageous men and women who shared their stories and are allowing the reader to learn from their experiences. While twenty-one stories are captured in *Undaunted Hope*, I interviewed over thirty people who shared intimate details of their life. I hold your trust in me sacred. It has been my honor to work with you all.

It is with gratitude I thank the Senior Fellows and administrative and clinical staff that so eagerly agreed to participate. Thank you as well for your many contributions to the behavioral healthcare field.

While my name is on the cover, I could not have written this book without the teamwork that included Carrie Cyrus, who amongst her many projects for Meadows Behavioral Healthcare was the book's project manager. As well, developmental editor Marisa Solis was invaluable capturing the essence of people's lives to be able to be told in just a few words. Working with the stories of lives impacted by such pain, and then recovery, has touched all three of us immensely.

Sean Walsh, CEO of Meadows Behavioral Healthcare, thank you for trusting me to capture not only the spirit of the contributors but the spirit of all the Meadows' programs. Jim Dredge, your feedback and support has been invaluable. In addition, Patty Evans, Aleah Johnson, Wendy Lee Nentwig, and Cherie Carter, your support that occurred during this process also was significant in shaping this book. It has been my privilege to author *Undaunted Hope*.

Central Recovery Press team, thank you for believing in my work, and Valerie Killeen, a special thanks for leading this publication. Sandi Klein, my assistant of over twenty-five years, it is with gratitude that you one more time have kept me organized as I venture into another important piece of work.

And to Jack Fahey, you are always with me in spirit.

Thank you all for sharing this journey.

ABOUT THE COMMENTATORS

Meadows Senior Fellows who contributed to Undaunted Hope

Patrick Carnes, PhD, CAS, continues to be the leading voice in the field of sex addiction. The founder of Gentle Path, he pioneered the development of the International Institute for Trauma and Addiction Professionals (IITAP). He is also the founder of Gentle Path Press, the American Foundation of Addiction Research, and has been awarded the Fulbright-Canada-Palix Foundation's Distinguished Visiting Research Chair in Brain Science. Dr. Carnes is the author of twenty books, most notably the groundbreaking *Out of the Shadows: Understanding Sexual Addiction,* and *The Betrayal Bond: Breaking Free of Exploitive Relationships.* Learn more at www.drpatrickcarnes.com, www.iitap.com, or www.afar.com.

Stefanie Carnes, PhD, LMFT, CSAT, is the clinical architect of Willow House. She is president of the International Institute for Trauma and Addiction Professionals (IITAP) and the author of numerous publications including her premier book, *Mending a Shattered Heart: A Guide for Partners of Sex Addicts,* and her latest, *Courageous Love: A Couples Guide to Conquering Betrayal.* Learn more at www.IITAP.com or www.stefaniecarnes.com.

Tian Dayton, PhD, TEP, is the developer of RTR Sociometrics and one of the foremost authorities on J.L. Moreno's psychodrama model. A prolific author of more than a dozen books, her latest releases include *Sociometrics: Embodied, Experiential Processes for Relational Trauma*

Repair, and *Treating Adult Children of Relational Trauma.* Learn more at www.tiandayton.com.

Kristin Kirkpatrick MS, RDN, is a consultant of Wellness Nutrition Services at the Cleveland Clinic Department of Integrative and Lifestyle Medicine. Her bestselling books include *Skinny Liver: A Proven Program to Prevent and Reverse the New Silent Epidemic—Fatty Liver Disease* and *Regenerative Health: Discover Your Metabolic Type and Renew Your Liver for Life.* Learn more at www.kristinkirkpatrick.com.

Peter Levine, PhD, is the developer of Somatic Experiencing® (SE), a naturalistic body-awareness approach to healing trauma, and the founder of the Ergos Institute of Somatic Education. An accomplished author, Dr. Levine penned the bestselling books *Waking the Tiger* and *In an Unspoken Voice: How the Body Releases Trauma and Restores Goodness.* Learn more at www.somaticexperiencing.com or www.traumahealing.org.

Kevin McCauley, MD, MPH, is an expert on the neuroscience of addiction and recovery management and served as a flight surgeon in the US Navy. Dr. McCauley is also an award-winning filmmaker, writing and directing *Memo to Self,* about the concepts of recovery management, and *Pleasure Unwoven,* about the neuroscience of addiction. Learn more at www.kevinmccauley.com or www.addictioneducationsociety.org.

Pia Mellody, RN, LISAC, is a preeminent authority and educator in the fields of addictions and relationships. Her Model of Developmental Immaturity is the cornerstone of all Meadows Behavioral Healthcare programs. She is also the author of several extraordinary books, including *Facing Codependence, Facing Love Addiction,* and *The Intimacy Factor.* Learn more at PiaMellody.com.

Resmaa Menakem, SEP, LICSW, MSW, is chaperone of the somatic abolitionism philosophy and practice and a leading voice in today's conversation on racialized trauma. He is the founder of Justice Leadership Solutions as well as the author of the *New York Times* bestseller *My*

Grandmother's Hands: Racialized Trauma and the Pathway to Mending Our Hearts and Bodies and *The Quaking of America*. Learn more at www.Resmaa.com or www.centralrecoverypress.com.

Jenni Schaefer is a sought-after speaker on eating disorders and recovery. Her breakthrough bestseller, *Life without ED: How One Woman Declared Independence from Her Eating Disorder and You Can Too,* changed the way people look at eating disorders. A recovery advocate, she is the author of two other books: *Goodbye Ed, Hello Me* and *Almost Anorexic*. Learn more at www.jennischaefer.com.

Richard Schwartz, PhD, is the developer of the Internal Family Systems (IFS) model of therapy and the founder of the IFS Institute. A faculty member of the department of psychiatry at Harvard Medical School, he is also the author of over fifty articles on IFS and nine books, most notably, *Internal Family Systems Therapy* and *No Bad Parts: Healing Trauma and Restoring Wholeness with the Internal Family Systems Model.* Learn more at www.ifs-institute.com.

Bessel van der Kolk, MD, is one of the world's foremost authorities on post-traumatic stress disorder (PTSD) and other related disorders as well as professor of psychiatry at Boston University School of Medicine. The past president of the International Society for Traumatic Stress Studies, Dr. van der Kolk initiated the process that led to the establishment of the National Child Traumatic Stress Network (NCTSN), and in 2018 he established the Trauma Research Foundation. He is best known as the author of the *New York Times* bestselling book *The Body Keeps the Score: Brain, Mind,* and *Body in the Healing of Trauma*. Learn more at www.traumaresearchfoundation.com or www.besselvanderkolk.com.

Meadows Executive and Clinical Staff

Jennifer Angier, MS
Vice President of Addiction Services

Kevin Berkes, MA
Director of Spiritual Services at The Meadows

Jean Collins, LCSW, MSW, CSAT
Clinical Consultant to Meadows Behavioral Healthcare, Former Executive Director of Rio Retreat Center

Michael Denicole, DO
Fellow of the American Society of Addiction Medicine, Medical Director at The Meadows

Kara Fowler, LPC-S, RD
Executive Director of The Meadows Ranch

Christine Herrera, MA, LPC
Clinician at Rio Retreat Center

Whitney Howzell, PhD, MPH, LCSW, CSAT
Executive Director of Claudia Black Young Adult Center

Havi Kang, LPC, CSAT-S, CPTT-5
Former Clinical Director of Willow House

Jerry Law, D. Ministry, CSAT, MDAAC, CMAT, CIP
Executive Director of The Meadows

Jack Register, LCSW, MSW
Former Clinical Director of Claudia Black Young Adult Center

Deirdre Stewart, MS, LPC, SEP, BCN
Vice President of Trauma Resolution Services

ABOUT MEADOWS BEHAVIORAL HEALTHCARE PROGRAMS

Meadows Behavioral Healthcare Programs referred to in Undaunted Hope

- **The Meadows (TM)** offers inpatient treatment for adults struggling with trauma, mental health, and/or various addictions. www.themeadows.com

- **Claudia Black Young Adult Center (CBC)** is an inpatient treatment program for young adults struggling with trauma, mental health, and/or various addictions. www.claudiablackcenter.com

- **The Meadows Ranch (TMR)** provides inpatient eating disorder treatment for pre-teen, teen, and adult females with anorexia, bulimia, and other eating disorders. www.meadowsranch.com

- **Gentle Path (GP)** is an inpatient program designed to treat all aspects of male sex addiction. www.gentlepathmeadows.com

- **Willow House (WH)** provides inpatient treatment for women struggling with relationship issues, love addiction, sexual compulsivity, sexual trauma, and other intimacy disorders. www.willowhouseforwomen.com

- **Rio Retreat Center (RRC)** offers intensive workshops to help those wanting to address unresolved childhood trauma, relationship problems, grief, and more. www.rioretreatcenter.com

For more information about all Meadows Behavioral Healthcare programs throughout the country, including outpatient, partial-hospitalization, and virtual treatment, go to www.meadowsbh.com. A complete list of Senior Fellows to include Bruce Perry, MD, and Laurence Heller, PhD, can be found at https://meadowsbh.com/senior-fellows/.

For information on the alumni program MBH Onward and the MBH podcasts *Recovery Replay* and *Beyond Theory*, go to www.meadowsbh. com. To order many of the titles mentioned in this book, visit The Meadows Bookstore at www.themeadowsbookstore.com.

ABOUT THE AUTHOR

Claudia Black, PhD, is the clinical architect of the Claudia Black Young Adult Center. She serves as a Senior Fellow and has been a clinical consultant to Meadows Behavioral Healthcare since 1998.

Internationally recognized for her pioneering and cutting-edge work with family systems and addictive disorders, Dr. Black's work with children impacted by drug and alcohol addiction in the late 1970s fueled the advancement of the codependency and developmental trauma fields.

She was the first to name and coin the dysfunctional family rules, Don't Talk, Don't Trust, Don't Feel. She broke the barrier and openly discussed physical and sexual abuse in the context of addictive families. She utilized art therapy in the context of group work with young children, which offered a model for children's programs for the past four decades. She described the phenomena of delayed stress, emotional trauma, the child's denial process, the phenomena of 'looking good' kids as they relate to growing up with addiction, and hence the meaning and phraseology of "Adult Children of Addiction." Her writings and teachings have become a standard in the field of addictions.

Claudia holds a Doctorate of Philosophy in Social Psychology from Columbia Pacific University, and a Master's Degree in Social Work and Bachelor of Arts Degree in Social Welfare from the University of Washington.

She is one of the original founders and serves on the Advisory Board for the National Association of Children of Addiction and the Advisory Council of the Eluna Foundation and its development of Camp Mariposa, a camp for children impacted by addiction.

She is the recipient of a numerous national awards including the Marty Mann Award, the Distinguished Alumni Award from the University of Washington School of Social Work, the Father Joseph Martin Professional Excellence Award, the NAADAC Lifetime Achievement Award, and the American Society of Addiction Medicine Media Award.

She is the author of more than sixteen books, including *It Will Never Happen to Me, Deceived: Facing the Trauma of Sexual Betrayal,* and *Unspoken Legacy.* Her work and her passion has been ageless and offers a foundation for those impacted by addiction to recover, and gives the professional field a library of depth and breadth.

The Claudia Black Library is available through Central Recovery Press on their website www.centralrecoverypress.com.

Printed in the USA
CPSIA information can be obtained
at www.ICGtesting.com
JSHW081701220324
59686JS00002B/19

9 781949 481853